Interculturality in International Education

This comprehensive volume provides a state-of-the-art survey of key issues and developments in study abroad research and practice with a specific focus on the intercultural and language learning dimensions of study abroad experience. Rather than looking at individual studies in detail, the book seeks to capture the full complexity of the language learning and intercultural dynamics of study abroad by exploring a wide range of topics of particular interest to study abroad researchers and practitioners, including the role of individual differences and external elements, identity reconstruction and interculturality, the challenges of assessing learning outcomes, and pedagogical interventions designed to enhance and extend language learning and intercultural engagement in study abroad contexts. The volume also takes a step back to look at future directions for study abroad research and offers suggestions for innovative interventions in study abroad programming that emphasise intercultural elements. This book is an authoritative resource for study abroad scholars and researchers in such fields as intercultural communication, applied linguistics, sociolinguistics, international education, and language education.

Jane Jackson is Professor of Applied Linguistics in the English Department at the Chinese University of Hong Kong where she teaches language and intercultural communication/transitions courses at the undergraduate and postgraduate levels, including a fully online course for study abroad students. An active intercultural educator and study abroad researcher, recent publications include *Intercultural Interventions in Study Abroad* (with Susan Oguro, 2018), *Introducing Language and Intercultural Communication* (2014), and *The Routledge Handbook of Language and Intercultural Communication* (2011). In preparation is *Online Intercultural Education and Study Abroad: Theory into Practice* (Routledge).

Interculturality in International Education

Jane Jackson

NEW YORK AND LONDON

First published 2018
by Routledge
711 Third Avenue, New York, NY 10017

and by Routledge
2 Park Square, Milton Park, Abingdon, Oxon OX14 4RN

Routledge is an imprint of the Taylor & Francis Group, an informa business

© 2018 Taylor & Francis

The right of Jane Jackson to be identified as author of this work has been asserted by her in accordance with sections 77 and 78 of the Copyright, Designs and Patents Act 1988.

All rights reserved. No part of this book may be reprinted or reproduced or utilised in any form or by any electronic, mechanical, or other means, now known or hereafter invented, including photocopying and recording, or in any information storage or retrieval system, without permission in writing from the publishers.

Trademark notice: Product or corporate names may be trademarks or registered trademarks, and are used only for identification and explanation without intent to infringe.

Library of Congress Cataloging-in-Publication Data
A catalog record for this book has been requested

ISBN: 978-1-138-59249-0 (hbk)
ISBN: 978-0-429-49002-6 (ebk)

Typeset in Sabon
by Apex CoVantage, LLC

Contents

List of Illustrations	vi
Abbreviations	vii
Acknowledgements	ix
1 Introduction	1
2 Research Paradigms and Issues	17
3 Acculturation, Socialisation, and Translanguaging	38
4 Language, Identity, and Interculturality FRED DERVIN AND JANE JACKSON	63
5 Individual Differences and Environmental Factors	82
6 Assessment and Evaluation	102
7 Intercultural Interventions	129
8 Taking Stock and Looking Ahead	157
References	169
Glossary	204
Index	222

Illustrations

Figures

3.1	The U-curve Adjustment Model	53
3.2	The W-curve Adjustment Model	54
6.1	The Developmental Model of Intercultural Sensitivity (DMIS)	112
6.2	The Process Model of Intercultural Competence	115

Table

2.1	Common Paradigms in Intercultural Study Abroad Research	21

Abbreviations

AAAL	American Association for Applied Linguistics
AAC&U	Association of American Colleges and Universities
ABC model	Affect–Behaviour–Cognition model
AILA	International Association of Applied Linguistics
APAIE	Asia-Pacific Association for International Education
BEVI	Beliefs, Events and Values Inventory
CARLA	Center for Advanced Research on Language Acquisition
CCAI	Cross-Cultural Adaptability Inventory
CEFR	Common European Framework of Reference for Languages
CERCLL	Center for Educational Resources in Culture, Language, and Literacy
CIEE	Council on International Educational Exchange
COST	European Cooperation in Science and Technology
DMIS	Developmental Model of Intercultural Sensitivity
EAIE	European Association for International Education
ECML	European Centre for Modern Languages
ERASMUS	European Region Action Scheme for the Mobility of University Students
FEA	Forum on Education Abroad
GCAA	Global Competence Aptitude Assessment
GPI	Global Perspective Inventory
IaH	Internationalisation at home
IAICS	International Association for Intercultural Communication Studies
IAIR	International Academy for Intercultural Research
IALIC	International Association for Languages and Intercultural Communication
ICC	Intercultural communicative competence
ICI	Intercultural Communication Institute
IDC	Intercultural Development Continuum
IDI	Intercultural Development Inventory
IES	Intercultural Effectiveness Scale

IoC	Internationalisation of the curriculum
IEREST	Intercultural Education Resources for Erasmus Students and their Teachers
ITI	Intentional, Targeted Intervention
MAXSA	Maximising Study Abroad
NAFSA	NAFSA Association of International Educators
OBA	Outcomes-based Assessment
PLATO	Project for Learning Abroad, Training & Outreach
PluriMobil	Plurilingal and Intercultural Learning through Mobility
ReN	Research network (International Association of Applied Linguistics)
SAREP	Study Abroad Research in European Perspective
SIETAR	Society for International Education, Training and Research
SNS	Social Networking Site
TCK	Third culture kid
WISE	Workshop on Intercultural Skills Enhancement

Acknowledgements

First, I would like to thank my PhD students, past and present, who inspired me to write this volume. I also appreciate the anonymous reviewers of the book proposal and manuscript who offered valuable criticism and suggestions. Fred Dervin, from the University of Helsinki, contributed to the writing of the chapter that centres on identity-related issues and provided helpful feedback on some of the other chapters. I would also like to express appreciation for the editorial assistance provided throughout this process by Elysse Preposi, Alexandra Simmons, and other members of the Routledge team. The preparation of the book was supported by the Hong Kong Research Grants Council (RGC) Prestigious Fellowship under the Humanities and Social Science Panel (HSSPFS) (Project code 2190404; CUHK 34000616). I sincerely hope that readers of this volume will be inspired to enhance international educational experience through intercultural theory-building, research, and/or practice.

The author and publisher appreciate the permission granted to reproduce the copyright material in this book: Figure 6.1 The developmental model of intercultural sensitivity (DMIS) and Figure 6.2 The process model of intercultural competence.

1 Introduction

The idea for this book emerged from several extended discussions that I had with my PhD students in Hong Kong about recent advances in international education, especially in relation to the language and intercultural learning of second language sojourners. We noted that the number of conferences that centre on international education has increased in recent years, with many more opportunities for PhD students and seasoned academics to present the findings of their study abroad research to a wider audience. My students were especially excited about the international gatherings that they would soon attend in different parts of the world as these events would include many presentations and workshops about study abroad learning, including their own talks. I am also frequently on the move to keep abreast with the latest developments in our field and share my work in conferences and other professional meetings. When I travel (in person or virtually online), like my students, I am exposed to new ideas and understandings, which often inspire me to think more deeply about my own language and intercultural research and practice, especially in relation to study abroad. Engaging with other scholars, especially those who embrace criticality, has raised my awareness of the importance of critical reflexivity in all areas of my work in international education.

In the past decade, many of my postgraduate students have been investigating the language and intercultural development of second language learners/users who are gaining some form of international education (e.g., short-term language and cultural immersion, a semester or year abroad for international exchange students, service-learning, study abroad for pre-service English as a Second Language (ESL) teachers). As one might expect, my research students are often searching for critical reviews of scholarly work that is concerned with interculturality and language learning in study abroad contexts. There are many publications about intercultural competence development in general as well as edited collections that showcase research on language and intercultural learning in international education; however; there was no single monograph that my students and I could point to that presented a comprehensive state-of-the art review of the intercultural dimension of study abroad research, theory, and practice.

With this gap in mind, I decided to write a critical review of recent developments in this burgeoning field of study, drawing on my own work as well as the contributions of many other scholars in different parts of the world. In the chapters that follow, due to space limitations, I have necessarily been very selective and have primarily focused on the major conceptual frameworks, research traditions, methodologies, issues, and practical concerns that have emerged in intercultural research in international higher education, citing relevant examples as needed. While I have aimed to present multiple perspectives and experiences, I have been increasingly embracing critical notions of interculturality and reflexivity in my work and this will be evident as you read the chapters that follow. As a consequence, throughout the book I encourage readers to adopt a critical, reflexive stance in their own research and practice to further enhance the field of international education.

Who Is This Book for?

This monograph addresses issues of importance to professionals in international education research and practice (e.g., study abroad) as well as intercultural education, more broadly. It is also relevant for scholars who are interested in second language acquisition, global citizenship, sociolinguistics, sociopragmatics, psycholinguistics, second or foreign language teaching, cross-cultural psychology, speech communication, and related fields.

For those who organise, supervise, or teach in study abroad programmes or other forms of international education, it is vital to have a firm grasp of the many complex factors that can influence the language and intercultural development of study abroad students and result in differing learning outcomes. These understandings can guide the planning and implementation of appropriate and effective pedagogical interventions (e.g., pre-sojourn orientations, intercultural transition courses, re-entry debriefings). Enhanced knowledge of core issues in international education can also assist the work of individuals who are called upon to document and assess the intercultural learning of student sojourners. An awareness of developments in the field (e.g., theory-building, research designs, methodologies, the growing emphasis on criticality and reflexivity in study abroad research and practice) benefits both novice and experienced international education researchers and practitioners.

When writing this book, I had graduate students in applied linguistics and/or intercultural communication in mind as well as international educators from diverse backgrounds who have a particular interest in study abroad. While I aimed to write in a style that would be accessible to newcomers in our field, I have also provided a review that should be comprehensive and substantive enough to enhance the understanding of experienced researchers and practitioners in international higher education, including individuals who are developing intercultural interventions to support and extend the intercultural learning of student sojourners. As well as reviewing existing work, this book aims to help novice and experienced international education scholars become more aware of limitations and gaps in the field (e.g., underrepresented populations and issues). In the last chapter I offer suggestions for future developments in study abroad research and practice. I hope this will inspire innovative projects that will enhance the international educational experience of many future study abroad participants in different parts of the world.

The introductory chapter offers definitions of core constructs in this field of study and draws attention to some of the key publication outlets (e.g., book series, journals) and professional organisations that are contributing to our understanding of interculturality in relation to international education. As interculturality is a central theme of this volume, I discuss contemporary understandings of its meaning and explain its importance in study abroad research and practice. I also discuss the notion of global citizenship as this construct is increasingly intertwined with interculturality and international educational experience. Finally, after citing the specific aims of the volume, I conclude this introductory chapter with an overview of the remaining chapters.

Core Terms and Constructs

Throughout the book, as in any field of study, readers are exposed to many terms and constructs. In some situations, scholars use the same term and mean different things or they use different terms for the same phenomenon. To help make sense of the dizzying array of terms and constructs, I have prepared a glossary that you may access at the end of the book. To get started, in this chapter I offer definitions of core elements related to international education and interculturality.

What Is International Education?

Before defining what I mean by interculturality, it is necessary to say a few words about internationalisation, international education, education abroad, and study abroad. One of the most widely quoted definitions of internationalisation was put forward by Knight (2004:11), who refers to it broadly as the integration of 'an international, intercultural or global dimension into the purpose, functions, or delivery of post-secondary education'. Building on Knight's work, a project commissioned by the European Parliament formulated a more comprehensive definition of internationalisation: 'the **intentional** process of integrating an international, intercultural, or global dimension into the purpose, functions and delivery of post-secondary education, **in order to enhance the quality of education and research for all students and staff, and to make a meaningful contribution to society**' [emphasis in original] (de Wit, Hunter, Howard and Egron–Polak 2015: 29). This definition encompasses international education, and, more specifically, education abroad and related sub-areas, including study abroad.

As a field, international education is concerned with the facilitation and support of the movement of students and scholars across geopolitical borders. It includes international student recruitment, study abroad programmes, international exchange programmes for faculty and students, and English as a Second Language (ESL) classes and other support services for non-local students in higher education, among others (Forum on Education Abroad 2011; Savicki 2008). In general terms, international education refers to 'any international activity that occurs at any level of education (K-12, undergraduate, graduate, or postgraduate)', and encompasses 'the knowledge and skills resulting from conducting a portion of one's education in another country' (Forum on Education Abroad 2011).

Education abroad refers to education that is obtained outside the student's home country. 'Besides study abroad, examples include such international experiences as work, volunteering, non-credit internships, and directed travel, as long as these programs are driven to a significant degree by learning goals' (Forum on Education Abroad 2011: 12). Some scholars simply refer to 'international educational experience' or 'education abroad' when discussing the experiences of students who spend part of their academic studies outside their home country.

The term 'study abroad' may be defined in a number of ways, depending, in part, on the context. For this book, it refers to 'a subtype of education abroad that results in progress toward an academic degree at a student's home institution', excluding 'the pursuit of a full academic degree at a foreign institution' (Forum on Education Abroad 2011: 12). In European contexts this form of education abroad is generally referred to as 'credit mobility' (European Commission 2015). An example is the ERASMUS (European Region Action Scheme for the Mobility of University Students) programme which enables European students to study in another European country for a semester or academic year and transfer credits back to the home institution (European Commission 2015).

What Is Interculturality?

Interculturality is a difficult construct to pin down and many scholars have offered different conceptions and definitions. Much of the confusion stems from ideas about culture. This book's approach to interculturality takes on a critical and reflexive stance. Inspired by, among others, Holliday's perspective on intercultural communication (2010, 2011), I consider interculturality to be ideological in the classical Marxist sense; thus, it is an evaluative, rather than a neutral or descriptive concept. Interculturality translates a process and something in the making when two individuals from different backgrounds meet. As suggested by Dervin (2016, 2017), the prefix *inter*-requires that we pay attention to the symbolic violence of interaction, context, the recognition of power relations, simplexity (the inevitable combination of the simple and the complex), and intersectionality (how different identities beyond race, ethnicity, nationality and language also contribute to interculturality). The idea of multiple identities, beyond the national, is central to this perspective (Abdallah-Pretceille 1986; Piller 2010, 2017; Dervin 2016; Zhu 2016a). The combination of all of these dimensions makes the notion of interculturality very unstable, political, and ideological. It is, thus, important to consider the ideologies and ensuing moralistic judgements that accompany or underpin discussions of interculturality. The second part of the notion, the 'cultural', needs to be unpacked and revised to reflect the malleability of interculturality. To sum up, the preferred approach to interculturality in this book represents an attempt to avoid easy formulas and ready-made clichés which ignore power relations in intercultural encounters and associate culture with nation, ignoring the diversity within. This goes well beyond the simplistic approach of 'tighten(ing) up a linguistic screw here and loosen a cultural bolt there' (Shi-xu 2001: 287).

What Is Global Citizenship?

Understandings of what it means to be a global citizen vary. For Olson and Kroeger (2001), globally-competent individuals possess enough global knowledge (e.g., understanding of cultures, languages, global events, and concerns), perceptual understanding (e.g., open-mindedness, sophisticated cognitive processing, resistance to stereotyping), and intercultural communication skills (e.g., empathy, adaptability, cross-cultural awareness, intercultural conflict mediation, intercultural sensitivity) to interact appropriately and effectively in multicultural contexts in our globally interconnected world. Thus, closely intertwined with the notion of global citizenship is interculturality or intercultural competence, which Chen and Starosta (2006: 357) define as 'the ability to acknowledge, respect, tolerate, and integrate cultural differences that qualifies one for enlightened global citizenship'. Accordingly, through various means including study abroad, institutions of higher education that seek to foster global citizenship encourage students to develop an understanding of global interdependence, appreciate cultural diversity, combat racial discrimination, protect the global environment, understand and respect human rights, accept basic social values that protect the rights and dignity of all human beings, and work towards social justice (Jackson 2018a; Patel, Li and Sooknanan 2011; Sorrells 2012, 2013). With these aims in mind, more and more study abroad programmes include pedagogical interventions that seek to promote the mindset, skills, and practices associated with ethical intercultural-global citizenship.

Rationale for the Volume

As internationalisation efforts intensify across the globe, the number of students who are participating in some form of international education has increased exponentially. In Europe, between 1987 and 2013 more than three million tertiary students joined the Erasmus programme to study outside their home country (European Commission 2015: 4). In the United States, one in ten undergraduates study abroad before they graduate (Institute of International Education 2016). Further, according to a report issued by the British Council in October 2013, approximately 3.85 million higher education students will take part in a study abroad programme by 2024, up from 3.04 million in 2011, with China and India accounting for 35 percent of the growth during this time period. The vast majority of students from East Asian nations (China, Hong Kong SAR, Japan, Korea, Taiwan, Macau SAR) study in a second language or a lingua franca while abroad, with English the most common medium-of-instruction (Jenkins 2013; Kirkpatrick 2009), and the United States the most popular host destination (British Council 2013).

For many international students, their sojourn experience involves a second language as well as exposure to a potentially unfamiliar physical and sociocultural environment. Even when students study in a host country where their first language is spoken, they are apt to be exposed to different accents, vocabulary, and communication styles (e.g., differing degrees of directness). Thus, language and intercultural dimensions feature in all study abroad experience, to varying degrees.

As a consequence of implicit or explicit internationalisation policies and a myriad of 'push and pull' factors, more and more institutions of higher education across the globe are taking steps to increase participation rates in study abroad programmes. Similar advances are also happening in secondary schools in some regions, with more opportunities for students to gain international educational experience.

For many years, administrators, educators, and students often naively assumed that study abroad experience would bring about advances in intercultural sensitivity, language proficiency, and global-mindedness, and other skills or attributes associated with global citizenship. Progressively, however, the 'immersion myth' is being debunked and questions are being raised about what participants actually gain from stays abroad when there is no intervention. Accordingly, a growing number of institutions of higher education and decision makers are calling for systematic research that documents and assesses the intercultural learning of participants. Partly in response to these calls, more applied linguists and scholars from other fields (e.g., psychology, teacher education, business education, speech communication, sociology) are conducting studies that investigate the intercultural development of student sojourners, including second language speakers.

With more awareness of variability in sojourn outcomes, institutions of higher education are becoming more cognisant of the need to intervene in study abroad. In view of that, in many parts of the world, more and more educators are developing and systematically assessing innovative, research-driven pedagogical interventions with the aim of enhancing the intercultural development of participants at various stages of the study abroad cycle: pre-sojourn, sojourn, and post-sojourn (Jackson and Oguro 2018a; Savicki 2008; Vande Berg, Paige and Lou 2012a). I was inspired to write this book as I believe that it is helpful and important for both novice and experienced study abroad scholars (PhD students, researchers, and practitioners) to become more familiar with current theory and practice in this dynamic field.

Publications on Study Abroad Research and Practice

Following the publication of Freed's (1995) seminal volume on second language acquisition in study abroad contexts, a number of books have appeared that centre on the learning of second language sojourners. Notably, Kinginger's (2009) volume reviews and critiques research on language learning through study abroad from an applied linguistics perspective. Freed's (1995) and Kinginger's (2009) books have made a significant contribution to the field; however, they pay little attention to the intercultural dimension of study abroad experience, including the development of interculturality. Moreover, since these books appeared in print, there have been many advances in study abroad research and practice. In the past decade, in particular, there has been tremendous growth in the number of research projects and publications that centre on educational sojourns in various parts of the world. More and more postgraduate students from different regions (e.g., Greater China) are undertaking research on intercultural learning in study abroad and contributing to theory-building. Many of them are or have been study abroad students themselves. Their voices are certainly enriching the field and raising awareness of elements and issues that have previously been overlooked. Today, there are also more studies that are examining the impact of social media and other forms of communication technologies on sojourn learning and intercultural pedagogy in study abroad contexts.

Multiple edited collections present research on second language sojourners. Some centre on second language acquisition (e.g., DuFon and Churchill 2006; Regan, Howard and Lemée 2009), whereas others describe studies that have explored language and intercultural learning (e.g., Byram and Feng 2006; Ehrenreich, Woodman and Perrefort 2008;

Lewin 2009; Savicki 2008; Vande Berg, Paige and Lou 2012a). More recently, edited volumes by Deardorff and Asaratnam-Smith (2017), Jackson and Oguro (2018a), and Plews and Misfeldt (2018) describe pedagogical interventions designed to enhance intercultural learning and engagement. The last two volumes focus solely on study abroad (e.g., cultural mentoring, pre-sojourn workshops, an online sojourn intervention, a telecollaborative exchange project, re-entry, interventions that span the full study abroad cycle).

A number of monographs (e.g., Dervin 2008; Jackson 2008, 2010, in preparation; Kinginger 2008; Papatsiba 2006; Patron 2007; Pellegrino Aveni 2005; Taguchi 2015) have also been published that examine the study abroad learning of second language sojourners. Most describe investigations of a small number of student sojourners who are studying in a particular host country (e.g., Australia, England, France, Japan, Russia). Although Jackson (in preparation) investigates the intercultural learning and engagement of a group of international exchange students from the same Hong Kong university, they are in different host countries while enrolled in an online intercultural transitions course.

In past decades, books concerned with international education research and practice generally appeared as independent volumes. With mounting interest in study abroad learning and research, a number of publishers are now supporting book series that are devoted to the publication of monographs or edited collections that explore issues relevant to our field (e.g., internationalisation, international education, study abroad, global citizenship, intercultural communication or language/intercultural education in study abroad contexts). (See Appendix A for a list.) The number of journals that are publishing articles on international education in relation to language and culture learning is also on the rise. (See Appendix B.) All of these developments offer evidence of the growing maturity of our field of study and the timeliness of the present volume.

The Sharing of Research and Pedagogical Advances Through Professional Organisations

International education scholars also share their research findings and pedagogical expertise within professional organisations devoted to the enhancement of international education, such as the Council on International Educational Exchange (CIEE), the Forum on Education Abroad (FEA), the National Association of International Educators (NAFSA), the European Association for International Education (EAIE), and the Asia-Pacific Association for International Educators (APAIE). (See Appendix C for a list.) Annual conferences, seminars, webinars, workshops, and other events afford scholars the opportunity to discuss their intercultural interventions and learn from each other. These organisations encourage interaction between study abroad administrators and advisors, international student and scholar directors and advisors, and educators interested in improving the intercultural skills of students studying outside their home country. Many publish newsletters or books that showcase study abroad research and practice.

In addition to the international education organisations cited in Appendix C, a number of professional bodies that are devoted to intercultural communication research and practice host annual or biennial meetings or workshops that provide opportunities for interculturalists to share their study abroad research findings and lessons learned from pedagogical interventions.

The Intercultural Academy for Intercultural Research (IAIR) organises a biennial conference, which typically includes multiple presentations and/or colloquia that focus on empirical research and intercultural pedagogical interventions in study abroad. The International Association for Intercultural Communication Studies (IAICS) also regularly hosts conferences which bring together international educators and scholars from diverse disciplines to share their research findings and views about intercultural communication issues in various contexts, including study abroad. Since 2013, Wake Forest University in North Carolina in the United States has organised the 'Workshop on Intercultural Skills Enhancement' (WISE). This interactive event provides an opportunity for study abroad programme coordinators, administrators, and educators to come together to discuss ways to advance the intercultural awareness and skills of student sojourners. The Society for Intercultural Education, Training, and Research (SIETAR) has various branches in different parts of the world (e.g., SIETAR India, SIETAR Japan, SIETAR Europa, SIETAR USA). Most of them host annual meetings that include presentations of relevance to international educators.

In addition, interculturalists who have a special interest in the language and intercultural development of student sojourners may enhance their professional development by attending language-oriented conferences. The International Association of Language and Intercultural Communication (IALIC) is a professional body that brings together interculturalists and applied linguists to critically engage with the notion of mediating between languages and cultures. The annual conference provides a forum for researchers and practitioners to explore ways in which research into language and culture mediation can inform practice, including intercultural interventions in study abroad contexts.

In the United States, the Center for Educational Resources in Culture, Language, and Literacy (CERCLL) at the University of Arizona hosts a biennial conference that focuses on the development and assessment of intercultural competence. The plenaries and many of the other sessions (e.g., workshops, academic paper presentations) are often devoted to some discussion of intercultural research and pedagogy in study abroad contexts.

Within the field of applied linguistics, in the past decade, much more attention is being paid to study abroad learning and research and this is bringing about a stronger presence in regional and international meetings of applied linguists. For example, the American Association of Applied Linguistics (AAAL) usually hosts at least one colloquium or panel that focuses on the study abroad learning of second language speakers and/or pedagogical interventions that seek to enhance the language and intercultural development of student sojourners. AILA, the International Association of Applied Linguistics, also hosts a major international conference every three years, and this event provides another opportunity for study abroad researchers to share their discoveries about the language and intercultural learning of student sojourners.

In 2012, AILA approved the creation of the Research Network (ReN) 'Study abroad and language learning', which was proposed by Carmen Pérez Vidal (Universitat Pompeu Fabra) and Martin Howard (University College Cork). This network links study abroad researchers from many parts of the world and provides another means to promote and disseminate research findings in our field. At AILA conferences, a ReN meeting showcases innovative study abroad research and practice. Innovative work is also disseminated through specialised ReN conferences/symposia and related publications (e.g., books, special journal issues). To date, there have been three ReN-affiliated study abroad conferences. In 2013, the University of Southampton, UK convened a meeting with the theme 'Residence abroad, social networks, and second language learning'; in 2015, Saint Mary's University in Canada hosted a conference with the theme 'the culture of study abroad for second languages', and in 2017, the Rice Center for Languages and Intercultural Communication in Houston, Texas hosted a conference with the theme 'Understanding the study abroad experience'.

Also, noteworthy is the creation of a European COST Action Network called *Study Abroad Research in European Perspective* (SAREP) whose objective is to jointly develop new initiatives in study abroad programming and close the gap between science, policy-makers, and society throughout Europe and beyond. Devoted to the enhancement of multilingual development and intercultural awareness among European citizens, this interdisciplinary network brings together researchers from the fields of second language acquisition, applied linguistics, language testing, language education, psychology, and sociology and statistics. SAREP has organised workshops and other activities to disseminate their findings. (See www.cost.eu/COST_Actions/ca/CA15130?)

In addition to the organisations cited above, other national and regional applied linguistics and international education conferences around the world provide avenues for scholars to present the findings of pedagogical research and practice that are concerned with the language and intercultural learning of student sojourners.

Aims of the Present Volume

With the above advances in mind, I aimed to fill a gap in the literature by presenting a state-of-the-art review of international education research and practice, with an emphasis on the intercultural dimension in study abroad contexts. *Interculturality in International Education* highlights key issues and developments in the field and offers suggestions for current and future researchers and practitioners. Reflecting the complex nature of international education, the chapters address a broad range of topics and concerns, including the complex relationship between language, interculturality, and study abroad; theories, methodologies and findings in recent international education research; adjustment and intercultural language learning; individual and environmental factors that impact intercultural language learning; identity reconstruction and interculturality in study abroad contexts; interventions designed to enhance and extend the intercultural/language learning and engagement of sojourners; the challenge of assessing intercultural competence in international education; and future directions in research and practice.

This book aims to contribute to the literature on interculturality, international education, language/intercultural development, the adjustment/learning of study abroad students, second language identities, internationalisation, intercultural education, and global citizenship. In addition to providing insight into relevant theories, methodologies, and current research findings, I review practical, pedagogical interventions designed to enhance the intercultural development of study abroad students, especially second language speakers. By its very nature as a complex social phenomenon, study abroad requires interdisciplinary discussion; therefore, in this book, I draw on knowledge from more than one academic discipline or school of thought.

Throughout this volume, readers are challenged to re-examine long-held assumptions and beliefs about international educational experience. Employing a critical lens when digesting publications and presentations can help to raise awareness of the ways in which differing conceptions of culture and interculturality have shaped research and practice in our dynamic field of study.

Overview of Content

Eight chapters, dealing with different topics related to interculturality, language and international education (especially study abroad), compose the book. The chapters are complementary and interrelate with each other. It is recommended that they be read in order of appearance.

Chapter 2 surveys the major research paradigms that underpin current investigations of interculturality in study abroad contexts, namely: (post-)positivism, interpretativism, constructivism, critical theory, and pragmatism. I also examine the relationship between these paradigms and the research designs and methodologies that are commonly employed in intercultural study abroad research. This review serves as a foundation for Chapters 3–7, which explore in more detail core intercultural themes, theories, and issues in study abroad research and practice.

Chapter 3 focuses on adjustment, second language socialisation, and contemporary notions of translanguaging in relation to study abroad. Challenging common assumptions about study abroad learning, including expectations of 'full immersion' in the host environment, I critically review research that has investigated the adjustment and adaptation of sojourners, including those who reside in homestays. Issues such as readiness for international/intercultural experience, language and culture shock, acculturation, accommodation, sociopragmatic awareness, second language socialisation, translanguaging, and re-entry culture shock are examined, with an emphasis on current studies that point to variability in sojourn experience and learning outcomes.

Chapter 4, which was co-authored by Fred Dervin from the University of Helsinki, addresses identity issues and the construct of interculturality within the context of study abroad. After describing common conceptions of 'identity', discussion centres on what researchers have discovered about the influence of identity elements (e.g., gender, age, language, cultural, sexual orientation, national, regional, social) on interculturality in terms of the positioning and learning of student sojourners. For example, the potential impact of social networks and social identities on intercultural competence development is discussed. Our review highlights the complex and highly contested relationship between language and identity in intercultural communication, drawing attention to the relational and discursive nature of identity, the use of language in identity negotiations, the 'dark' sides of identity (e.g., biases, Otherisation, ethnocentrism, stereotyping), the challenge of contested identities, and the potential for identity reconstruction/expansion (e.g., hybrid selves, global selves) through intercultural engagement, critical reflection, and study abroad experience. Suggestions are offered for researchers of identity and interculturality in study abroad contexts.

Chapter 5 identifies and discusses external or environmental factors and individual differences that can lead to profound differences in sojourn learning and engagement. After underscoring the need to pay close attention to 'whole person' development in study abroad investigations, I review programme features (e.g., duration, format) and other environment elements (e.g., the degree of host receptivity, access to communities of practice, the host–sojourner power imbalance) that can result in different developmental trajectories among student sojourners. I then identify and examine some of the many individual differences that researchers have discovered can impact language and intercultural learning on stays abroad, including self-efficacy, degree of intercultural competence/

ethnocentricism, willingness to communicate, second language proficiency, intercultural attitudes, motivation, anxiety, goal-orientation, degree of investment, personality, etc.

Chapter 6 explores recent developments in the assessment of intercultural learning in study abroad contexts. In particular, I discuss the nature of intercultural competence and its components, and highlight the complexity of defining and assessing interculturality. I then describe and critique multiple assessment modes and strategies that are being used to assess the intercultural learning and engagement of sojourners in a range of study abroad programmes and contexts. I also discuss the critical importance of programme evaluation in study abroad to enhance the design and delivery of intercultural interventions.

Chapter 7 is concerned with intercultural pedagogical interventions in study abroad programming (e.g., the fostering of interculturality, global citizenship, and a deeper level of engagement in the host environment through guided, critical reflection). Drawing on recent publications, I review various approaches and strategies that are being employed in study abroad programmes to scaffold, deepen, and extend the intercultural language learning and global-mindedness of participants (e.g., pre-sojourn orientations, ethnography projects, online intercultural transition courses for international exchange students) at various stages of the study abroad cycle: pre-sojourn, sojourn, post-sojourn.

Finally, in Chapter 8, I review and summarise the key issues and perspectives that have been presented in the book, and discuss interculturality in relation to future study abroad theories, research, and practice. As I have done throughout this volume, I emphasise the pressing need for criticality and reflexivity in work in our field. After identifying concerns facing contemporary study abroad researchers, I offer a number of suggestions to guide future investigations and pedagogical interventions in study abroad programming, with an emphasis on the intercultural dimension.

I sincerely hope that the chapters that follow will help readers to become more informed, critical consumers of presentations and publications on international education, especially work that centres on interculturality in relation to second language sojourners. From a practical standpoint, I am also optimistic that this review will inspire further contributions to study abroad theory-building, research, and practice so that future sojourners will more fully benefit from international educational experience. The field will certainly be enriched by the voices of postgraduate students and scholars from diverse parts of the world who are concerned about the quality of study abroad.

Appendix A
International-Intercultural Education Book Series

Education Beyond Borders: Studies in Educational and Academic Mobility and Migration (Fred Dervin, Series Editor), Peter Lang

Intercultural Communication and Language Education (Stephanie Houghton and Melina Porto, Series Editors), Springer

Internationalization in Higher Education (Elspeth Jones, Series Editor), Routledge

Post-Intercultural Communication and Education (Fred Dervin, Series Editor), Cambridge Scholars

Routledge Studies in Language and Intercultural Communication (Hua Zhu and Claire Kramsch, Series Editors), Routledge

SIETAR Europa Intercultural Book Series (Elisabeth Hansen, Barbara Covarrubias Venegas, and Carla Cabrera Cuadrado, SIETAR Europa Book Team)

Appendix B
International-Intercultural Education Journals

Frontiers: The interdisciplinary journal of intercultural relations

Intercultural communication studies

Intercultural education

Interdisciplinary journal on global research and study abroad

International education studies

International journal of intercultural relations

Journal of international education research

Journal of research in international education

Journal of studies in international education

Language and intercultural communication

Study abroad research in second language acquisition and international education

Appendix C
Professional Organisations in International-Intercultural Education

Alliance for International Educational & Cultural Exchange (The Alliance)

Asia-Pacific Association of International Education (APAIE)

Association of International Education Administrators (AIEA)

Australian Education International (AEI)

Canadian Bureau for International Education (CBIE)

China Education Association for International Exchange (CEAIE)

Council for International Education UK (UKCOSA)

Council on International Educational Exchange (CIEE)

Diversity Abroad Network

European Association for International Education (EAIE)

The Forum on Education Abroad (FEA)

Institute for International Education (IIE)

Institute of International Education Generation Study Abroad (IIE)

International Association for Intercultural Communication Studies (IAICS)

International Association for Languages and Intercultural Communication (IALIC)

International Education Association of Australia (IEAA)

International Education Association of Canada (IEAC)

International Education Association for New Zealand and Australia (ISANA)

International Education Association of South Africa (IEASA)

Japan Network for International Education (JAFSA)

Mexican Association for International Education (AMPEI)

NAFSA—Association of International Educators

Netherlands Organization for International Cooperation in International Education (NUFFIC)

Society for Intercultural Education, Training, and Research (SIETAR)

2 Research Paradigms and Issues

Introduction

This chapter is devoted to research that centres on interculturality in international education. To make sense of contemporary studies, it is helpful to have an understanding of developments over time. In the past few decades, scholars from a number of disciplines and traditions have been investigating the language and intercultural learning of student sojourners, including applied linguists, interculturalists, cross-cultural psychologists, social psychologists, second language teachers, and international educators, among others. Not surprisingly, in this multidisciplinary field of study, multiple approaches to research have emerged, due, in part, to differing conceptual frameworks, aims, foci, definitions of core constructs (e.g., culture intercultural competence), and methodological expertise. Scholars are shaped by their disciplinary roots, (potential) interdisciplinary interests as well as the breadth of their knowledge and experience. All of these factors affect the way they design and conduct research.

As questions are increasingly being raised about the effectiveness of study abroad programmes, in recent years, more and more institutions of higher education are calling for the systematic documentation and assessment of sojourn outcomes (e.g., second language proficiency, intercultural competence, global-mindedness) (Deardorff 2015a; Ogden 2015; Savicki and Brewer 2015a; Vande Berg, Paige and Lou 2012b). Further, a growing number of intercultural education scholars are advocating research-driven interventions (e.g., intercultural transition courses, workshops) to enhance learning in study abroad contexts (e.g., Jackson and Oguro 2018a, Lou, Vande Berg and Paige 2012; Savicki and Selby 2008) (see Chapter 7). These developments are inspiring the creation and refinement of numerous theories, research tools, and methodologies, and fueling a significant rise in inquiries, publications, and presentations that centre on international educational experience. This work is helping us to better understand interculturality at all stages of the study abroad cycle: pre-sojourn, sojourn, post-sojourn, and post-post sojourn (six months and longer after study abroad experience).

To date, the majority of studies have focused on American or Anglo-European students abroad (Coleman 2013; Hoffa 2007; Jackson 2012; Kinginger 2009; Paige and Vande Berg 2012). This is changing as more researchers across the globe, including PhD students, are tracking the intercultural learning of student sojourners of diverse ethnic and linguistic backgrounds in a wide variety of study abroad situations and locations, including non-traditional settings (e.g., African, Asian, Latin American and Middle Eastern regions) (Coleman 2013; Paige and Vande Berg 2012; Plews and Jackson 2017; Wells 2006). This development, coupled with advances in theories, research design and methodology, is enriching our field and broadening our understanding of the language and intercultural dimensions of study abroad.

As worldviews guide the way scholars make decisions and carry out research, in any field of study it is essential to have some knowledge of the ones that are the most influential. Therefore, in this chapter I review the major research paradigms that underpin investigations of interculturality in study abroad contexts: (post-)positivism, interpretivism, constructivism, critical theory, and pragmatism. I also take a closer look at the connection between these paradigms and the research designs and methodologies that are commonly employed in intercultural study abroad research. This review serves as a foundation for Chapters 3–7, which explore in more detail core intercultural themes and issues in study abroad research and practice.

Ontology, Epistemology, and Paradigms

In order to make sense of the frameworks that influence intercultural communication research in study abroad contexts it is helpful to have a basic grasp of ontology and epistemology. Ontology (from the Greek *on/ontos*, essence or being and the suffix *logy* for study of) is concerned with the philosophy or study of existence and the assumptions and beliefs that we have regarding the nature of knowledge (Burrell and Morgan 1988; Guba and Lincoln 1994). Basically, ontology addresses philosophical questions such as the following: What is the meaning of life? What constitutes reality? What is truth? How can we make sense of our existence?

Epistemology (from the Greek *episteme* knowledge, science and *logos* study) refers to the study or science of knowledge examined from a philosophical point of view (Audi 2011; Guba and Lincoln 1994). Essentially, this branch of philosophy is concerned with the theory of knowledge and the assumptions or beliefs that we have about the nature of knowledge. Thus, while ontology deals with 'reality', epistemology is preoccupied with the relationship or connection between that reality and the researcher, and the methodology employed in a study refers to the techniques and approach used by the researcher to investigate that reality. As epistemology is concerned with sources of knowledge, it addresses such questions as: How do we perceive the world? How do we gain knowledge? Does knowledge represent reality as it really is? What is the relationship between the researcher and the known?

A paradigm is a model or framework that is derived from a belief system or worldview. Simply put, it is a way of looking at or thinking about something. Guba and Lincoln (1994: 105) refer to it as the 'basic belief system or worldview that guides the investigator'. For Weaver and Olson (2006: 460) paradigms are 'patterns of beliefs and practices that regulate inquiry within a discipline by providing lenses, frames and processes through which investigation is accomplished'. These worldviews are shaped by ontological (the nature of reality or existence), epistemological (the nature of knowledge), and methodological queries (how the researcher should seek knowledge) (Creswell 2014; Kuhn 1970, 2003; Ulysse and Lukenchuk 2013). Paradigms drive research questions, and subsequently the design and methods adopted in a study. In our field, paradigms also influence how intercultural education (or training) is designed, implemented, and evaluated in international education (see Chapter 7). Therefore, it is imperative to develop an understanding of the most influential frameworks in intercultural study abroad research and practice.

I must also acknowledge that these paradigms are not always clear-cut and it is actually quite rare for researchers to identify the worldview that is guiding their work. Further, to complicate matters, researchers may draw on multiple paradigms and not even realise it. This, in turn, can lead to contradictory, and somewhat confusing, outcomes. It is therefore important for researchers to be fully aware of the paradigm that they are embracing and to make an effort to adhere to its tenets so that their work is more coherent.

Key Paradigms in Intercultural Study Abroad Research

Within a particular scientific community, a belief system or worldview about the nature of knowledge and human existence affects the way researchers make decisions and carry out their investigations. In a multidisciplinary field of study such as intercultural communication, more than one paradigm may influence the work of researchers and at particular times in history some frameworks may be more dominant than others. To complicate matters, the ways in which paradigms are labeled, defined, and categorised varies somewhat among researchers and in some cases the differences among paradigms are subtle.

Drawing on the work of leading scholars in education, psychology, speech communication, linguistics, and sociology (e.g., Burrell and Morgan 1988; Creswell 2014; Guba and Lincoln 1994), a number of interculturalists have written about the paradigms that have guided and continue to influence work in intercultural communication studies (e.g., Dahl, Jensen and Nynäs 2006; Bennett 2012; Martin and Nakayama

20 *Research Paradigms and Issues*

2013; Martin, Nakayama, and Carbaugh 2012; Zhu 2016b) and study abroad research, more specifically (e.g., Paige 2015a; Vande Berg et al. 2012b). While some of their descriptions and categories overlap, there are also differences in the ways the paradigms are conceptualised. For this chapter, in relation to interculturality and study abroad, I focus on the following frameworks: positivist, interpretivist, constructivist, and critical paradigms (see Zhu 2016b). I also discuss pragmatism or multi-paradigmatic research as it is becoming more prevalent in international educational contexts. (See Table 2.1 for an overview of the paradigms.)

For each paradigm, I take a look at underlying conceptions of culture, assumptions about the relationship between culture and communication and/or other core beliefs, commonly addressed questions and themes, and related research designs and methodologies. I also provide relevant examples of intercultural study abroad research related to each paradigm.

The (Post-)Positivist Paradigm

In the 1970s, speech communication specialists, anthropologists, and sociologists who conducted intercultural communication research were mainly guided by the culturalism paradigm, that is, a focus on people's experience of culture (cultural texts and practices) (Hall 1980; Scannell 2015). In their work, culture was generally viewed as encompassing meaning and values as well as lived traditions and practices (Leeds-Hurwitz 1990; Martin et al. 2012). By the 1980s, communication specialists in the United States began to draw heavily on the work of behavioural social psychologists. At this juncture, scholars also took inspiration from social theorists such as Auguste Comte and Emile Durkheim, who viewed the social world as 'composed of knowable empirical facts that exist separate from the researcher' (Martin et al. 2012: 21). This led to the emergence and subsequent dominance of the positivism paradigm in the 1970s and 1980s, with scholars seeking to apply models and methods of the natural sciences to investigations of intercultural behaviour (Burrell and Morgan 1988; Mumby 1997).

Within the context of intercultural study abroad, researchers who follow the positivist paradigm embrace the 'scientific method', that is, '[a] way of knowing that is characterized by the public nature of its procedures and conclusions and by rigorous testing of conclusions' (Fraenkel and Wallen 2008: G-8). This paradigm seeks to provide an objective reality against which researchers can compare their claims or assertions and establish 'the truth' about the subject matter under investigation.

In their intercultural communication studies, positivists seek to answer questions such as:

- In a particular study abroad context, what are the culture-specific routines for speech acts such as greetings, refusals, requests, and apologies?

Table 2.1 Common Paradigms in Intercultural Study Abroad Research

Paradigm	Ontology	Epistemology	Conceptions of culture	Aims of research	Common methodologies
(Post-)positivism	Implicit or hidden rules or cultural norms impact communicative behaviours and practices; Reality is objective and tangible	Objective; The researcher employs reliable and valid tools to measure behaviour	Singular, static, product-oriented, measurable; emphasis on 'large' or national cultures	To identify patterns and the causal effect of cultural norms on behaviour; to offer strong predictions about (inter) cultural interactions	Quantitative (surveys: longitudinal, cross-sectional, correlational; experimental and quasi-experimental design studies); hypothesis-generating, testing
Interpretivism	Reality is created inter-subjectively through social interaction	There is a clear link between the researcher and the researched	Dynamic, process-oriented	To explore and understand why people behave the way they do; to discover the meaning of activities	Naturalistic: Qualitative (e.g., diaries, interviews, participant observation) (ethnographical, biographical, phenomenological, case study design studies)
Constructivism	There are multiple local and specific, socially-constructed realities	The researcher is an active participant within the world being investigated	Socially constructed through discourse/social interactions	To identify and make sense of developmental trajectories (e.g., identity construction)	In-depth, unstructured interviews, field-based participant observation, audio or video recordings; action research, grounded theory research
Critical (transformative)	The real world is replete with inequities and social injustice	The researcher changes the social world within which participants live	Co-created, dynamic, emphasis on 'small cultures'	To identify and address injustice; to empower people	Ideological critique/review, action research, participant observation, text analysis, civil actions
Pragmatism (multi-paradigmatic)	Not limited to one system of reality; emphasis on practicality	Objectivity and subjectivity are dependent on the problem or issue under study	Pluralistic conceptions of culture	To problem-solve; to adopt the most appropriate methods to address issues	Mixed-methods (sequential, concurrent, transformative)

- How do cultural values influence communicative behaviours in particular study abroad contexts and situations? How does the concept of 'face' influence intercultural communication and intercultural conflict situations?
- What cultural differences serve as barriers in intercultural interactions? What are the implications for the preparation of student sojourners?

Positivists tend to view culture as somewhat static and unitary. Cultural values, norms (e.g., rules for behaviour in social situations) and communicative actions (e.g., verbal and nonverbal communication strategies) are regarded as variables that can be identified and measured (Martin et al. 2012). In their work, scholars who follow this tradition may seek to determine how cultural values or norms influence the ways in which people behave (e.g., communicate verbally and nonverbally) in particular cultures. Drawing on their findings, they may make generalisations about values and patterns of behaviour within cultures (e.g., conflict communication styles, sociopragmatic norms of politeness in discourse, degree of directness) and then make comparisons between cultures.

Emphasising an objectivist orientation to studying social phenomena, positivism tends to rely on research methods that involve the collection and analysis of quantitative data (e.g., large-scale questionnaire surveys) and the implementation of controlled experiments (e.g., experimental design studies). For example, study abroad researchers who work within this paradigm may administer a large-scale questionnaire survey about values in both home and host countries and then compare and contrast the findings to identify cultural differences that may impede intercultural communication. They may also survey student sojourners to ascertain their perceptions of the host culture and their study abroad situation.

In this paradigm, mis-and non-communication and misunderstandings in intercultural interactions are often attributed to cultural differences, such as conflicting cultural values, differing sociopragmatic norms, or divergent communication styles. Cross-cultural pragmatics specialists, for example, maintain that a lack of understanding of commonly accepted and expected behaviour in certain social situations can lead to pragmatic failure in individuals who find themselves in an unfamiliar cultural context (LoCastro 2003; Thomas 1983).

Challenging the belief in the absolute truth of knowledge, post-positivism, 'a milder form of positivism', emerged in the 1980s. It follows the same principles but permits more interaction between the researcher and the participants under study and acknowledges some limitations in the findings of studies of this nature (Riazi 2016; Taylor and Medina 2013). For example, while positivists believe in an objective reality which is identifiable and predictable, post-positivists maintain that social reality is so complex that the interpretation of findings is affected by the researcher's theoretical understandings, background, and values. A post-positivist begins with a theory, gathers data that either supports or disputes the theory, and then makes adjustments and carries out additional tests (Creswell 2014). Similar to the work of positivists, much of this research entails the collection and analysis of quantitative data and quasi-experimental design studies, whereby the treatment and control groups may not be fully comparable at baseline.

A number of intercultural communication models and theories have been developed by positivists and post-positivists that are particularly relevant to study abroad contexts, including notions of acculturation/cultural adaptation (Gudykunst 2004; Kim 2012), anxiety/uncertainty management (Gudykunst, Lee, Nishida and Ogawa 2005), communication accommodation theory (Giles, Bonilla and Speer 2012), conflict management (Ting-Toomey 2012), cultural dimensions theory (Hofstede 1980, 1991, 2001), identity negotiation (e.g., Ting-Toomey 2005), intercultural communication competence (Wiseman and Koester 1993), and intercultural sensitivity theory (Chen and Starosta 2000), to name a few. Much of this work has been conducted by speech communication specialists and cross-cultural psychologists. Within applied linguistics, speech act theory (Austin 1962) and the sub-fields of intercultural/cross-cultural /interlanguage pragmatics, which centre on pragmatic norms in social discourse (Kecskes 2012, 2014), have also been influenced by (post-)positivism.

In recent years, the positivistic paradigm has been rebuked for essentialising cultures, that is, promoting national culture as the 'default signifier' of who people are (MacDonald and O'Regan 2012), largely ignoring the (inter-)subjective, unique character of individuals (Dervin 2012; Holliday 2011, 2012). Critics argue that study abroad research that reduces student sojourners and host nationals to fixed sets of characteristics and attributes (e.g., values, communication styles) can lead to stereotyping and Otherisation, impeding the development of constructive intercultural relations. Stressing the need to acknowledge subjectivity and diversity within cultures, detractors of this paradigm call upon researchers to recognise the agency or free will of individuals as well as the potential impact of the power dimension (e.g., degree of host receptivity) on intercultural learning and engagement. When researching individuals in real-world situations, they argue that it is impossible to determine an absolute truth as so many variables influence people's thoughts and actions.

Examples of (Post-)Positivism Research in International Education

- Pedersen, E.R., Neighbors, C., Larimer, M.E. and Lee, C.M. (2011) 'Measuring sojourner adjustment among American students studying abroad', *International Journal of Intercultural Relations*, 35: 881–9.

    This article centres on the acculturation or sociocultural and psychological adjustment of study abroad students who temporarily reside in a foreign country. The authors designed and investigated the usefulness of a multi-component measure of sojourner adjustment, which they labeled the 'Sojourner Adjustment Measure'. In their study, they surveyed 248 American study abroad students and through factor analyses of the data they established a theoretically-driven, 24-item measure of sojourner adjustment, which was composed of four positive factors (host language development and use, social interaction with host nationals, cultural understanding and participation, host culture identification) and two negative factors (social interaction with co-nationals, homesickness/feeling out of place).

- Yang, M., Webster, B. and Prosser, M. (2011) 'Travelling a thousand miles: Hong Kong Chinese students' study abroad experience', *International Journal of Intercultural Relations*, 35: 69–78.

    This largely quantitative study focused on a questionnaire survey of the sojourn goals, experiences, and learning outcomes of 214 undergraduates from a Hong Kong university who studied abroad or took part in an overseas internship or volunteer programme. Correlation analysis identified a close link between the achievement of study abroad goals (e.g., personal development, intercultural learning) and host country experiences (i.e., intercultural, second language interactions). Personal changes were also found to correlate with intercultural experiences. The researchers concluded that students should be encouraged to set specific sojourn goals related to intercultural, personal and academic/career development and be prompted to focus on them during their stay abroad.

The Interpretive Paradigm

Naturalistic inquiry and the interpretivist paradigm emerged in the 1970s as an alternative to positivism and static, prescriptive notions of culture. Proponents of interpretivism argue that there is a fundamental difference between the nature of the phenomena investigated by the natural sciences and human behaviour, and this necessitates a different approach to research. Scholars who follow the anti-positivist or interpretivist paradigm focus on 'learning and understanding the personal motives and reasons that shape the way a person or a group of people act in particular ways in certain contexts' (Riazi 2016: 156). Interpretivists maintain that people are shaped by the particular cultures in which they live and this influences the way they interpret their environment and themselves. As interpretivists ask different questions than positivists, this brought about a shift in methods (e.g., from quantitative to largely qualitative studies).

Study abroad scholars who conduct interpretivist studies seek to answer questions such as:

- In a particular study abroad context, how do people (e.g., hosts-sojourners) communicate with each other verbally and nonverbally?
- What do the communicative actions of the host nationals reveal about their culture?
- What are the perceptions and mindsets of student sojourners towards their hosts in homestay situations and how do they change as they develop an interpersonal relationship?
- From the perspective of these individuals, why do they communicate or behave the way they do in particular situations and contexts? What are the implications for hosts and newcomers?

In contrast with positivism, in the interpretivist paradigm, culture is viewed as dynamic, relational, and co-constructed through the communicative behaviours of individuals within particular sociocultural contexts (Geertz 1973; Hall 1959/1973, 1966/1990). Adopting an exploratory orientation, interpretivists typically engage in prolonged observation to develop a holistic picture of the culture under study instead of generating a list of cultural norms (e.g., do's and don'ts for behaviour in that context). For example, in study abroad contexts, interpretivists may examine how people (e.g., host families, student sojourners) use language and nonverbal codes within specific sociocultural settings (e.g., informal conversations, academic seminars, intercultural interactions, homestays).

As the interpretivist paradigm stresses the subjective dimension of social phenomena, researchers often draw on qualitative data generated by ethnographic research methods (Gumperz and Hymes 1972; Hymes 1974). Ethnography refers to

> ... the study of people in naturally occurring settings or 'fields' by means of methods which capture their social meanings and ordinary activities, involving the researcher participating directly in the setting, if not also the activities, in order to collect data in a systematic manner but without meaning being imposed on them externally.
> (Brewer 2000: 10)

In their fieldwork, ethnographers may employ multiple methods of data collection, such as ethnographic conversations; qualitative interviewing; focus groups; participant observation; videotaping; and the collection and analysis of documents, visual materials, and artefacts to better understand the behaviour (e.g., linguistic, sociocultural) from inside the event or setting. The ultimate aim is to develop thick, rich descriptions of cultural scenes, events, or behaviour rather than make generalisations that extend beyond the scene under study (Brewer 2000; Jackson 2006, 2016a). While primarily seeking out an 'emic' or insider perspective, ethnographers typically include an 'etic' (outsider or researcher) stance in the analysis of data of this nature and also declare elements of their background and experience that could influence their selection and interpretation of the data.

Since the 1980s, within the field of international education, a growing number of investigations of sojourn learning have been adhering to an interpretivist paradigm. In particular, we have witnessed a rise in the number of ethnographic studies that build on the work of anthropologists, applied linguists, sociologists, communication specialists, and scholars in other fields. The ethnographic investigations of the American anthropologist Edward T. Hall (Hall 1959/1973, 1966/1990), which focused on verbal and nonverbal patterns of behaviour in cultures, have been particularly influential. The ethnography of speaking (ethnography of communication), a branch that centres on the examination of ways of speaking within a particular speech community (Hymes 1974: Martin et al. 2012), has also inspired interpretivist research in international education. As well as ethnographies, interpretivist studies may take the form of biographies, case studies, or phenomenological accounts, that is, the study of consciousness as experienced from the first-person point of view.

Interpretivist research is not without critics. (Post-)positivists note the lack of generalisability and scientific verification of findings. Uncomfortable with the subjective nature of interpretivist studies, they point to the potential for researcher bias and argue that reliability is undermined. In response, interpretivists stress the deeper level of insight that can be gained through richly detailed qualitative studies. They maintain that the data can have a high level of validity as efforts are made to build trust with the participants, who are then more apt to freely disclose their views and experiences.

Examples of Interpretivist Research in International Education

- Beaven, A. and Spencer-Oatey, H. (2016) 'Cultural adaptation in different facets of life and the impact of language: a case study of personal adjustment patterns during study abroad', *Language and Intercultural Communication*, 16(3): 349–67.

  As part of a longitudinal study of 21 Erasmus students from Italy, Beaven and Spencer-Oatey (2016) examined the sojourn adaptation of one of the participants. The case study explored how this young woman coped over time with the adaptation demands that she faced in her social–personal life as well as in the academic domain. Data was gathered by way of pre-departure and post-return interviews, weekly 'diary-tables' and monthly sojourn interviews. The findings revealed that the case participant's adaptive journey differed in the personal and academic areas of her life, and language learning/use was also viewed differently in these domains. The researchers concluded that adaptation can evolve at different rates in different domains throughout a stay abroad. They called for more studies that investigate individual and contextual differences in the developmental trajectories of student sojourners in various domains.

- Chambers, A. and Chambers, K. (2008) 'Tuscan dreams: Study abroad student expectation and experiences in Siena', in V. Savicki (ed.) *Developing Intercultural Competence and Transformation: Theory, Research, and Application in International Education*, Sterling: Stylus, pp. 128–53.

   This chapter presents an ethnographic case study of student experience in an 11-week study abroad programme for Americans in Italy. In addition to participant observation (in the Italian language classes, the programme office, and on excursions), the researchers collected data from a variety of other sources (application essays, assignments in a cross-cultural communication course, questionnaires, open-ended interviews, and informal conversations with the students and staff). When triangulating and reviewing their data, the authors took an anthropological look at the goals, motivations, and assessments that students made of their sojourn adjustment and learning. An emic perspective dominated the presentation and analysis of their data.

The Constructivist Paradigm

Whereas the focus of (post-)positivist research is on objective reality, constructivism seeks to develop 'an understanding of the *participants'* subjective experiences as they interact with others and construct meaning (reality) and the multiple interpretations it implies' (Riazi 2016: 54). Scholars who follow the constructivist paradigm may develop theories or conceptual models from the data that they collect.

Within a study abroad context, intercultural researchers who embrace the constructivist paradigm, may begin their study by asking such questions as:

- In what ways are intercultural differences socially constructed (e.g., developed and sustained through the use of discourse, but also potentially contradicted by actions)?
- How are the preferred self-identities of the interlocutors (e.g., student sojourners, host families) changed through intercultural interactions during stays abroad?

Within this paradigm, culture and intercultural communication are viewed as socially constructed and research primarily centres on 'the internal, cognitive process of individuals' (Zhu 2016b: 13). Different from (post-)positivism, the agency of individuals is more fully recognised; that is, the researcher views individuals as actively involved in the construction of their own social world rather than as passive representatives of a national culture. The constructivist researcher relies on the participants' interpretations of situations and seeks to capture their perceptions of their experiences. In the process of carrying out their studies, researchers may examine the language that is used in relation to the social construction of meaning in particular contexts and situations.

Constructivist researchers in the field of intercultural communication have examined the impact of discourse and interaction in the construction of an individual's cultural and ethnic identities (Zhu 2016b). A number of studies on interculturality have drawn on this paradigm to investigate how individuals view themselves and their place in the world and make creative and perhaps strategic use of linguistic resources to express certain identities in particular situations and contexts (e.g., Zhu 2014).

In international education, the construction and evolution of identities has become a significant issue for investigation and a number of study abroad researchers are now drawing on the constructivist paradigm to track the developmental trajectories of student sojourners (e.g., the cultivation of a more intercultural, global mindset while in the host country).

Examples of Constructivist Research in International Education

- Harvey, L. (2016) '"I am Italian in the world": a mobile student's story of language learning and ideological becoming', *Language and Intercultural Communication*, 16(3): 368–83.

    This article centres on the language learning experiences of Federica, an Italian student sojourner in the UK. Drawing on a Bakhtinian dialogic perspective, Harvey (2016) examined the relationship between language and intercultural learning in the young woman's story. The researcher maintains that the application of dialogism in study abroad research offers a relational perspective on the self and the other. In this approach, as illustrated in Federica's story of learning English, intercultural learning is viewed as a process of ideological becoming with the other, enacted in, with, and through language.

- Virkkula, T. and Nikula, T. (2010) 'Identity construction in ELF contexts: A case study of Finnish engineering students working in Germany', *International Journal of Applied Linguistics*, 20(2): 251–73.

    Centring on identity and language use in lingua franca contexts, the researchers investigated the identity construction of second language speakers of English who took part in an internship in

Germany. In their study, Virkkula and Nikula (2010) conducted interviews with seven engineering students from Finland before and after their sojourn. When analysing the transcripts that centred on the students' language use and learning, the researchers drew on poststructuralist notions of identity as multiple, dynamic, and relational. Virkkula and Nikula paid close attention to the discursive construction of the students' identities in settings where they had been using English as a lingua franca. This article illustrates how language users may actively draw on different discourses when constructing their identities as second language users.

The Critical (Transformative) Paradigm

In intercultural communication research, critical scholars emphasise that 'human behavior is always constrained by societal ideological superstructures and material conditions that privilege some and disadvantage others' (Martin et al. 2012: 28). Researchers who embrace critical theory are driven by the desire to document and find ways to overcome social injustice that stems from a power imbalance. As noted by Riazi (2016: 73), critical theorists seek 'to change the status quo in favour of the disadvantaged and marginalised groups by unfolding the power relations that permeate the underlying social structures'. Thus, social change is a primary motive of their research, which is why this paradigm is sometimes referred to as transformative.

Critical researchers strive to address questions such as the following:

- What impact do ideology and power have on intercultural communication in a particular study abroad context?
- In what ways are (cultural) differences accentuated or ignored by individuals in positions of power?
- In the host environment, how do the actions of the people who are in power influence newcomers' access to local communities of practice?

Within this paradigm, culture is deemed a site of struggle for power and positioning rather than a benign entity as in (post-)positivist orientations (Holliday 2011). The primary aim of critical scholars is to identify and problematise systems of oppression in order to effect meaningful change (e.g., promote equality). Critical cosmopolitanism refers to a sociological framework or paradigm in which culture is viewed as being politically constructed; scholars who embrace this perspective strive to view the cultural Other with respect and empathy (Delanty 2009; Holliday 2011). When investigating intercultural interactions, critical researchers pay close attention to contextual elements that may be influencing the communication process, including linguistic, social, political, religious, historical, and geographical dimensions, among others. To promote and achieve social justice and equality, critical scholars call upon researchers to recognise the complex relationship between power, culture, and communication when carrying out intercultural communication research or interpreting the work of other scholars (Holliday 2011, 2012; Sorrells 2012, 2013; Sorrells and Sekimoto 2016).

Critical perspectives are not new as some researchers who work within the interpretivist tradition (e.g., ethnography of communication scholars) have examined their data through a critical lens and, in the process, raised awareness of injustice and an imbalance of power. The difference is that the primary mission of interpretivists has not been to investigate critical issues and effect social change, although they may make some recommendations of this nature.

Within the context of international education, contemporary critical researchers are examining a wide range of issues (e.g., the proliferation and implications of the use of English as the de facto medium or language of internationalisation (Englishisation in international education), the power imbalance of second language sojourners in the host community, host receptivity, the impact of a dramatic increase in the number of English-speaking international students on the local language and community in non-English-speaking countries, the fostering of critical cosmopolitanism in student sojourners). Critical intercultural communication researchers may carry out studies that entail ideology critique, participatory action research, critical discourse analysis, or critical ethnography. Through their work, they draw attention to power and positioning in language and intercultural communication within a particular context.

Examples of Critical Research in International Education

- Raymond, P. M. and Parks, S. (2004) 'Chinese students' enculturation into an MBA program: Issues of empowerment', *Critical Inquiry in Language Studies*, 1(4): 187–202.

    In a 20-month qualitative study in a Canadian university, Raymond and Parks (2004) investigated issues of empowerment in relation to the experiences of Chinese students who completed English for Academic Purposes courses prior to enrolling in a Master of Business Administration programme. Employing a critical lens, the researchers explored (a) the literacy demands and socialisation processes enacted within the educational institution, particularly with regard to professors' epistemological stances, (b) students' resistance in regard to certain aspects of their graduate programme, and (c) education as commodity for both administrators and students. They suggested that some conflicts could be mitigated by the stance adopted by professors and called on other researchers to pay more attention to empowerment issues in international education.

- Müller, M. and Schmenk, B. (2017) 'Narrating the sound of self: The role of pronunciation in learners' self-constructions in study-abroad contexts', *The International Journal of Applied Linguistics*, 27(1): 132–51.

  This article reports on an empirical study that investigated the relationship between study abroad experience, learner identity, and pronunciation. Using a critical discourse analysis approach, Müller and Schmenk (2017) scrutinised the narratives of Canadian learners of German who were participating in a study abroad programme in Germany. The analysis of data gained from semi-structured interviews and e-journals focused on discourses of language learning, culture, and identity. The researchers discovered that the learners' views about pronunciation, including their own, were closely tied to their perceptions of the 'native-speaker ideal'. This influenced their perceptions of Self and Other, and their interpretations of their learning experience. The researchers concluded that pronunciation is a key element in language learning in study abroad contexts and called for more research of a critical nature that centres on emic perspectives and the potentially inhibiting effect of the 'native speaker' image.

Pragmatism (Multi-Paradigmatic Research)

Nowadays, there is more recognition of the complexity of our social world and pragmatic or multi-paradigmatic investigations of language and intercultural learning are becoming more commonplace and sophisticated. Instead of adhering to a single worldview, pragmatists borrow from more than one paradigm (e.g., post-positivist and constructivist approaches) and employ multiple methods within the same study to address complex problems or issues (Phakiti and Paltridge 2015). In their work, they face the challenge of developing a consistent and coherent approach while employing diverse theories, instrumentation, procedures, and/or analyses.

Pragmatists may mix quantitative and qualitative modes of data collection and analysis, even though they stem from different assumptions about reality and are associated with differing conceptions about the roles and objectivity of the researcher. Creswell (2015) defines mixed-methods research as:

> [a]n approach to research in the social, behavioral, and health sciences in which the investigator gathers both quantitative (closed-ended) and

qualitative (open-ended) data, integrates the two, and then draws interpretations based on the combined strengths of both sets of data to understand research problems.

(p. 124)

Eschewing the paradigmatic war of the 1980s that pitted quantitative researchers against qualitative scholars, advocates of pragmatism or multi-paradigmatic research point out that it is the research questions that should dictate what methods are followed in a study and this may necessitate a pluralistic approach. As Wiersma and Jurs (2009: 11) note, '[t]he wording of the research question will probably imply the paradigm that best suits the situation'. Pragmatists argue that it is only natural for some inquiries to incorporate questions that are best suited to the collection and processing of mixed-method data. For example, in some investigations of interculturality in study abroad contexts, one research question may require the collection of qualitative data, while others are best addressed through quantitative measures. (See Clark and Ivankova 2016 or Creswell 2015 for a more in-depth discussion of mixed-methods research.)

Examples of Multi-Paradigmatic Research in International Education

- Bloom, M. and Miranda, A. (2015) 'Intercultural sensitivity through short-term study abroad', *Language and Intercultural Communication*, 15(4): 567–80.

    In a mixed-methods study, Bloom and Miranda (2015) tracked the intercultural sensitivity development of 12 students from an American university who were taking part in a four-week summer study abroad programme in Salamanca, Spain. The Intercultural Sensitivity Instrument (ISI) was administered before and after the sojourn to measure the participants' perceptions of their intercultural sensitivity at these stages. Their linguistic proficiency in Spanish was measured by an oral and written placement test administered by the host institution. While in the host environment the students took language and cultural enhancement courses and wrote reflective journal entries in Spanish about their language and intercultural experiences. The authors coded the qualitative data and then compared the qualitative findings with the pre- and post-ISI results. They discovered that the cohort changed little in terms of their degree of intercultural sensitivity as measured by the Intercultural Sensitivity Index and as reported in the qualitative data; however, these methods produced conflicting indications of the students' stages of intercultural sensitivity development.

- Schartner, A. (2016) 'The effect of study abroad on intercultural competence: A longitudinal case study of international postgraduate students at a British university', *Journal of Multilingual and Multicultural Development*, 37(4): 402–18.

    In this longitudinal case study, the researcher viewed intercultural competence as individual abilities and attributes needed to 'perform effectively and appropriately when interacting with others who are linguistically and culturally different from oneself' (Fantini and Tirmizi 2006: 12). A mixed-methods sequential explanatory design was employed to track the intercultural competence development of a multinational group of 223 international postgraduate students at a British university. In stage one, quantitative questionnaire data were collected from the full cohort and, in the second stage, qualitative data was collected from a sub-sample ($N = 20$) by way of semi-structured interviews conducted throughout the academic year. This data was then analysed to help account for and expand on the results of the first stage. The researcher concluded that intercultural development involves a 'dynamic and continual process'.

Paradigms, Research Designs and Methodologies

The paradigms that I have described in this chapter are typically not identified in research projects or subsequent publications; however, as I have explained, they profoundly influence the way studies are conducted even if the researchers are not fully aware of it. In investigations of interculturality in international education it is especially important to pay attention to the way in which researchers define culture and intercultural competence.

Researchers usually begin their studies by asking questions that they wish to address through the collection and analysis of data. A research question is 'a theoretical question that indicates a clear direction and scope for a research project' (Walliman 2011: 177). In quantitative studies the researcher also identifies the proposed variables of interest (e.g., independent, intervening, dependent, control) (Creswell 2014). Whereas research questions ask what relationships exist between the different variables in the project, a hypothesis predicts the relationship between them. An hypothesis is 'a theoretical statement that has not yet been tested against data collected in a concrete situation, but which is possible to test by providing clear evidence for support or rejection' (Walliman 2011: 172). In qualitative or exploratory studies, instead of asking very specific research questions or stating hypotheses, the researcher may indicate the objectives, aims, or broad questions that will guide the study.

Research design is fundamental because everything that happens in a study is ultimately affected by the design choice, which is, in turn, closely linked to the investigator's worldviews, research questions or hypotheses and theoretical understandings. Hittleman and Simon (2006: 309) describe research design as 'the overall strategy or plan used by researchers for answering their research questions'. The design of a study defines the study type (descriptive, correlational, experimental, quasi or semi-experimental, review) and sub-type (e.g., descriptive-longitudinal case study), and, if applicable, data collection methods and modes of analysis (e.g., a statistical analysis plan, thematic analysis in qualitative studies).

Intercultural study abroad researchers draw on a wide variety of designs to answer their research questions and test their hypotheses (Zhu 2016c). There are numerous ways to classify research designs (e.g., quantitative vs. qualitative, single vs. mixed-methods, experimental vs. non-experimental, longitudinal vs. non-longitudinal, case study vs. cross-sectional). Some research designs centre on primary data (the collection of original data by the researcher for a particular study), while others involve secondary data (existing sources of information, such as documentaries, historical archives, published reports) (Vanderstoep and Johnston 2009; Walliman 2011).

Research methods are the activities researchers employ within their research design (e.g., conduct direct observations, administer questionnaire surveys, carry out semi-structured interviews). As is evident in the review of common paradigms, study abroad researchers who are concerned with intercultural issues may make use of various methodologies (e.g., ethnography, narrative analysis, critical discourse analysis) and instruments (e.g., questionnaires and surveys, interviews) to collect qualitative, quantitative, or mixed-method data depending on their research questions and research design. In coherent studies, the mode of analysis is in sync with the research questions, hypotheses, and/or objectives and fits with the research design that has been adopted.

Issues Which Divide Contemporary Intercultural Researchers in International Education

As the field of international education is multidisciplinary and researchers have differing backgrounds, aims, and understandings, it is not surprising that differences in worldviews and research approaches are prevalent. As one might expect, there are many questions that inspire spirited debate among researchers concerned with the intercultural dimension of international education, including the following:

Aims and Scope

- Should research on interculturality in international educational contexts aim to produce knowledge about the intercultural learning of participants (e.g., theory-building) or should the main mission be

the enhancement of international educational experience (e.g., implications for practice)? Or both? Should investigations seek to identify what works and what does not work in study abroad contexts?
- What issues should be addressed in future research in international educational contexts? What are the gaps in the field?

Researchers and Collaboration

- Should the process and product of research on interculturality in study abroad contexts be carried out solely by professional researchers or should there be collaborations with other stakeholders (e.g., staff in international offices, student sojourners)? What role should action research play in intercultural study abroad research?
- In studies of interculturality in intercultural education should there be collaboration between researchers in both home and host institutions (e.g., inter-institutional studies)?

Methodological Issues

- Is qualitative evidence of intercultural learning in study abroad superior to quantitative measures, or vice versa? If both quantitative and qualitative data are collected, how should they be connected?
- Is it possible for researchers to explain and predict the quality and outcomes of intercultural interactions in study abroad contexts (e.g., conflict situations) or is it only feasible to describe interactions? If attempts are made to explain intercultural interactions, should it be through causal accounts or by other means?

Quality Assurance

- What criteria should be used to judge the quality of studies that investigate interculturality in study abroad contexts? If so, what are they?
- How can and should study abroad scholars respond to pressures to demonstrate the intercultural learning of participants in various forms of international education?

Theoretical Underpinning

- How should intercultural competence be defined and measured?
- Do the theories employed in a study fit with the paradigm that has been adopted?

Research–Teaching Nexus

- Should research-based knowledge drive intercultural interventions in study abroad programming or vice versa? What should the connection be between research and practice?

- What is the desired relationship between study abroad researchers and practitioners? What is the preferred relationship between study abroad researchers and student sojourners?

Ethics and Social Responsibility

- What ethical issues and concerns should be addressed in contemporary international education research that centres on interculturality?
- Should research be neutral in political orientation or should it strive to identify and challenge inequalities in study abroad contexts with regard to such aspects as language, gender, social class, sexual orientation, disability, ethnicity, religion, underrepresented minorities, etc.?

Responses to these questions will depend on the researcher's worldview and this, in turn, will affect the research questions that are posed in a study, the research design that is adopted, and the choice of methodology. In the remainder of the book and as you digest publications that address interculturality in study abroad contexts, it is helpful to keep these complex issues in mind.

Conclusion

In this chapter, I reviewed the major conceptual frameworks and research traditions that are employed in intercultural study abroad research today. Although worldviews are often not spelled out clearly in publications and presentations, they should not be ignored as they influence both study abroad research and practice. Reflexivity and transparency should be expected of researchers.

I hope that the review will help you to be a more informed critical consumer of published and unpublished research in our field of study and serve as a foundation and inspiration for your own investigations. The chapters that follow explore the dominant themes, issues, and controversies that have emerged in key studies in this exciting area of research.

Further Reading and Resources

Martin, J.N., Nakayama, T.K. and Carbaugh, D. (2012) 'The history and development of the study of intercultural communication and applied linguistics', in J. Jackson (ed.) *The Routledge Handbook of Language and Intercultural Communication*, Abingdon: Routledge, pp. 17–36.

    In this chapter the authors draw on their experience with different research paradigms (functionalist/post-positivist, interpretive, critical) to survey the major strands of research that have influenced the historical foundations of contemporary intercultural communication and applied linguistics.

Vande Berg, M., Paige, R.M. and Lou, K.H. (2012) 'Student learning abroad: Paradigms and assumptions', in M. Vande Berg, R.M. Paige and K.H. Lou (eds) *Student Learning Abroad: What our Students Are Learning, What They're Not and What We Can Do about It*, Sterling, VA: Stylus Publishing, pp. 3–28.

In this publication, the authors suggest that US-sponsored study abroad has largely been influenced by three paradigms: positivism, relativism, and constructivism. Their examples illustrate how worldviews and theory-building provide direction for study abroad practice.

Zhu, H. (2016) 'Identifying research paradigms', in H. Zhu (ed.) *Research Methods in Intercultural Communication: A Practical Guide*, Chichester: John Wiley and Sons, pp. 3–22.

After providing an overview of the multidisciplinary nature of intercultural communication as a field of enquiry, this chapter reviews positivist, interpretative, critical, constructivist, and realist paradigms that have guided intercultural communication research.

3 Acculturation, Socialisation, and Translanguaging

Introduction

When students leave the familiarity of their home country and enter a region that is new to them, they may be exposed to unfamiliar languages or dialects, values, norms, beliefs, educational practices, notions of friendship, and other 'ways of being' (e.g., verbal, nonverbal), which can be both exciting and confounding, at times. Although I concentrate on such differences in this chapter, it is important to note that similarities with what the students know and have experienced in their home country (or elsewhere) will also be part of their international experience.

Researchers from a number of disciplines have explored the intercultural transitions of students who are gaining some form of international educational experience (e.g., a semester abroad, summer language immersion, an internship). Cross-cultural psychologists and international educators with diverse backgrounds have identified and investigated elements that can lead to variations in the adjustment and intercultural learning of student sojourners. Applied linguists have also explored adjustment issues that can influence the language and intercultural socialisation or translanguaging of students who participate in study abroad programmes. In their work, scholars have identified an array of psychological, cultural, linguistic, physiological, and social factors that can impact border crossings. This has also brought about the development of numerous theories that seek to account for individual differences in the ways sojourns unfold.

This chapter begins with definitions of core terms and concepts associated with the adjustment, second language socialisation, and translanguaging of student sojourners in the host environment. After discussing some of the transition issues that have been identified in study abroad research, I cite potential benefits of the adjustment process. I then review and critique several of the most well-known models of sojourner adjustment. Drawing on recent research findings, I conclude the chapter by briefly summarising the pedagogical implications for the preparation and support of international students. This chapter underscores the need for two-way adjustment, involving changes on the part of both newcomers and hosts.

Acculturation and Second Language Socialisation: The Dangers of Essentialism

There are many concepts and terms associated with the process of adjusting and adapting to a new environment. Most stem from the work of psychologists and are aligned with a (post-)positivistic worldview and essentialist notions of culture (see Chapter 2). Whereas enculturation is defined as the process of learning one's own culture (Kirshner 2012), John Berry, a cross-cultural psychologist, refers to acculturation as 'the process of cultural and psychological change that takes place as a result of contact between cultural groups and their individual members' (Berry 2015: 1). Berry, Poortinga, Breugelmans, Chasiotis and Sam (2011) observe that intercultural interactions may serve as a catalyst for changes in both newcomers and members of the host community (e.g., student sojourners as well as host nationals). Kirshner contrasts the constructs of 'enculturation' and 'acculturation' in this way:

> In relation to each other, enculturation generally signals the case in which the newcomer is an immature member of the cultural community into which she or he is being socialised (e.g., a child); acculturation signals the case in which the newcomer is not a member of the cultural community (e.g., an immigrant).
> (Kirshner 2012: 1148)

With reference to long-term settlers (e.g., immigrants), Berry et al. (2011) describe adaptation as the process of coping with the experiences and strains of acculturation (e.g., different food, weather, routines, values, languages, communication styles). For Kim (2012: 233), cross-cultural adaptation is 'the phenomenon in which individuals who, upon relocating to an unfamiliar cultural environment, strive to establish and maintain a relatively stable, reciprocal and functional relationship with the environment'. Kim (2012, 2015b) maintains that this process may be experienced by both short-term and longer-term border crossers, including study abroad students.

Some cross-cultural psychologists distinguish between psychological adaptation (feelings of personal well-being and self-esteem) and sociocultural adaptation (competence in dealing with life in the larger society) (Berry 2015; Ward et al. 2001; Ward 2015), noting that multiple internal and external elements are involved in the acculturation process (Berry 2006, 2010). Drawing on the work of acculturation specialists,

Komisarof and Zhu (2016: 4) explain the multifarious nature of the transition process:

> Acculturation is complex — shaped by social, political, economic, cultural and linguistic factors in the societies of origin and settlement as well as individuals' stress levels; skill deficits; affective, behavioral, and cognitive responses; and demographic factors such as age, socioeconomic class, and gender.
> (Van Selm, Sam and Oudenhoven 1997; Ward 1996)

Underscoring the complexity of acculturation, in their ABC model of adaptation, Ward et al. (2001) include the following dimensions: affective ('stress and coping'), behavioural ('culture learning'), and cognitive ('social identity and cognition') and 'highlight the shift from the negative and reactive features of culture contact towards its adaptive, active coping aspects' (p. 39) (see also Ward 2015). In the adjustment process, individuals may experience varying degrees of acculturative stress, that is, 'a negative psychological reaction to the experiences of acculturation, often characterized by anxiety, depression, and a variety of psychosomatic problems' (Berry et al. 2011: 465). They may then employ a range of acculturation strategies (e.g., avoidance, mastery of the host language) to cope in the new environment.

When border crossers, including study abroad students, move to an environment where their first language is not widely spoken, acculturation is apt to encompass the learning and use of another language. Even if newcomers have an advanced level of proficiency in the host language in relation to the academic domain, it is important to recognise that they may be unfamiliar with the way it is used in informal, social situations in daily life.

The term 'second language socialisation' refers to the process whereby newcomers gain familiarity with and may gradually adopt some of the language conventions, sociopragmatic norms, cultural scripts, communication styles, and other language-related behaviours, that characterise the new linguistic environment (Duff 2010; Ochs and Schieffelin 1984; Taguchi 2018). As Kinginger (2015) explains, through exposure to local practices (e.g., greetings, communication styles, idiomatic expressions), 'novices are socialized to use language and at the same time are socialized through language toward community activities and worldview' (p. 57). Over time, through second language socialisation, 'newcomers in a community or culture gain communicative competence, membership, and legitimacy in the group' (Duff 2007: 310) provided they wish to do so and there is adequate access to local communities of practice. (See Chapter 5 for a discussion of internal and external elements that can influence sojourn experience, including host receptivity.) As individuals experiment with new ways of being in the host environment, they may experience a broadening of their sense of self or identity reconstruction, a phenomenon which is discussed in Chapter 4.

From Acculturation/Socialisation Perspectives to Languaging and Translanguaging

The literature on adaptation and second language socialisation which depicts culture as static and unitary is criticised by critical theorists (Komisarof and Zhu 2016; Holliday 2011). The 'culture as nation' approach is defined by Martin, Nakayama and Carbaugh (2012) as 'a view of peoples within national boundaries as essentially homogeneous, possessing certain core characteristics' (p. 18). This contentious issue is closely linked to Holliday's (1999, 2011, 2012) concept of 'small and large cultures', whereby 'large' refers to generalised, monolithic concepts of ethnic, national or international cultures and 'small' signifies the multiple cohesive social groupings individuals engage with on a daily basis and which are 'the basic cultural entities from which all other cultural realities grow' (Holliday 2011: 3). Holliday (2011, 2012) and other critical scholars warn that when diversity within 'cultural or national groups' is ignored, essentialism and reductionism ensue (e.g., the stereotyping of host nationals or members of a particular discourse community).

Critical theorists also object to the portrayal of language learners or sojourners as 'passive recipients of cultural influence' (Chiu and Hong 2006: 18–19). Instead of assuming that 'every person has an essential unique, fixed and coherent "core" (introvert/extrovert; motivated/unmotivated)', poststructuralists conceptualise individuals as 'diverse, contradictory, dynamic and changing over historical time and space' (Norton and Toohey 2002: 121). Accordingly, contemporary critical theorists may refer to language learners as 'active social agents', 'language activists, 'languagers', 'translanguagers' or other terms that stress the dynamic, agentive nature of human experience (e.g., Canagarajah 2014; García and Li 2014; Mazak 2017; Phipps 2006).

Contrasting formal and informal language learning, Phipps and Gonzalez (2004) employ the term 'languaging' to refer to the process whereby learners use their second language 'to make sense of and shape the world' around them (e.g., the host environment, homestay life). These applied linguists explain that '[l]anguaging is a life skill. It is inextricably interwoven with social experience—living in society—and it develops and changes constantly as that experience evolves and changes' (ibid.: 2–3). Through the use of their second language in various contexts and situations in the host environment, sojourners have 'an opportunity to enter the languaging of others, to understand the complexity of the experience of others to enrich their own' (ibid.: 3). Phipps (2006) offers further insight into this interactive process, as follows:

'Languagers', for us, are those people, we may even term them 'agents' or 'language activists', who engage with the world-inaction, who move in the world in a way that allows the risk of stepping out of one's habitual ways of speaking and attempt to develop different, more relational ways of interacting with the people and phenomena that one encounters in everyday life. 'Languagers' use the ways in which they perceive the world to develop new dispositions for peptic action in another language and they are engaged in developing these dispositions so that they become habitual, durable. Languaging, then, is an act of dwelling.

(Phipps 2006: 12)

More recently, García (2009) refers to 'translanguaging 'as the constant, active envisioning of new realities through social action and the use of a second language'. Li (2011) muses about the potentially transformative dimension of 'translanguaging space':

The act of translanguaging then is transformative in nature; it creates a social space for the multilingual language user by bringing together different dimensions of their personal history, experience and environment, their attitude, belief and ideology, their cognitive and physical capacity into one coordinated and meaningful performance, and making it into a lived experience. I call this space 'translanguaging space,' a space for the act of translanguaging as well as a space created through translanguaging.

(p. 1223)

García and Li (2014: 21) further explain that translanguaging involves 'new language exchanges among people with different histories, and releases histories and understandings that had been buried within fixed language identities constrained by nation-states'. This conception draws attention to the political, social, and historical dimensions of language practices and their interconnectedness with ideology. (See Chapter 4 for a fuller discussion of identity-related issues.)

As newcomers in an unfamiliar setting, study abroad students may initially find it difficult to express themselves through the host language in daily life, especially if they have had little or no exposure to informal, social discourse prior to venturing outside their home country. In the host culture some sojourners ('social actors') may decide to learn and use the host language only to a certain extent (e.g., to express their basic needs and wants), avoiding new ways of being in the world. Some may resist the language of the host community, believing that it positions them unfavourably or disrespects their first language. As they will only spend a short time in the host environment, sojourners may choose not to invest in the learning of informal expressions in the host language. In contrast, others may embrace the new linguistic community, frequently initiate intercultural interactions in their second language, actively engage in the act of 'translanguaging', pick up colloquialisms in the host language, and experience a broadening or reconstruction of their multilingual sense of self, a phenomenon that is described in Chapter 4.

The process of settling into a new environment is highly idiosyncratic and much more complex than is presented in some publications that centre on international educational experience. When reading materials that focus on adjustment, adaptation, and socialisation, it is important to be mindful of the ways in which culture, interculturality, and individuals (e.g., student sojourners, hosts) are portrayed. As noted in the previous chapter, the worldviews of study abroad scholars impact how the language and intercultural transitions of student sojourners are described and interpreted.

The Challenges of Adjustment

Many of the investigations of short-term border crossers (e.g., international exchange students, summer language immersion students) that have been conducted by applied linguists and intercultural scholars have focused on internal and external barriers to a smooth transition, with the practical aim of identifying ways to help sojourners quickly adjust to the new environment and optimise their temporary stay abroad (e.g., learn the host language, cope with culture difference, communicate in culturally appropriate ways with host nationals). Work of this nature also seeks to reduce attrition (limit the number of students who return to the home country before completing their study abroad programme).

International education researchers from diverse backgrounds in various geographic locations have employed a variety of methodologies (e.g., mixed-method case studies, ethnographic investigations, questionnaire surveys) to identify and better understand the adjustment challenges that student sojourners may face before, during, and after their stay abroad. Their discoveries have helped to provide direction for the intercultural interventions that are described in Chapter 7. To better understand the rationale for these schemes, we will take a closer look at past and current understandings of intercultural transitions.

For J. M. Bennett (1998), 'transition shock' broadly refers to the state of loss, disorientation, and identity confusion that can happen when individuals move to a new situation and find themselves confronted with the strain of adjusting to unfamiliar ways of being. Adjustment issues, of course, can also arise in one's home environment (e.g., the transition from one's family home to a college dormitory for the first time). Over decades of research, scholars have found that transitioning from one linguistic and cultural environment to another has the *potential* to cause varying degrees of anxiety, confusion, and elevated levels of stress (Arthur 2004; Savicki

2015; Ward 2015; Ward et al. 2001). In some cases, border crossers may experience little or no malaise, especially if they have very little contact with host nationals (or other people who have a different linguistic and cultural background) during their stay abroad.

While living and studying abroad can have emotional, psychological, behavioural, cognitive, and physiological consequences, in most cases the effects are temporary and acculturative stress subsides when the newcomers find their feet in the new environment. In some situations, difficulties persist throughout the stay abroad and this sense of disequilibrium may endure after the sojourner returns home. Individuals who suffer from severe adjustment issues may even leave the host environment much earlier than originally planned.

Scholars (e.g., Arthur 2004; Duke 2014; Furnham and Bochner 1986; Jackson 2014, 2016b; Klopf and McCroskey 2007; Nolan 1999; Oberg 1960; Ward 2015; Ward et al. 2001) have identified numerous sources of transition malaise in student sojourners: inadequate preparation, loss of the familiar, unrealistic expectations, abrupt changes (e.g., diet, weather, routines), daily exposure to new signs and symbols (verbal and nonverbal), unexpected differences in sociopragmatic norms of behaviour, sensory overload (e.g., new sights, sounds, smells), exposure to unfamiliar practices (e.g., different ways of teaching and learning), ambiguity and uncertainty, inadequate socio-emotional support, standing out (e.g., being a visible minority for the first time), discrimination or perceptions of discrimination, weak host receptivity (e.g., unfriendly hosts), language fatigue (e.g., the use of a second language in daily life for the first time), frequent miscommunication, conflict in values, change in status or positioning in the new environment (e.g., not performing as well as usual in an unfamiliar academic environment), among others. Several subcategories of 'transition shock' have been identified in the study abroad literature, namely: culture shock, role shock, language shock, and identity or self shock.

Culture Shock

When sojourners cross borders, they travel with the language, values, beliefs, and habits that they developed in their home culture through the process of enculturation or primary socialisation. In a new linguistic, physical, and social environment, it is not unusual for newcomers to experience stress and confusion when confronted with unfamiliar worldviews and behaviours (verbal and nonverbal), just as they may feel some discomfort in new situations in their home country. For some border crossers, this experience can be very unsettling and how they respond can affect the quality of their stay abroad and their willingness to initiate intercultural interactions.

In 1950 anthropologist Cora DuBois coined the term 'culture shock' to refer to the disorientation that anthropologists often experience when entering a new culture to conduct field work (Furnham 2015; Furnham and Bochner 1986; La Brack and Berardo 2007; Ward 2015; Ward et al. 2001). Kalvero Oberg (1960) extended the term to include the transition of any individuals who venture outside their home environment and experience difficulties adjusting to the new culture. Fifteen years later, Adler (1975: 13) described culture shock as 'a set of emotional reactions to the loss of perceptual reinforcements from one's own culture, to new cultural stimuli which have little or no meaning, and to the misunderstanding of new and diverse experiences'.

While the term 'culture shock' is still widely used today, critics maintain that the word 'shock' is too jarring and pejorative. For example, Coleen Ward, a cross-cultural psychologist who has extensively researched and written about intercultural transitions, explains her reservation about the use of this term:

> the term *culture shock* is very limiting in terms of advancing our understanding of the process and outcomes of cross-cultural transition. 'Shock' overemphasizes the negative and threatening aspects of novel situations and the pathological reactions to the unfamiliar. It also ignores the positive growth experiences that can result from intercultural contact and change.
>
> (Ward 2015: 209)

Nonetheless, as this term still frequently appears in orientations for student sojourners as well as in the literature in our field, I will examine some of the dimensions commonly associated with it, especially in relation to study abroad.

Shifting Roles

When students study abroad they are apt to be exposed to roles, procedures, and responsibilities that diverge from what they have grown accustomed to in their home country. Role shock can arise when newcomers experience an abrupt change in status (Arthur 2004; Jackson 2014) and are confronted with unfamiliar norms of behaviour in the new environment (e.g., unwritten 'rules' of politeness in social and academic situations such as norms about when to speak and for how long) (Byrnes 1966; LoCastro 2003; Timpe 2014). Arthur (2004: 17) explains the potential challenges and effects of this aspect of border crossings for student sojourners:

> Role changes and loss of status in the new culture can have a profound impact on the sense of security felt about one's personal identity. Crossing cultures may mean shedding prior roles, usual ways of operating in those roles and building new sources of personal identity.

the new culture in order to meet role expectations.

International students may discover that there are expectations for the behaviour of males and females in the academic arena in the host environment that differ from what they are used to. In some situations, on the basis of their gender (or other personal characteristics), they may be denied access to contexts that are routinely open to them in their home environment; alternatively, domains that are forbidden at home, may be accessible in the host setting. For some newcomers, these differences may be difficult to process and accommodate, at least at first, and for some, role shock can threaten their emotional security, self-identities, and overall sense of well-being.

International exchange students may also find that they are expected to assume more (or less) responsibility for their own learning than what they have grown accustomed to in their home university (e.g., Cortazzi and Jin 2011; Jackson 2013, 2016b; Jin and Cortazzi 2016). For example, in contemporary discussion-based pedagogy or 'flipped classrooms' in the host country, students may be required to view short videotaped lectures (or other multi-media material), digest assigned readings, and then come to class prepared to discuss and apply what they have learned (Carbaugh and Doubet 2016). For study abroad students who are more familiar with didactic or transmission modes of teaching, whereby the lecturer assumes much of the responsibility for student learning, these new expectations may be daunting, at least initially (Jackson and Chen 2017).

The open expression of ideas in fast-paced discussions (often in a second language) and the acceptance of multiple viable solutions to problems may be commonplace in host institutions. These aspects, however, may be disquieting for newcomers who are more familiar with teacher-directed learning and firm conclusions (e.g., the identification of a single best solution to a problem at the end of a lecture or case discussion). New arrivals may also be shocked by differences in the degree of formality in teacher–student relationships (e.g., calling professors by their first name—a practice that would be regarded as overly familiar and rude at home). Without adequate pre-sojourn preparation and support, student sojourners who have a low tolerance for ambiguity and weak coping strategies may find the transition to the new environment unduly stressful and this may adversely impact their learning.

Language Challenges

International educational experience often involves exposure to a language that is not one's mother tongue, especially since the majority of study abroad students are second language speakers of English. Smalley (1963) defines language shock as the difficulties second language speakers may experience when they find themselves in an unfamiliar linguistic environment especially if they are not fluent in the host language. Hile (1979) describes this form of transition shock as 'the frustration and mental anguish that results in being reduced to the level of a two-year-old in one's ability to communicate'. When their language skills are not sufficient to perform basic daily tasks, it can be very frustrating for newcomers. Even if they speak the same first language as host nationals, variations in accent, vocabulary, slang, cultural scripts, norms of politeness, dialects, humour, and communication styles can impede communication, at least initially (Komisarof and Zhu 2016). In the host environment, nonverbal behaviours (e.g., body language, paralanguage, the use of space) can also be confusing for student sojourners. Language and culture-related differences can result in disorientation and discomfort in new arrivals, including student sojourners.

Identity Challenges

Moving to another country to study can also heighten awareness of one's identities and place in the world. Identity or self shock refers to 'the intrusion of inconsistent, conflicting self-images', which can involve 'loss of communication competence', 'distorted self-reflections in the responses of others', and 'the challenge of changing identity-bound behaviors' (Zaharna 1989: 501). As international students encounter unfamiliar values, worldviews, and ways of being, they may experience some confusion about who they are and how they fit into the world around them. Significant events like border crossings (e.g., encountering unfamiliar ways of being, frequently being asked where you are from) can trigger reflection on one's life and positioning (Furnham 2015; Mezirow 1994, 1996, 2009; Zaharna 1989). As students try to make sense of their new environment and communicate their preferred identities and personality in a second language, they may be dismayed to discover that they are not perceived as they would like. Newcomers can easily be misunderstood just as they may misinterpret their local interlocutors. To exacerbate the situation, when students realise that their usual ways of conveying their personality and identities are misunderstood by others, they may not know how to change the situation and enhance their intercultural communication, especially in the first part of their sojourn.

When an individual's preferred self-identity labels are not understood or accepted, it can be very unsettling and even shocking for some newcomers (Iedema and Caldas-Coulthard 2008; Jackson 2014). For example, Korean students may be mis-identified as Chinese when abroad and vice versa, and this can put them in an uncomfortable situation. Second language speakers who perceived themselves to be fluent in the host language before going abroad may be discouraged when they are constantly reminded that they are foreigners because of their accent, vocabulary choice, or physical appearance. (See Chapter 4 for more on contested identities.) Situations like this can result in a bumpy transition to the host environment.

Acculturative Stress

An interesting finding in research on sojourner adjustment is the discovery that individuals do not experience acculturative stress in exactly the same way or to the same degree. Some student sojourners maintain that they have not experienced any transition shock, especially if they have spent most of their free time with co-nationals, conversing in their first language.

Researchers who have examined the adjustment of student sojourners (e.g., Adler 1975; Arthur 2004; Furnham 2010, 2015; Furnham and Bochner 1986; Gebhard 2010; Ward 2015; Ward et al. 2001) have identified multiple factors that help to account for differing responses to an unfamiliar linguistic and cultural environment.

- *Quality of preparation* (degree and quality/accuracy of fact-finding, knowledge about new environment, awareness of the process of intercultural adjustment). Individuals who enter a new environment armed with current information about the host country (e.g., language, history, climate, 'cultures of learning', politics, religious practices, customs, transport system, etc.), and at least a basic understanding of the process of adjustment, are better prepared to face transition issues than those who arrive without having done any groundwork and perhaps have idealised (or overly negative) images of the host country in their heads. International students who have a deeper sense of their positioning as 'temporary strangers' in the host society are apt to be better equipped to deal with the impact of this identity on their intercultural interactions and adjustment in the host environment (Dervin 2013; Murphy-Lejeune 2002).
- *Cultural similarity* (the degree of similarity between one's home culture and the host culture in terms of values, beliefs, language, nonverbal behaviours, customs, 'cultures of learning', etc.). Culture distance refers to 'the degree to which interacting people share meanings. The fewer meanings that are mutually shared, the greater is the cultural distance' (Grove 2015: 195). When there are major cultural differences between one's home country and the host environment, culture shock may be more severe (Ting-Toomey and Chung 2012). For example, students from Wuhan, China may find it more challenging to adjust to Berlin than Singapore. Similarly, a Brazilian may find it easier to adjust to Lisbon than Nairobi, although there are no guarantees that this will be the case as many other factors can affect the adjustment process.

- *Linguistic similarity* (the degree of similarity between one's first language and the host language). Sojourners who speak a romance language like French may find it easier to cope in a Spanish-speaking environment than in a host community where a Semitic language (e.g., Arabic) or East Asian language (e.g., Korean) is the dominant medium of communication. When the language or dialect is from the same family, it is easier to pick up the rhythm of the language as well as the script (written form).
- *Congruence of communication style* (the degree of similarity between one's communication style and those that are widely used in the host culture). Individuals who are most familiar with an indirect style of communication, for example, are apt to find it less challenging to move to an environment where a similar style is widely used (Jackson 2014, 2015a; M.-S. Kim 2015; Nam 2015). If Japanese students opt to study in the Netherlands or another country where more direct styles of communication are favoured, they may find this aspect of their adjustment more difficult, especially if they were not aware of this difference prior to their arrival.
- *Interpersonal dimensions* (e.g., age, fortitude, independence, previous travel, proficiency in the host language, resourcefulness, tolerance for ambiguity). All of these individual traits or personal characteristics can impact one's ability to deal with difficulties that arise in the new environment. Individuals who are more resilient and possess a high tolerance of ambiguity are better positioned to cope with the strains of adjustment (Arthur 2004; Benson 2012; Gao 2015; Ward 2015).
- *Physiological elements* (mental strength and physical condition, medical or dietary issues, ability to tolerate changes in temperature/time zones, resilience). Individuals who are less physically robust (e.g., become ill easily, susceptible to changes in the weather/diet) and not emotionally stable may be more adversely affected by the adjustment process (Arthur 2004; Furnham 2015; Pedersen 1991; Pedersen, Neighbors, Larimer and Lee 2011). Resilience, that is an individual's ability to cope with stress and adversity, can account for differences in the developmental trajectories of student sojourners.
- *Intensity of experience* (the degree of stress related to the border crossing). Intensity factors, that is, 'the set of characteristics related to the person and the context that can intensify the experience of living and working in cultures other than one's own' (Paige 2015a: 444), can bring about differing degrees of acculturative stress and influence the quality of adjustment in the host environment. Personal characteristics may include such aspects as the sojourner's degree of ethnocentrism, host language proficiency, previous international/intercultural experience, personality, and sojourn expectations and aspirations. Situational

factors may include the degree of language and cultural immersion in the host environment, the visibility (or invisibility) of the newcomer in the host environment (e.g., the ability to blend in or stand out due to being ethnically different from the majority), and changes in status and positioning (Paige 2015a; Ward 2015; Ward et al. 2001).

- *Socio-emotional support* (friendship circles, intracultural and multicultural relationships, family support). The strength of a sojourner's bonds with other people (e.g., friends in the host environment) and the amount of socio-emotional support (warmth and nurturance) provided can have a significant impact on how the sojourn unfolds (Y.Y. Kim 2001, 2012, 2015b; Rienties and Jindal-Snape 2016a, 2016b). Newcomers who spend nearly all of their time with co-nationals may benefit from the camaraderie and suffer less acculturative stress; however, this can limit their second language/culture learning and personal growth (e.g., maturity, autonomy). Initially, those who make more of an effort to develop friendships with host nationals may experience more transition stress due to more exposure to new ways of being (e.g., ideas, communication styles, values) but, ultimately, they may benefit much more from the sojourn, especially if the locals they befriend help them to make sense of unfamiliar practices in the host environment. Sojourners who develop meaningful ties with host nationals may become more proficient in the host language, gain a deeper understanding of the host environment, and become more self-reliant and confident (Gareis 2012; Hendrickson et al. 2010; Jackson 2012; Kinginger 2009). Individuals who forge satisfying relationships with international students from other parts of the world may also enhance their linguistic and intercultural communication skills. Shared experiences may help them to understand and support each other. Thus, the diversification of social networks can be an influential element in study abroad adjustment and learning.
- *Agency* (the capacity of individuals to make choices). Learner agency can play a major role in determining how sojourns unfold. Two students with a similar background may be in the host environment at the same time. While one takes advantage of every opportunity possible to interact with locals and practice the host language, the other person constantly pines for home and spends all of his/her free time on Skype complaining to friends and family about the weather, food, local people, etc. in his/her first language. Some sojourners may be overwhelmed by homesickness and feel completely disconnected from local scenes, whereas others may be willing to try new things and invest more time and energy into making friends with host nationals. With a more diverse social network that includes locals, they may more quickly 'fit into' the new environment. Not surprisingly, agentive elements can lead to divergent developmental paths. (Agency is discussed further in Chapter 5.)

- *Degree of control* (amount of control over such aspects as one's move abroad, living conditions in the new environment, sojourn duration, free time, selection of courses, social networks, etc.). Individuals who have chosen to go abroad and wish to optimise their time in the host environment are apt to be more motivated than those who venture abroad for the sole purpose of fulfilling a programme or job requirement. One's degree of autonomy in other aspects (e.g., housing/roommates, selection of courses/host institution/destination) can also result in differences in the ways newcomers view and respond to acculturative stress. Individuals who feel disempowered and constantly under threat in the new environment may find adjustment more challenging (Paige 2015a; Savicki 2015).
- *Geopolitical factors* (relationship between the home country and the host nation; international, national, regional, or local tensions) If newcomers are studying in a region that has strong, favourable ties with their home country (and is portrayed in a positive light in the media in their home country), they may view the host country positively, and this may help them feel secure and well received by host nationals. Conversely, if the host country has tense or hostile relations with their home country, the sojourners may be apprehensive about entering and not be welcomed in the same way.
- *Duration of sojourn and spatial factors* (length of stay, location of residence, geographical locale) Sojourners who reside in an apartment with home nationals and only stay a short time in the host environment are likely to have less opportunity to develop interpersonal relationships with host nationals or other foreign students than those who stay for a longer period of time and live in a homestay or dormitory with locals, although they may not act on affordances. The amount and quality of exposure to the host culture can affect the degree of acculturative stress that sojourners experience (Benson 2017; Dwyer 2004; Furnham 2015; Nerlich 2016; Ward 2015).

A brief review of these elements points to the complexity of intercultural transitions and the adjustment process, and helps to explain variations in the developmental trajectories of student sojourners.

Positive and Negative Consequences of the Adjustment Process

Early conceptions of culture shock were largely negative. Oberg (1960: 177) described it as 'an occupational disease of people who have been transplanted abroad'. This 'disease'-oriented perspective endured for several decades and consequently, pre-sojourn orientations typically centred on ways to avoid this phenomenon. With more recognition of the potentially positive dimensions of the adjustment process, in some institutions of higher education, the focus of pre-sojourn orientations has shifted to productive ways to manage the acculturative stress that naturally occurs as one enters and adjusts to an unfamiliar environment (Furnham 2010, 2015; La Brack 2015; Mikk 2015; Ward 2015).

More scholars now recognise the potential for language and culture-related stress to spur deeper levels of 'whole person' development (e.g., emotional intelligence and resourcefulness, interpersonal communication skills, empathy, intercultural competence, independence, maturity) and identity expansion (e.g., a broadened, more inclusive sense of self, the development of a global outlook) (Jackson 2012; Kim 2001, 2012; Kinginger 2009). Dealing with the challenges of transitions can result in more profound understandings of oneself:

> In the encounter with another culture the individual gains new experiential knowledge by coming to understand the roots of his or her own ethnocentricism and by gaining new perspectives and outlooks on the nature of culture . . . Paradoxically, the more one is capable of experiencing new and different dimensions of human diversity, the more one learns of oneself.
>
> (Adler 1975: 22)

While language and cultural adjustment challenges can be overwhelming for some and, in extreme cases, lead to a hasty exit from the host environment, they also have the potential to bring about substantial learning and personal growth, as noted by Lantis and DuPlaga (2010: 60–1):

> By getting 'culture shocked,' you are challenging yourself, surpassing your comfort zone, and becoming much more aware of your identity and of the world around you. You are building skills, gaining confidence, and forging relationships that surpass your former boundaries. Ultimately, you are learning what it means to be a global citizen.

This notion is in accord with Mezirow's (1994, 2009) transformative learning theory, which suggests that individuals who face a significant event in their lives (e.g., the transition to an unfamiliar linguistic and cultural environment to study abroad) may experience significant personal growth if they take the time to engage in deep, critical reflection (Taylor 2015). (This phenomenon is explained in more detail in Chapter 7.)

When newcomers immerse themselves in the host environment, they have more opportunities to meet host nationals and observe local practices or ways of doing things. Significant contact with local language and cultural practices (as well as the values and ways of being of other international students) can be exhausting and stressful at times (Jackson 2008, 2010; Paige 2015a); however, study abroad researchers have found that the discomfort can also lead to more awareness and understanding of both Self and Other, especially when educators intervene to help sojourners make sense of critical incidents (Jackson 2015b, 2015c; Paige 2015b; Paige and Vande Berg 2012). Firsthand exposure to new communities of practice can compel individuals to reflect on and even question their behaviours, self-identities, values, and beliefs. It can motivate them to master the host language and enhance their intercultural sensitivity, which can ease their transition to the new environment. As sojourners become more tolerant of ambiguity, actively engage in translanguaging, and develop more sophisticated intercultural communication skills, they are apt to experience more satisfying intercultural interactions, which, in turn, can facilitate their adjustment. Successfully dealing with transition challenges can be a source of pride and can help sojourners become more self-confident and independent. This, in turn, can provide the encouragement and confidence they need to undertake longer-term sojourns.

Models of Culture Shock and Adjustment

The U-Curve Adjustment Model

Since the term culture shock was introduced, scholars have created various models to illustrate the process of adjusting to a new culture. One of the earliest and most well-known models is the U-curve adjustment model (Lysgaard 1955), which is illustrated in Figure 3.1.

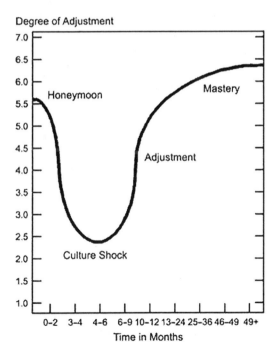

Figure 3.1 The U-curve Adjustment Model

54 Acculturation and Socialisation

This model includes four stages, which have been given various names by different scholars (e.g., Lysgaard 1955; Oberg 1960):

1. The honeymoon stage (initial euphoria): Fascination and excitement about the new culture, curiosity about linguistic and cultural differences, and interest in cultural similarities;
2. Culture stress and shock (crisis and frustration): Confrontation with different values and behaviours, confusion and anxiety, and criticism/rejection of the new language and culture;
3. Adjustment (integration or recovery): the learning of new linguistic, social, and cultural norms, an increase in one's level of comfort and well-being, and respect for the new culture (e.g., different ways of being) and language;
4. Mastery (adaptation and acceptance, biculturalism): awareness and understanding of cultural differences, an increase in autonomy and satisfaction, a dual cultural/linguistic identity.

Re-entry and the W-Curve Adjustment Model

Convinced that returnees often experience a period of adjustment when they return home, Gullahorn and Gullahorn (1963) extended the U-curve model by adding two stages: re-entry or reverse culture shock and resocialisation, the process of re-adjusting one's attitudes and behaviours to feel at ease in one's 'home environment' after a period away (see Figure 3.2).

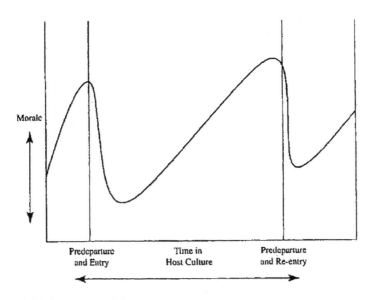

Figure 3.2 The W-curve Adjustment Model

Since then, many versions of their W-shape adjustment model have been proposed (e.g., Kohls 2001; Ting-Toomey and Chung 2012).

Before we review the mounting criticisms of these models, we will take a look at each phase in the W-curve model, since variations of it are still widely used in study abroad programmes.

The Honeymoon Phase (Initial Euphoria)

When sojourners first arrive in the host culture, the curve model suggests that they are generally excited and looking forward to what lies ahead. Similar to the early stage of a romance, newcomers may initially overlook negative aspects of the host culture and take delight in the new sights, sounds, and smells that they encounter.

Hostility Phase

In the model, the second phase is sometimes referred to as 'culture shock', 'crisis stage' or 'disintegration'. After the initial euphoria fades away, sojourners may feel uncomfortable in the host environment. Some may be overwhelmed by the psychological, cognitive, and physical demands of the new culture and the loss of the familiar. Bombarded by stimuli that are difficult to process, excitement may be replaced by disappointment and frustration. In an irritable state, differences between the home culture and host environment are viewed as problems and obstacles to overcome. For example, student sojourners may discover that their roommates have values and practices that they find difficult to accept (e.g., consumption of alcohol, casual sex). In this hostile phase, much of their discourse may be replete with 'us' vs. 'them' comments, with host nationals portrayed unfavourably.

Sojourners may also discover that their second language skills are not as well developed as they had assumed. Studying the language in formal classrooms in their home country may not have prepared them for interpersonal, social situations. Unexpectedly, they may experience difficulty communicating with people from the host culture, especially in informal situations where colloquialisms and humour are frequently used. As well as being mentally and physically exhausting at times, using a second language can make it more challenging to cultivate and sustain multicultural relationships.

When classes get underway, student sojourners may come face to face with differing expectations and learning/teaching styles and long for familiar 'cultures of learning' (Jackson 2013, 2016b; Jackson and Chen 2017; Ryan 2013). The concept 'cultures of learning' encompasses 'taken for granted frameworks of expectations, attitudes, values and beliefs about how to teach or learn successfully and about how to use talk in interaction' (Jin and Cortazzi 2006: 9). In the 'hostility stage', homesickness may set in and sojourners may question their decision to go abroad. A small number who suffer severe symptoms of language and culture shock may head home.

Humourous Stage

The third phase is sometimes termed the 'reorientation and re-integration phase' or 'adjustment and recovery'. The curve model suggests that sojourners in this stage have regained their sense of humour. They have begun to realise that many of the problems that they have experienced in the new environment are due to cultural difference (including their response to it) or language problems rather than deliberate attempts by locals to annoy them. While comparisons are still made between their home and host cultures, this model suggests that the sojourners are more balanced in their views by this stage and more aware of linguistic or cultural differences that may have led to misunderstandings.

With a more positive mindset, sojourners in this phase are better able to interpret subtle linguistic and cultural cues, and may find it easier to express themselves in the host language. At the host university, student sojourners may have started to form friendships with other international students and perhaps some local students as well. These interpersonal connections help them to feel a bit more connected to the local scene. Although better able to function in the host culture, they may still experience difficult days (e.g., occasional bouts of homesickness and malaise).

The 'At Home' Stage

This phase is sometimes referred to as 'adaptation' or 'resolution'. The curve model suggests that sojourners in this stage feel more at home and happy in the host environment. In a more relaxed frame of mind, they demonstrate more understanding and appreciation of the host language and culture and their new way of life. When using the host language in daily life, sojourners are better able to communicate their ideas and feelings in ways that are context-appropriate as their sociopragmatic awareness has increased (Taguchi 2015, 2018). They may actively participate in activities and have a circle of friends they can confide in, which boosts their self-confidence and sense of belonging in the new environment.

By this time, student sojourners may have become more receptive to new 'cultures of learning' as they better understand what lies behind different practices (e.g., fast-paced, discussion-based pedagogy, autonomous learning). With enhanced self-confidence, sojourners in this stage may employ more culturally appropriate problem-solving and conflict mediation techniques. They are more adept at coping with challenges that come their way.

This model also suggests that some sojourners may feel that they have developed a bilingual and bicultural identity by this stage. Biculturalism is

Acculturation and Socialisation 57

characterised by proficiency and comfort with both one's original culture and the culture of the new country or region (Berry 1997; Byram 2012; Fantini 2012a). As noted by Kanno (2003: 3), bilingual individuals may 'incorporate these languages and cultures into their sense of who they are'. (See Chapter 4 for a fuller discussion of the relationship between language, culture, and identity.)

Re-entry or Reverse Culture Shock

Re-entry refers to the process of returning home after spending time abroad (La Brack 2015; Martin and Harrell 2004; Niesen 2010; Smith 2002). The W-curve model suggests that many returnees experience ups and downs that are similar to what they experienced abroad. Re-entry or reverse culture shock may be defined as 'the process of readjusting, reacculturating, and reassimilating into one's own home culture after living in a different culture for a significant period of time' (Gaw 2000: 83–4).

Returnees may experience disorientation, surprise, and confusion when they do not easily fit back into their home environment. This malaise may be due to a variety of reasons (e.g., a shift in perspectives, boredom with the familiar, appreciation of the host country's customs or values, idealised images of the home country formed while abroad). The shock of re-entry can sometimes be more severe than the malaise that the individual experienced while adjusting to the host country, in part because it is not expected (Kartoshkina 2015; La Brack 2015; Martin and Harrell 2004; Smith 2002; Szkudlarek 2010). After all, the sojourner is returning 'home'.

In the beginning, those who more fully integrated into the host culture (e.g., made close friends with host nationals or other international students) and functioned well in the host language in their daily life, may find it more difficult to re-adjust to their home culture and first language use in daily life. They may miss their more independent lifestyle and friends made abroad, and find it difficult to fit back into the rhythm of local life.

While excited to share their experiences, returnees may find that their friends and family quickly tire of their international stories. Disillusioned, returnees may consider host nationals boring and provincial; they may long for the life they had during the sojourn and view it through rose-coloured glasses. They may miss not being able to converse as much in their second language as they did while abroad. Their discourse may be full of complaints about their home culture. This time, 'us' vs 'them' discourse may elevate all aspects in the host culture and denigrate local ways of being.

Returnees may realise they have changed but find it difficult to put into words. They may feel torn between the values and behaviours of the host country and their home environment. Some may suffer from identity confusion, that is, they may feel as if they are caught between two distinct worlds, the one they left behind and the one they have returned to. They may not feel that they fit into either.

Resocialisation Stage

The final phase in the model is sometimes referred to as 're-integration', 'the independence stage' or 'acceptance and understanding'. In this stage, returnees are beginning to feel more at home and are better able to communicate effectively and appropriately with their family members, friends, and colleagues. Similar to recovery and adjustment phases in the host country, the returnees start to re-adjust to the home country and reintegrate into the local way of life. The initial re-entry shock has subsided and they are better able to find a sense of balance between their 'new old' home and the culture they have just left.

Returnees may take pride in having developed a hybrid, multicultural identity and display more interest in both international and local happenings. The W-curve model suggests that returnees in this stage are able to identify and appreciate multiple ways in which they have changed for the better due to their international and intercultural experiences. They may make an effort to diversify their social networks to include both local and international friends, and maintain contact with friends made abroad. Feeling more stable and self-confident, they may make plans for further stays abroad.

Criticisms of the U-and W-Curve Adjustment Models

In addition to the criticisms of the term 'culture shock' that were explained earlier in the chapter, a number of scholars have identified problems with the use of the curve models of adjustment. While the U-curve and W-curve adjustment models (or variations of them) are still employed in some programmes to prepare students for study abroad, researchers have discovered that many people experience developmental trajectories that differ from what is portrayed in these models. As many scholars point out (e.g., Berardo 2006, 2012; Church 1982; La Brack 2010, 2011, 2015; La Brack and Berardo 2007; Machart and Lim 2014; Ward 2015; Ward, Okura, Kennedy and Kojima 1998; Ward et al. 2001), the curves of adjustment models are not backed up by empirical research. While some study abroad students may experience the phases that they depict, the reality is that these models cannot accurately predict the occurrence or degree of culture shock.

Questions are also being raised about the applicability of the curved models of adjustment for several sub-types of study abroad students: heritage students, individuals who have had considerable international experience before studying abroad, and refugees. The term 'heritage students' refers to those who study abroad in an environment that is associated (e.g., culturally, linguistically, historically) with their family or cultural background (Forum on Education Abroad 2011: 34), whereas 'global nomads' are individuals who live a mobile and international lifestyle. 'Third culture kids' are students who have spent a significant part of their developmental years outside their parent's culture or country of birth (Pollock and Van Reken 2009; Schaetti 2015; for a critical review of the notion see Benjamin and Dervin 2015). In La Brack's (2011) estimation, the W-curve model 'does not fit the global nomads and third culture kids (TCKs) very well, nor does it fit "heritage-seeking" students or education abroad populations from refugee/immigrant backgrounds' (p. 2).

In mixed-method and ethnographic investigations of student sojourners (summer immersion, semester-and year-long sojourners) from Greater China, Jackson (2008, 2010, 2012, 2013, 2016c, 2016d, 2017a) found that some sojourners endured significant ups and downs while abroad, whereas others did not. Some experienced acculturative stress during their sojourn, while others claimed that their transition to the new environment had been smooth and stress-free. Some suffered from identity confusion and disequilibrium while abroad, whereas others felt confident about their sense of self and positioning throughout their sojourn. The amount and quality of contact with the host language and culture (e.g., access to local communities of practice) varied considerably among the student sojourners and this affected the quality and amount of their language and intercultural learning. Some sojourners formed close bonds with host nationals, benefited from translanguaging, and became more fluent in the host language while their peers clung to friends from their home country and returned home with less desire to initiate intercultural interactions or use their second language outside of class. Their developmental trajectories varied considerably, providing further evidence of the idiosyncratic nature of study abroad.

The degree of re-entry culture shock also varies among student sojourners. Some return home with higher levels of intercultural sensitivity and a strong desire to use their second language in intercultural interactions; they may continue to seek out opportunities to initiate intercultural dialogue. Convinced that they have developed a more cosmopolitan, multicultural persona, they may take pride in the acquisition of characteristics and behaviours commonly associated with global citizenship (Byram and Parmenter 2015). With heightened interest in international affairs, they may take further steps towards a global sense of self. In contrast, other returnees are very negative about their sojourn experiences; they may have become even more ethnocentric and hyper nationalistic during their stay abroad. Overwhelmed by culture difference and ill-equipped to manage language and culture shock, they may have returned home with reinforced stereotypes of host nationals, heightened xenophobia, and little interest in further developing the social dimension of their second language proficiency (Coleman 2013; Jackson 2008, 2010, 2012; Kinginger 2009).

A complicated mix of individual elements (e.g., agency, sojourn aims, adaptive stress, personality, resilience, mindset, awareness of language and culture learning strategies), level of intercultural competence, and external factors (e.g., degree of host receptivity, housing arrangement, exposure to host culture, power imbalance) account for differences in the developmental trajectories of sojourners and significant variations in sojourn outcomes (Y.Y. Kim 2001, 2005, 2012, 2015b). (See Chapter 5 for more discussion on individual differences and environmental factors that can impact study abroad.)

As noted by Coleman (2009); Benson (2012); Jackson (2012); Kinginger (2009); Härkönen and Dervin (2015) and other language and study abroad researchers, the experience of sojourners is much more complex and variable than what is suggested by the curves of adjustment models. Consequently, study abroad scholars call for more longitudinal, mixed-methods research or ethnographic (and other qualitative) studies that capture the 'whole person' development of sojourners before, during, and after stays abroad (Coleman 2013; Jackson 2012). We also need more studies that adopt a critical perspective and eschew 'the culture as nation' orientation, which all too often dominates the literature on sojourner adjustment and adaptation.

Despite the limitations detailed above, variations of the U-and W-curve adjustment models remain popular in pre-sojourn orientations, sojourn support programmes, and re-entry debriefings as they are simple to grasp and seem plausible. In light of recent research, however, more educators regard these models as 'useful heuristic devices to raise issues related to cultural adjustment but no longer present them as phases that everyone will automatically experience' (Forum on Education Abroad 2011: 41). Although the curves models cannot accurately predict the developmental trajectories of sojourners, educators who use them maintain that they can help to raise awareness of the *potential* ups and downs that students might experience in the host environment and after they return home.

Implications for Study Abroad Programming

For decades, many institutions of higher education focused their attention and resources on increasing participation rates in study abroad programmes to meet their internationalisation agenda. Administrators and educators generally assumed that participants would quickly adjust to the host environment and become fully immersed in the host environment. Myths of study abroad have long promoted the idea that students will become more global-minded, develop fluency in the host language, and cultivate meaningful multicultural friendships (Abdallah-Pretceille 1999; Dervin 2008, 2013; Coleman 2013; Härkönen and Dervin 2015, 2016; Holmes et al. 2015; Jackson 2012); as a consequence, institutions of higher education have been sending many students abroad with little or no guidance or intercultural preparation.

Nowadays, systematic investigations of the learning and intercultural experiences of student sojourners are raising more awareness of differences in the ways sojourns unfold. Some students gradually feel at ease in the host environment, take an active role in local communities of practice, and experience significant growth in intercultural sensitivity, global-mindedness and second language proficiency. In contrast, others may be overwhelmed by the move abroad and retreat to the safety of their in-group. While some take full advantage of affordances in the host environment, others miss out on opportunities for personal growth, meaningful multicultural relationships, and identity expansion. A number of studies have heightened awareness of the limited meaningful intercultural interactions on campus, suggesting that many of the common aims of internationalisation are not being realised simply by increasing participation in study abroad programmes (Brown 2009; Jackson and Oguro 2018b; Leask 2009; Montgomery 2010).

More aware of the adjustment challenges facing student sojourners, educators in many parts of the world are developing creative intercultural interventions to better prepare and support students at all stages of the study abroad cycle (e.g., Carroll 2015; Jackson 2015b, 2015c; Jackson and Oguro 2018a; Lou, Vande Berg and Paige 2012; Plews and Misfeldt 2018). Efforts are also being made to enhance the intercultural sensitivity and receptivity of host nationals. (See Chapter 7 for descriptions of innovative intercultural interventions in international education and more information about internationalisation at home initiatives.)

Conclusion

I began this chapter by defining terms and concepts associated with the adjustment process and drew attention to various factors that can lead to differences in the acculturation and second language socialisation of study abroad students. Researchers from diverse disciplinary backgrounds have identified a number of internal and external factors that can lead to differences in the adjustment process and the quality of international educational experience and, ultimately, result in disparate sojourn outcomes (e.g., differing degrees of translanguaging and intercultural competence development).

In this chapter, I also critiqued some of the well-known models of sojourner adjustment and highlighted the idiosyncratic, multifarious nature of study abroad. To ease the adjustment of student sojourners and optimise their learning in the host environment, more and more educators and administrators are recognising the need for research-driven, theory-based pedagogical interventions in study abroad programmes.

Many of the studies that were cited in this chapter have drawn attention to the various ways in which identity elements can influence the adjustment, sense of belonging, and second language socialisation of student sojourners. International students who open themselves up to affordances in the host environment and actively engage in translanguaging may broaden their social networks and experience a broadening of their sense of self. In the next chapter, identity issues in relation to international educational experience are discussed in more detail.

Further Reading and Resources

Kim, Y.Y. (2001) *Becoming Intercultural: An Integrative Theory of Communication and Cross-Cultural Adaptation*, Thousand Oaks, CA: Sage Publications.

In this monograph, the author draws on research findings to create a theory that draws attention to multifarious internal (e.g., psychological) and environmental factors (e.g., host receptivity) that can influence the intercultural transitions and cross-cultural adaptation of border crossers (e.g., immigrants, refugees, sojourners).

Kinginger, C. (2009) *Language Learning and Study Abroad: A Critical Reading of Research*, Basingstoke, UK: Palgrave MacMillan.

In this volume, the author reviews investigations of language learning in study abroad settings, noting the advantages and constraints of various research designs. In the process, readers develop awareness of multiple elements that can foster or hinder sojourner adjustment and language learning.

Kinginger, C. (ed) (2013) *Social and Cultural Aspects of Language Learning in Study Abroad*, Amsterdam and Philadelphia: John Benjamins Publishing Company.

This edited collection includes case studies that offer insight into the language and intercultural adjustment issues that study abroad students may face.

Vande Berg, M., Paige, R.M. and Lou, K.H. (eds) (2012) *Student Learning Abroad: What our Students Are Learning, What They're Not and What We Can Do about It*, Sterling, VA: Stylus Publishing.

In this edited collection, many of the chapters describe the challenges student sojourners may encounter as they prepare for international educational experience and adjust to the host environment. Some chapters also explain re-entry challenges.

4 Language, Identity, and Interculturality

Fred Dervin and Jane Jackson

Introduction

The concept of identity is probably one of the most important and researched concepts in the social and human sciences today. It has also received widespread interest by the public and titillated the media (Sen 2006: 1). In many studies of interculturality, identity has taken over and somewhat substituted the contested concept of *culture* in order to reflect 'critical questions to do with access, power, desire, difference and resistance' (Pennycook 2001: 6). Identity goes hand in hand with other concepts, which affect all societies: inclusion, equality/equity, and social justice. It is thus a very relevant concept for study abroad. Besides potentially transforming students, study abroad inevitably leads to implicit/explicit involvement with these phenomena.

Identity is a highly interdisciplinary concept. Sociologists, philosophers, anthropologists, and linguists, among others, have discussed, debated, and analysed identity. Identity has been central in the so-called 'hard sciences', in, for example, research on genetics and epigenetics (Mukherjee 2016). Psychologists have also extensively addressed identity issues. Erikson's (1968) seminal work on ego identity deals with a subjective feeling of consistency and continuity of self across situations. Social psychologists such as Moscovici (1961/1976) have insisted on the importance of belonging to groups in strengthening people's identity. For Sen (2006: 1) 'a sense of identity can [thus] be a source not merely of pride and joy, but also of strength and confidence'. Yet, as we shall see in this chapter, identity is an unstable process which is context-and interlocutor-dependent, of which one is not always in control. Identity has been described as *imagined, transformed, repositioned, affiliated, disaffiliated, brought about, contested* and *resisted*—sometimes with all of these elements simultaneously (Benson, Barkhuizen, Bodycott and Brown 2013; Dervin and Risager 2015; Jackson 2014). Identity can also lead to conflict, unequal power relations, and forms of discrimination (the 'dark' sides of identity) (Jackson 2014; Samovar, Porter and McDaniel 2010).

This chapter helps the reader to reflect on what is meant by identity and discusses what researchers have discovered about the influence of identity elements (e.g., gender, age, language, cultural, sexual orientation, social) on interculturality in relation to the positioning and learning of student sojourners. We discuss the potential impact of social networks and social identities on intercultural competence development. Our review also highlights the 'dark' sides of identity, the challenge of contested identities, and the potential for identity reconstruction/expansion (e.g., hybrid selves, global selves, multilingual selves) through intercultural engagement, reflection, and study abroad. We also problematise imaginaries about identity in study abroad research and practice. In our discussion, we underscore the multifarious nature of language, identity, and interculturality in relation to study abroad. We conclude the chapter with suggestions for researchers of identity and interculturality in study abroad contexts.

Positioning Language and Identity

Identity refers to one's self-concept or sense of self. Simply put, it defines how individuals view themselves or imagine their positioning in the world. Understandings of identity have evolved over time. In contrast with early identity theorists who portrayed identity as fixed and unitary (Erikson 1968; Joseph 2016), poststructuralists tend to use the plural form 'identities' in recognition of the complex, multiple strands of selfhood (Baxter 2016). Norton and Toohey (2002) offer examples to highlight differences in the ways individuals are conceived.

> While humanist conceptions of the individual—and many definitions of the individual in SLA research—presuppose that every person has an essential, unique, fixed and coherent 'core' (introvert/extrovert; motivated/ unmotivated), poststructuralism depicts the individual—the subject—as diverse, contradictory, dynamic and changing over historical time and space.
>
> (Norton and Toohey 2002: 121)

Poststructuralist orientations position individuals (e.g., student sojourners) as 'social agents' who have some responsibility for their own learning. Drawing attention to the fluid or dynamic nature of identity, cultural theorist and sociologist Stuart Hall (1990: 222) writes:

> Identity is not as transparent or unproblematic as we think. Perhaps instead of thinking of identity as an already accomplished fact, which the new cultural practices then represent, we should think instead of identity as a 'production,' which is never complete, always in process and always constituted within, not outside representation.

Poststructuralists observe that people have many dimensions to their sense of self (e.g., linguistic, personal, social, cultural, gender) that may change as they mature and gain life experience, such as exposure to multiple languages and diverse ways of being while studying abroad. Students who are members of the majority group in their home environment may give little thought to their identities until they travel or study abroad and/or experience life as a minority for the first time. Being different from the majority may stimulate deeper contemplation about multiple dimensions of their identities (e.g., cultural, ethnic, linguistic, religious, national) and lead to a higher level of self-awareness. Hence, the phenomenon of identity change or reconstruction is often associated with transformative experience, that is life events that may provoke reflection on one's sense of self (Mezirow 2009; Ting-Toomey 2015). (Chapter 7 explains that this 'transformation' may not occur in study abroad students without some form of intercultural intervention; international experience alone may be insufficient to propel students to a higher level of intercultural awareness and competence.)

Depending on the situation and context, individuals may stress different dimensions of their sense of self. Identity salience refers to 'the degree to which an identity is prominent or stands out to us in a given situation' (Oetzel 2009: 59). The prominence of a particular identity can influence an individual's affective state and behaviour as each identity carries with it certain understandings (e.g., knowledge), beliefs, associations (e.g., memories) and expectations. Some elements of an individual's identity may become more salient or meaningful in particular social situations, depending, in part, on the communication partner(s), the discourse, and the context. For example, the quality of the relationship between interlocutors can impact which aspects of an individual's self are emphasised at a particular point in time.

The relationship between identity, language, and culture is multifarious. As Baxter (2016) explains, 'reciprocally, identities are constructed by and through language but they also produce and reproduce innovative forms of language' (p. 34). Many dimensions of our social and cultural identities (e.g., gender, class, nationality, ethnicity) are shaped by the language(s) we speak. During the socialisation process (enculturation), self-identities emerge through linguistic practice and performance, and are reinforced through social interactions with people in one's family and the wider community. Identities continue to evolve as people experience life (e.g., gain study abroad experience).

National Affiliation and the Instability of Identity

National identity and culture have been the centre of attention in study abroad since the 20th century. When students cross national borders, they are often considered representatives of a nation state, symbolised by the passport they carry. Many contemporary institutions of higher education and organisations that fund international educational experience stress this dimension in their websites and related materials that promote their study abroad programmes. While in the host country, student sojourners may see themselves as 'cultural or national ambassadors' (Dolby 2004, 2005, 2007; Jackson 2015d; Patron 2007) and feel under some pressure to convey a positive image of their home country and home institution, even if they have not been prodded to assume these roles. In contrast, other student sojourners may reject this identification and prefer to be viewed as independent from a regional or national affiliation and the baggage that comes with it (e.g., political, religious, social, linguistic, ethnic).

The idea of national identity and culture is a remnant of Modernity which emerged in the 18th century. National borders started to be established then and passports and national identity cards began to serve as 'proofs of identity' for cross-border activities. For Zygmunt Bauman (2004: 23), national identity was never treated like other identities. He adds (ibid.): 'Unlike other identities that did not demand unequivocal allegiance and exclusive fidelity, national identity would not recognize competition, let alone an opposition' (p. 23). This has led to two world wars and to the extermination of those who did not fit into the national 'boxes' determined by this identity in the 20th century. Although the end of the Second World War marked the beginning of a postmodern and postcolonialist world (Maffesoli 1988), national identity and its spectres are enmeshed in today's globalisation. In her book *Internationalism, National Identities, and Study Abroad: France and the United States, 1890–1970*, Walton (2009) offers a diachronic study of educational travel between a European country (France) and the United States. The author charts the meanings and changing purposes of study abroad in this crucial modern and emerging postmodern era. She also shows how the issue of national identity has evolved in relation to study abroad in the last 100 years.

The emphasis on national identity in the research methodologies employed in cross-border studies is referred to as 'methodological nationalism' or the use/naturalisation of the nation state as the principal and only identity marker to examine intercultural encounters (Amelina, Devrimsel, Faist and Schiller 2012). Methodological nationalism represents a bias which can lead to essentialism (Holliday 2010), which Gelman (2003: 3) defines as 'the view that categories have an underlying reality or true nature that one cannot observe directly but that gives an object its identity'. In other words, essentialism makes us believe that individuals and groups have 'essences' that dictate who they are, how they behave, and what they think. Sen (2006: xv) summarises well the idea of essentialism with the expression 'the illusion of a unique and choiceless identity'. For de Singly (2003: 81) methodological nationalism represents a potential 'abuse of power' or a 'form of totalitarism', which rids individuals of their agency.

The sociologist Zygmunt Bauman (2004) has characterised identity as being 'solid' and/or 'liquid', referring to people's essentialist tendencies (solid) and more open and constructionist aspects of identity (liquid). In fact, we could use the metaphor of 'liquid crystals' to characterise identity. Liquid crystals have both properties of liquids and solid crystals. Our times of accelerated globalisation, whereby individuals, ideas, objects, technologies, etc. circulate faster than ever, have led to many people losing their bearings in their own society thus, often, resorting to 'solidify' their national identity (Appadurai 1996, 2006). Like Berthoz (2009: 8), we could compare this to the Ancient Greek hero Theseus who is lost in a labyrinth without a clew (a ball of thread) to find his way out. The clew represents the nation state that can save people from being crushed by complexity. At the same time, accelerated globalisation allows people to explore their identity and to renegotiate it almost unceasingly (Amselle 2010). This leads us to several important characteristics of identity: It is always emergent, contradictory, and performed and thus 'inescapably diverse' (Sen 2006: 4).

In their 2014 article, Young, Barrett, Young-Rivera, and Lovejoy maintain that study abroad experience has a clear impact on students' self-images that are associated with personal identity (see self-transformations in Ellwood 2009, 2011) but very little about the way they identify with their home country. Interestingly, in contrast, other studies (e.g., with non-Europeans) have found that study abroad students may develop a stronger attachment to a national or regional identity (imagined conception of home nation or region) while in the host country especially if they do not feel welcomed or they spend all of their free time with co-nationals (e.g., Brown 2009; Hail 2015; Jackson 2015d). The disparate findings highlight the complexity of the relationship between self-identities (e.g., attachment to a national identity) and study abroad experience. (See Chapter 5 for more discussion on the many internal and external elements that can lead to differing sojourn outcomes, including variations in how students see themselves and their positioning in the world.)

To summarise, one could say that constancy and stability (national identity) as well as inconsistency and unpredictability (a dynamic quality) characterise identity (Lifton 1993: 1). In what follows we discuss how this contradiction occurs.

The Politics of Identity: Ascription and Avowal

As asserted earlier, identity is malleable. This does not mean, however, that people can change their identity the way they want to or always be viewed as they wish. The identities of individuals are affected by how other individuals or groups define or label them (e.g., 'put them into boxes'). An avowed identity is the one that individuals wish to present or claim in an interaction. As Oetzel (2009) explains, avowal refers to 'the process of telling others what identity(ies) you wish to present or how you see yourself' (p. 62). For example, when interacting with co-nationals abroad, student sojourners may prefer to converse in their common first language to signal the strength of in-group bonds and facilitate the communication process. In some situations, a student may also be reluctant to use the host language when in the company of 'ingroup members' for fear of being 'outgrouped' and labelled a show-off (Jackson 2014). The use of a particular language, dialect or communication style can serve as a powerful identity marker. Not surprisingly, the issue of language choice has captured the attention of many sociolinguists (e.g., Meyers-Scotton 2006).

Individuals and groups can freely select some dimensions of their identities that they wish to present to others. For example, people may convey a particular image of themselves through adornments, speech, communication style, or dress; however, people are not entirely free to adopt any identities they want. The perception of others impacts how individuals are viewed and positioned in a specific situation and context. An ascribed identity is the one that other people assign or give to us. Oetzel (2009) defines ascription as 'the process of assigning in another person what you think his or her identity should be' (p. 62). Factors such as language, accent, ethnicity, age, dress, skin colour, social class, communication style, and gender, among others, can influence how others see and categorise us. Consequently, a sojourner's preferred identities may not be the ones that are recognised and respected by others, which can be an irritant in intercultural interactions. When attempts to express one's identity preferences are repeatedly overlooked, it can become a source of friction and a barrier to constructive intercultural relations.

The term 'contested identity' refers to facets or elements of one's identity that are not accepted by the people we are in contact with. In some circles, the identity an individual wishes to project (e.g., English language self) may not be fully recognised and accepted by locals (first language speakers). That is, it may be contested or challenged. For example, after living abroad for many months, an international exchange student may feel at home in the host environment and begin to feel a part of the local scene. Nevertheless, her accent, physical appearance, temporary status, and lack of familiarity with some of the local social norms may set her apart from locals who persist in viewing her as an outsider or foreigner.

It always takes the presence, influence and pressure of an Other to (re)position, resist, bring about and (dis-)affiliate identity—in other words, to 'do identity' (Howarth 2002). According to Gallagher (2011: 492), research on identity therefore should cover the aspects of *self-in-the-other* and *other-in-the-self*. R. D. Laing (1961: 81) argues that, without these continua, identity is 'distorted'. He adds (ibid.: 86):

A person's own 'identity' cannot be completely abstracted from his identity-for-others. His identity-for-himself; the identity others ascribe to him; the identities he ascribes to them; the identity or identities he thinks they attribute to him; what he thinks they think he thinks they think.

The extent to which identity is 'done' also depends on the context: (macro level) one's country, a foreign country, a 'third' country; (micro level) a pub, a shop, a university lecture hall, a dorm room, a homestay, etc. Depending on these contexts and the interlocutor(s), identity might be triggered in different ways: to one's benefit or detriment (stereotypes, positive/negative evaluations, xenophobia/xenophilia and even racism, evoking the 'dark' sides of identity). The interdependence with the other for identity work is often referred to as the 'politics of identity' (Kaufmann 2014; Khan 2005). The very root of the word interculturality, *inter-*, reflects this central aspect of identity. When two people from different countries meet, like in any other form of human interaction, they negotiate different kinds of identities, often starting from their national identity ('Where are you from?'). At first, individuals might reveal a preference for their own national group and employ comparative discourses about cultures that position their group as 'superior' to others. This phenomenon, which is characterised by frequent 'us vs. them' discourse is called 'ethnocentrism'. In this monocultural orientation, 'one's own culture is central to reality and serves as the point of reference for evaluating and interpreting other cultures' (Paige and Bennett 2015: 521).

Social Networks and the Social Dimension of Identity

For the social psychologist Tajfel (1981: 256) an individual from a particular group might 'seek membership of new groups if these groups have some contribution to make to the positive aspect of his social identity'. In the context of study abroad this might be a group representing the 'local' identity, other national groups or a mix of these groups. Thus, the evolving social networks of study abroad students are a subject that has garnered the attention of a growing number of contemporary researchers (e.g., Mitchell 2015; Rienties and Jindal-Snape 2016b). A social network may be defined as 'a structure comprised of individuals who are connected with others by one or more specific types of interdependence, such as friendship, kinship, or common interests' (Dewey, Ring, Gardner and Belnap 2013: 114).

Research on the social networks of student sojourners has underscored the need to pay close attention to the relationship between language identity, community involvement (e.g., friendship ties, access to local communities of practice), second language socialisation, and translanguaging

(Li 2011; Mitchell 2015; Pérez-Vidal and Howard 2014; Shiri 2015). A 'community of practice' refers to 'an aggregate of people who come together around mutual engagement in some common endeavour. Ways of doing things, ways of talking, beliefs, values, power relations—in short, practices—emerge in the course of their joint activity around the endeavour' (Eckert and McConnell-Ginet 1992: 464). Within this framework, the second language socialisation of newcomers is regarded as a process of gradually gaining competence and membership in a given community (e.g., a student organisation at the host institution, homestay), provided there is adequate access.

Within study abroad contexts, investigations in the United States and the UK have found that the quality and diversity of the social networks that student sojourners develop can affect their academic, intercultural, language, psychological, and social development (Dewey et al. 2012, 2013; Mitchell 2015). Similarly, Kinginger's (2010, 2011) investigations of American learners of French in France, Trentman's (2015) study of American learners of Arabic in Egypt, and Jackson's (2011, 2016c, 2016d, 2017a) investigations of Chinese study abroad students in English-speaking countries are just a few of the many studies that have sought to better understand how social networks can play a role in the language and intercultural development and identity reconstruction of student sojourners.

Dervin (2008) notes a tendency amongst Erasmus students to avoid contact with people from their own national group, believing that such contact is counterproductive for language and culture learning. Härkönen and Dervin (2015) observed a clear hierarchy in the desire to mix with the Other, whereby the 'local' is a priority, other international students hold a second place and people of the same nationality represent the least desirable individuals who seem to provide students with a negative identity (e.g., they are not open-minded and/or curious enough).

The Erasmus programme has explicit goals, with a clear emphasis on intercultural interactions, and this may help to explain why Härkönen and Dervin's (2015) findings differ from many other studies that have examined the social networks of study abroad students. While it is common for students to express the desire to make friends with host nationals prior to venturing abroad, researchers in many parts of the world have discovered that study abroad students often spend nearly all their free time with co-nationals and end up having a 'bubble experience' abroad. Alternatively, student sojourners may seek out international students from different parts of the world due to common interests and experiences. A smaller number of newcomers cultivate meaningful relationships with host nationals, in part due to the difficulty of breaking into well-established social circles, especially since local students may not feel the need to develop relationships with them (Hendrickson, Rosen and Aune 2010; Jackson 2012; Montgomery 2010).

With more recognition of the potential impact of social networks (diversity, strength, quality of interactions) on the identities and sense of belonging of student sojourners, the number of researchers who are exploring this dimension in various study abroad contexts continues to grow (e.g., Hendrickson et al. 2010; Mitchell 2015; Mitchell, Tracy-Ventura and McManus 2017; Trentman 2015). (Chapter 5 explores some of the internal and external elements that can lead to varying degrees of exposure to local communities of practice, host nationals, and international students from home and other parts of the world. These factors, in turn, can influence how study abroad students see themselves and invest in language and intercultural learning and the diversification of their social networks.)

Much of the literature on study abroad centres on the importance of meaningful intercultural interactions between domestic and international students; however, it is also essential to recognise the value of social connections between international students from different parts of the world. Intercultural interactions of this nature can prompt newcomers to think more about their place in the world (e.g., how they are viewed by others, how they see themselves, how they are changing as they gain more real-world experience) and also provide additional practice in a second language (e.g, the use of English as a lingua franca among Korean and Malaysian international exchange students in Hong Kong). Interactions with co-nationals can also be beneficial; they can ease acculturative stress (e.g., provide socio-emotional support and camaraderie), and potentially provide encouragement for the seeking out of multicultural relationships in the host environment.

The Multifarious, Multifaceted Nature of Identity

At a more micro level of interpersonal encounters, identity is much more complex (see the aforementioned metaphor of the liquid crystal) as it is also often a matter of discovery. The notion of intersectionality is very useful here. For many scholars, examining identity from a predominating framework is somewhat inadequate (e.g., national or cultural identity) and simplifies identity work. As a stranger in a foreign land, the experience of a foreign student does not make sense if it is not examined within social structures that are interlocking (see Collins 1990). Dimensions such as gender, social class, religion, sexuality, but also race and ethnicity, are all social constructs that contribute to people 'doing' identity together, and in relation to larger structures of potential oppression and privilege. Wimmer and Glick Schiller (2002: 324) argue: '[m]uch of transnational studies overstates the internal homogeneity and boundedness of transnational communities; they overestimate the binding power for individual action; they overlook the importance of cross-community interactions as well as the internal divisions of class, gender, religion and politics'.

Researchers have concentrated on various aspects of identity and participation in study abroad research (Jackson 2008; Kinginger 2011, 2013, 2015; Patron 2007). For instance, Shames and Alden (2005) have examined the impact of short-term study abroad on the identity changes of students with learning disabilities and/or ADHD. Brux and Fry (2010) explain that students of colour (whom they refer to as 'multicultural students') rarely participate in study abroad programmes because of financial and administrative issues, amongst others. In another example, Bryant and Soria (2015) concentrate on the study abroad experience of bisexual, gay or lesbian, questioning, self-identified queer, transgender, and gender queer students (LGBTQQ).

The concept of power, another central concept in the human and social sciences today, thus becomes essential to pinpoint the interconnectedness of identities, privileges, and structures (Dill and Zambrana 2009). Several aspects of power relations in intercultural encounters need unpacking to understand what is happening. For instance, it is important to be aware of the ideologies, symbols, and images that each participant in an intercultural encounter holds of each other, in terms of different identities (male/female/other; atheist/Muslim/Lutheran; first language speaker/second language speaker, etc.) and to examine how these become relevant in the way they talk to each other and treat each other. Brah and Phoenix (2004: 76) refer to these as 'multiple axes of differentiation'. As identity in *inter*-culturality relies on the presence of two people *a minima*, in order to study it, 'what we must ask is "*Identity in whose eyes?*"' (Howarth 2002: 20). Dolby's (2005) study is interesting in this regard—although it has the potential to lead to some form of essentialising. In her article, she compares the impact of study abroad on Australian and American undergraduates. Because of their different symbolic power in the world—the author claims that American students have a strong national identity while Australians' national affiliation is weak—Australian students are more prone to a robust global sense of place. In her analysis, however, she also observes that they are less willing to tolerate racial and ethnic diversity than American students.

Imaginaries About Identity in Study Abroad

For better and/or worse, as far as we know, intercultural engagement during study abroad has the potential to lead to identity reconstruction and expansion (e.g., the cultivation of a cosmopolitan, global mindset, the strengthening a regional identification) and is part of the 'unstoppable experimentation' of people's identity building (Bauman 2004: 85). It is noteworthy that since the early 2000s the use of social media such as Facebook, WeChat or Twitter have become fully integrated into many study abroad contexts and they, too, contribute to identity experimentation abroad.

An increasing number of contemporary studies deal with social media in study abroad. In 2016 Forbush and Foucault-Welles published a paper that explored the impact of the use of Social Networking Sites (SNSs) by Chinese students in the US. They report that the more SNSs are used to link up with the host country before and during the stay, the more significant the levels of social and academic adaptation are. This, in turn, enables the students to negotiate more complex identities by the end of their stay abroad. In another similar study, Mikal, Yang and Lewis (2015) note that social media can alleviate stress, and support 'integration' and learning while abroad. In *'Oh, I'm Here!': Social Media's Impact on the Cross-cultural Adaptation of Students Studying Abroad* Sandel (2014) analyses in-depth interviews with students abroad about their use of social media and online communication. Interestingly the author notes that social media can serve as 'identity buffers' with both the host country and distant family members, and thus support their identity work.

Study abroad experience might also influence and shift students' 'habitual ego' (Wilkinson 1998: 2). Zamani-Gallaher, Leon and Lang (2016) talk about 'study abroad as self-authorship'. For instance, a student may usually identify as shy and modify his/her representation of self after some time abroad. It is vital to note, however, that this does not happen automatically. Further, Howarth (2002: 19) explains that 'there are limits to how far we can opt in and out of identities'. She gives the examples of skin colour and gender of which 'the gaze of the other makes these identities unavoidable' (ibid.). You may recall our earlier discussion of contested identities. Some studies have compared the self-identity shifts of students who have studied abroad with those who studied in their home country. For example, in Europe, Jacobone and Moro's (2014) compared the self-identities of Erasmus students with those who remained on the home campus and found that those with study abroad experience developed a stronger sense of a European identity and provided evidence of a deeper level of cultural and language learning.

Interestingly, there are also a certain number of (old and new) imaginaries about identity in discourses about the benefits of study abroad. Imaginaries correspond to the way(s) one imagines one's social existence (Taylor 2004). Imaginaries are often based on specific ideologies that represent how individuals view their 'real conditions of existence' (Althusser 1971: 162). One of the most widespread imaginaries is based on the idea that study abroad allows students to find their identity/their self. This very old ideology seems to relate to the Ancient Greek aphorism γνῶθι σεαυτόν ('know thyself') from the Temple of Apollo at Delphi. Another imaginary relates to national culture and identity; students are often reported to have become like the Other, to have acquired a culture and/or a language like a 'native'. Finally, related to intercultural learning, it is not unusual for study abroad returnees to assert that they have learnt to be open-minded, not to have stereotypes anymore or to have become 'citizens of the world' (see Dervin 2008; Härkönen and Dervin 2016; Jackson 2008, 2010, 2011; Kinginger 2013).

A number of scholars have dealt with study abroad as a promoter of global citizenry (see Lewin 2009 for an edited collection of papers on this topic). In their 2009 study of American undergraduates, Hendershot and Sperandio describe the importance given to the development of global citizen identities and the practice of cosmopolitan ideas by study abroad returnees. Using a pre-/post-test design to gauge the impact of study abroad, Tarrant, Rubin and Stoner (2013) found the fostering of global citizenry to be an important added value of international educational experience.

Within Europe, many scholars have attempted to evaluate the potential 'Europeanising impact' of the Erasmus programme ('the Erasmus Effect', see Mitchell 2015), which was created somewhat to boost European identity amongst the youth. In their 2003 article, King and Ruiz-Gelices analyse a large postal survey of Sussex graduates who had studied abroad in another European country. The authors found that the students developed a more 'European' identity or consciousness, although they warn of the need to nuance this result. Using a mixed-method approach, Van Mol (2013) discovered that after a stay abroad, students differ in the way they discuss their European identity. Drawing on a study involving 1,729 study abroad students from 28 universities in six countries, Mitchell (2015) contradicts previous studies by claiming that the Erasmus exchange programme provokes significant and positive identification with Europe. In all of these studies, there is a lack of critical engagement with what Europe is (the European Union? Europe as a historical, political, cultural, linguistic entity?), which makes the results problematic.

In terms of identity, these discourses represent neo-solid aspects of the liquid crystal. There is a shift, but it is one-dimensional/-directional (from one national/linguistic identity to another) and idealistic (can open-mindedness be achieved entirely?). These shifts also often appear to be self-sufficient ('I am now more tolerant than others'; 'I am interculturally competent because I know their culture', etc.) and can be counterproductive as they lead to essentialisation. In his article 'The Personal consequences of a year of study abroad', Nash (1976) notes that, over the long-term, such discourses of change (which he calls 'personality changes'), do not persist after the return home. There is thus a need for long-term research on these imaginaries.

Ideally, in order to reflect further on identity in relation to interculturality, Holliday, Hyde and Kullman (2004) suggest that one should 'respond to people according to how you find them rather than according to what you have heard about them'; 'avoid easy answers about how people are. Bracket—put aside simplistic notions about what is 'real' or 'unreal' in your perception of 'another culture'; 'appreciate that every society is as complex and culturally varied as your own' (among others).

Language Identity and International Educational Experience

The study of identity and language in international education has probably had the longest tradition, especially since the emergence of the 'social turn' in research (Block 2003). Identity is seen implicitly and explicitly as pivotal in *linguistic gain and use* (Benson et al. 2013; Carroll 1967; Freed 1995).

For applied linguist David Block (2007), language identity refers to 'the assumed and/or attributed relationship between one's sense of self and a means of communication which might be known as a language (e.g., English), a dialect (e.g., Geordie), or a sociolect (e.g., football-speak)' (p. 40). This notion of language identity is associated with language expertise (proficiency in a particular language), language affiliation (attitudes towards the language), and language inheritance (being born into a family or community where the language is spoken) (Block 2007). Language identity is also linked to the notions of avowal and ascription that were explained earlier in this chapter. For example, individuals may wish to be affiliated with a particular social or cultural group (e.g., host community) through the use of the host language (avowed identity) but first language speakers (host nationals) may continue to regard them as outsiders no matter how well they master the language and follow the prevailing sociopragmatic norms of politeness (ascribed identity).

It is essential to note here that while language use in international education does not systematically involve speaking a foreign language, the vast majority of student sojourners have to use linguistic forms that differ from those 'normally' used 'at home'. The model of reference for linguistic gains for those who have to learn to use a different language has often been that of the 'native speaker' (Magnan and Back 2007).

Benson et al. (2013) define second language identity broadly as 'any aspect of a person's identity that is connected to their knowledge or use of a second language' (p. 28). Interestingly, in their investigation of the second language identities of student sojourners, Benson and his colleagues found that '[t]here appears to be . . . a chain of variables in which the identities students bring to and imagine they will adopt in the study abroad setting lead to certain patterns of engagement, which in turn influence identity development' (p. 144). (See Chapter 5 for more discussion about variables that can impact the way sojourns unfold, including agency and self-efficacy.)

In recent years, the study of the processes and outcomes of second language use in international education has shifted from quantitative to qualitative perspectives (or a combination of both) and more attention is being paid to the complex connection between language, culture, and identity. With more awareness of the limitations of large-scale, product-oriented studies that rely on quantitative surveys, there is now a push for empirical study abroad research that incorporates multiple types of data (e.g., blogs, interviews, questionnaire surveys, digital images, sociograms/social network maps) to develop a comprehensive picture of international educational experience and identity reconstruction (Deardorff 2015a; Jackson 2012, 2016d; Kinginger 2013). Hence, we have noticed the publication of more case studies and narrativised accounts that centre on the language and intercultural development and identity expansion of student sojourners in various parts of the world (Benson et al. 2013; Jackson 2008, 2010, 2016d, forthcoming a; Kinginger 2008; Mitchell 2015). This is a welcome development as it is enriching our awareness and understanding of how diverse international educational experience can be.

In particular, the affective dimension has captured the attention of many study abroad researchers, who have discovered that student sojourners may feel differently depending on the language they use (e.g., first language, host language) and the context of the interaction (Jackson 2008, 2010). In some cases, study abroad students may change their perception of their second language as they become more fluent and gain experience with its use in social situations. If they have primarily used their second language in formal, academic contexts prior to going abroad, their feelings about the language may change after they become familiar with informal discourse and begin to build multicultural relationships through that language. They may move from a largely instrumental, detached orientation towards the language (e.g., perceptions of it as a tool for professional advancement) to one in which they feel that the language has become a part of themselves (e.g., Jackson 2008, 2010, 2011, 2016d). In this way, the sojourners may experience a broadening of their language identity.

In a 2013 chapter, Brown explored the use of Korean honorifics by advanced male second language learners who were studying in Korea. He noted a gap in their knowledge and usage of honorific norms at the end of their stay, which he related to their identities. In a similar vein, Iwasaki (2013) reported on the use of hedges by second language learners of Japanese. She found that after a sojourn in Japan, they employed a wider range of hedges, which had a positive influence on their identity making in this context. In an article that combines the social interactive and pragmatic dimensions of language, Kinginger (2015) argues that study abroad should stimulate students to reflect on linguistic choices in a variety of interpersonal, social, and cultural contexts. In another example, Müller and Schmenk (2017) explored the relationship between Canadian students' identity as learners of German and their pronunciation of that language while taking part in a study abroad programme in Germany. The researchers observed that the self-constructions of the learners were associated with the 'native-speaker' ideal and this constrained the development of their identity as German language users.

From a broader perspective, Pellegrino Aveni (2005) examined how second language use contributes to constructing self-presentation in study abroad. The author described the intersecting factors (e.g., self-esteem, anxiety, control, age, gender, etc.) that appeared to support and/or limit the sojourners' interactions and expression of their personalities in a second language. To better understand how one might improve the effectiveness of study abroad, Benson et al. (2013) employed a more specific approach (narrative research) and examined three interrelated dimensions of second language identity: identity-related second language competence (development of sociopragmatic competence), linguistic self-concept (the way the students see themselves as language learners), and second language-mediated personal competence (intercultural and academic competence). In *Language, Identity and Study Abroad: Sociocultural Perspectives*, Jackson (2008) drew on sociocultural and identity theories to explain the effect of study abroad on students' sense of self and perceptions of language and culture. She argued that knowledge of these perspectives can support students in their identity work abroad and help them to develop a more inclusive 'third kind' of identity or *intercultural personhood* (Kim 2001).

Also, informed by a sociocultural framework, amongst others, the UK Economic and Social Research Council-funded LANGSNAP project (Social Networks, Target Language Interaction and Second Language Acquisition during the Year Abroad: A Longitudinal Study), which is described in the volume *Anglophone Students Abroad* (Mitchell et al. 2017), followed 57 British undergraduate language majors over a period of 21 months. The main objective of the project was to examine the relationship between the students' identities, their social experiences, and their second language development (French and Spanish). The researchers tracked in detail how the students navigated through their changing sense of self, multiple identities (students, young adults, language learners, etc.), and evolving relationship.

One last strand of research relates to the use of lingua francas in study abroad. Today's major lingua franca is English, but any language in a study abroad context is a potential lingua franca (for French, see Behrent 2007; Dervin 2013). Research on the perception and use of English as a lingua franca (ELF) in study abroad is emerging. The issue of identity and ELF has been researched, for instance, in the UK (Jenks 2016), Germany and Finland (Virkkula and Nikula 2010), Hong Kong (Xie 2018), and the United States (Lee 2016). In Hong Kong, Sung (2014a) examined the development and perception of English as a second language learners' 'global identity' and discovered that they held different views as to what this desired identity meant and entailed. In another study, the same author (2014b) showed how the students dis-/identified with other English as a Foreign Language speakers—and made judgements about them—depending on their origins.

Multicultural/Multilingual Identities and International, Intercultural Education

Linked to the concept of transformation and identity reconstruction (or expansion) is the emergence of a multicultural identity, which Martin and Nakayama (2008: G-4) define as '[a] sense of in-betweeness that develops as a result of frequent or multiple cultural border crossings'. These interculturalists maintain that individuals with ample intercultural experiences may acquire 'an identity that transcends one particular culture', that is border crossers may gradually come to 'feel equally at home in several cultures' (p. 112) and languages. For example, study abroad students who fully immerse themselves in the host environment and open themselves up to new ways of being may develop hybrid (mixed) identities that integrate diverse cultural elements (e.g., multiple languages, local values, global perspectives) (Kraidy 2005; Kramsch 1993) that help them to function in today's multicultural world. In some cases, they may feel that they have nurtured both a global and a local self. A number of experienced intercultural educators argue that this is more likely to happen when guided, critical reflection (e.g., mentoring, experiential learning) is embedded into the study abroad programme (Jackson and Oguro 2018a; Paige 2013; 2015b).

Nguyen and Benet-Martínez (2010: 96) observe that '[t]he process of negotiating multiple cultural identities is complex and multi-faceted' and intense feelings of loss and inbetweeness may emerge in border crossers. Some international students, for example, may feel torn between different cultural worlds, identities, and languages. Suffering from identity confusion, they may experience difficulty functioning in daily life and feel on the periphery of the languages and cultures they are in contact with. A well-designed intercultural intervention (e.g., online course, series of workshops and debriefings) can help students make sense of their international experience and identity conflicts/awakenings.

International educational experience is variable. While some study abroad students may experience identity confusion and fragmentation, others may take full advantage of the opportunities that their mobility and multicultural, multilingual experiences afford them, especially when adequate support and encouragement are provided. With resilience, and a positive mindset, student sojourners may appreciate and embrace their ability to interact with growing ease in different cultural settings in multiple languages. (See Chapter 7 for more discussion about the ways in which pedagogical interventions may help prepare students for identity-related issues that may arise through study abroad. A review of contemporary schemes also points to diverse approaches that are being implemented in various parts of the world to optimise the identity expansion of students during and after study abroad.)

Researching Identity

In relation to power and positioning, when researching the identities, language learning, and intercultural development of study abroad students, it is essential to recognise how the status of the home country or region (e.g., messages in the media) may impact host receptivity and the degree of access to local communities of practice. It is also incumbent on researchers to become attuned to the expectations, concerns, and biases of the newcomers, which can also influence their reception in the new environment and, ultimately, their self-identities (e.g., openness to the process of identity reconstruction, including the cultivation of a more cosmopolitan, global self).

During the research process, it is also imperative for researchers themselves to question their own position in relation to 'doing identity'. Heightened self-awareness and reflexivity are crucial for scholars who seek to better understand the complex connections between interculturality and the 'doing of identity' in study abroad contexts. In her 1994 article 'Working the Hyphens—Reinventing Self and Other in Qualitative Research', Fine claims that '[m]uch of qualitative research has reproduced, if contradiction-filled, a colonising discourse of the "Other"'. She proposes to 'work the hyphen', or the relationships between researchers and their research participants, highlighting here again the interdependence between interlocutors and the *inter-*of the *intercultural*.

Research is also a form of interculturality, whereby two individuals meet to negotiate meaning and identity. Fine (1994: 72) maintains that we should create 'occasions for researchers and informants to discuss what is, and is not, "happening between", within the negotiated relations of whose story is being told, why, to whom, with what interpretation, and whose story is being shadowed, why, for whom, and with what consequence'. In a similar vein, Krumer-Nevo and Sidi (2012: 299) analyse how Othering takes place in research on women in poverty and proposes ways of avoiding it. They suggest fighting against objectification (turning participants into stereotypes 'composed of inferior, mostly negative, features'), decontextualisation (e.g., detachment from a general context of policy and socioeconomic structures), dehistorisation (only focus is the present) and deauthorisation (the article is presented as being autonomous, objective and authorless) (ibid.: 300). As solutions, the authors propose a concentration on three modes of writing that can remove some traces of Othering in publications: narrative, dialogue and reflexivity (ibid.).

Work on identity must pay attention to interdisciplinary discussions and debates in order to enrich theoretical, methodological and analytical aspects of study abroad research. It is also important to use more interactive research processes which fully include the researcher (e.g., provide details about his or her positioning, relevant prior experiences); this could make the reporting of research results fairer as potential researcher biases are more evident. The importance of language use is also essential when examining identity in study abroad contexts. Finally, intersecting different identity markers—rather than concentrating on the 'routine' issue of cultural and national difference—represents an important step in trying to identify complex facets of identity—bearing in mind that one will never be able to describe an identity in full. Related to this last point, it is more and more critical to include discussions of social justice in study abroad research. As a negotiated and power-laden phenomenon, 'doing' identity should entail resisting and navigating stereotypes, prejudice, and different forms of -ism (nationalism, ethnocentrism, linguism, racism, etc.).

Conclusion

This chapter emphasised important links between identity, interculturality, and international educational experience, and provided an overview of contemporary, poststructuralist notions that have implications for research and practice in the field of international education. We discussed the potential relationship between national or regional identity and study abroad, the politics of identity, the social dimensions of identity (e.g., the impact of social networks on study abroad), and the multifarious nature of identity and its relationship to language and culture. We also reviewed and contested multiple imaginaries about identity in study abroad and touched on some of the many factors that can influence identity development and lead to differences in how study abroad students see themselves and their positioning in the host environment.

Finally, in this chapter we discussed the potential benefits of pedagogical intercultural interventions to help students deal with identity-related issues in study abroad contexts and offered some advice for scholars who research interculturality and identity in study abroad contexts. The next chapter explores in more depth some of the many internal and external elements that can bring about variations in the imagined second language identities and intercultural developmental trajectories of student sojourners.

Further Reading and Resources

Benson, P., Barkhuizen, G., Bodycott, P. and Brown, J. (2013) *Second Language Identity in Narratives of Study Abroad*, Basingstoke: Palgrave MacMillan.

This book includes case study narratives that illustrate how diverse programme elements and individual differences can lead to variations in the second language identity development of study abroad students.

Dervin, F. and Risager, K. (eds) (2015) *Researching Identity and Interculturality*, New York: Routledge.

This edited collection focuses on advances in research methodology that centres on discourses of identity and interculturality. It includes a range of qualitative studies: studies of interaction, narrative studies, conversation analysis, ethnographic studies, postcolonial studies and critical discourse studies, and underscores the role of discourse and power in investigations of identity and interculturality. Critical reflexivity is emphasised throughout.

Jackson, J. (2008) *Language, Identity, and Study Abroad*, London: Equinox.
Drawing on sociocultural theories, this monograph centres on the language and intercultural learning and identity awakening of study abroad students from Hong Kong who took part in a study abroad programme in the UK. Case studies are provided that illustrate divergent developmental trajectories.

Kinginger, C. (2015) 'Student mobility and identity-related language learning', *Intercultural Education*, 26(1): 6–15. doi: 10.1080/14675986.2015.992199.
This journal article reviews some recent studies that problematise various dimensions of identity in relation to mobile students' encounters with the sociopragmatic aspects of language.

Mitchell, R., Tracy-Ventura, N. and McManus, K. (2017) *Anglophone Students Abroad: Identity, Social Relationships and Language Learning*, London and New York: Routledge.
Drawing on both quantitative and qualitative data, this volume presents the findings of a study that centred on the language learning, social networking, integration, and identity developments of British students of French and Spanish who were participating in a residence abroad programme.

5 Individual Differences and Environmental Factors

Introduction

International educational experience is often assumed to offer students the best opportunity to enhance their intercultural sensitivity, global-mindedness, and proficiency in the host language; however, as the introductory chapter noted, this expectation has increasingly been called into question in recent years. Researchers are finding that the relationship between language proficiency advancement, intercultural competence development, identity reconstruction, and international educational experience is far from straightforward. Not only are there multiple variations in programmes; a complex range of environmental elements can hamper or enhance the developmental trajectories of student sojourners. To complicate matters, individual differences among participants can also lead to strikingly different outcomes. Even when two individuals who have a similar background and attributes (e.g., language proficiency, intercultural competence, international experience) join the same study abroad programme, the way that their sojourns unfold is apt to differ. Study abroad learning is highly idiosyncratic.

As interest in sojourn learning has intensified, more and more study abroad scholars are conducting empirical research, including qualitative and mixed-methods inquiries as well as traditional quantitative studies. As explained in Chapter 2, researchers are drawing on different paradigms, theories, and methodologies in an effort to better understand the complexities inherent in study abroad experience. In particular, we have witnessed growth in studies that adopt interpretive, critical perspectives; their findings are shedding more light on what actually happens on stays abroad. The cumulative work of scholars from different regions of the world is debunking study abroad myths and enabling us to more fully grasp the complexity of study abroad learning. As our interdisciplinary field has matured, we have become much more attuned to the myriad of internal and external elements that can lead to differing sojourn experiences and learning outcomes.

Richly detailed, largely qualitative, case studies of individual second language sojourners are increasingly appearing in the literature on study abroad and they are helping us to make sense of some of the findings in large-scale, product-oriented studies (e.g., variations in learning outcomes). The longitudinal dimension in some inquiries is affording us additional insight into the developmental trajectories of student sojourners and alerting us to the potentially long-term impact of international educational experience.

In recent years, narrativised accounts have tracked the second language and intercultural learning of Erasmus students in European countries (e.g., Murphy-Lejeune 2002), American students in France (e.g., Kinginger 2004, 2008; Wolcott 2013), Asian students in English-speaking countries (e.g., Chik and Benson 2008; Jackson 2008, 2010, 2013, 2016d), and American students in China (e.g., Diao 2011), among others. These case studies have heightened our awareness of individual and environment variables that can lead to different learning paths and sojourn outcomes (e.g., varying degrees of intercultural competence and language proficiency). New understandings have contributed to theory-building and inspired pedagogical interventions that seek to enhance the second language learning and intercultural development of student sojourners. (See Chapter 7 for a review of innovative intercultural interventions in study abroad programmes.)

This chapter begins by drawing attention to the study abroad terminology that is used in different parts of the world. I then review historical developments and identify some of the many variations that exist in contemporary study abroad programmes. I also discuss other environmental elements that can influence the language and intercultural learning of student sojourners. Drawing on recent research findings, I highlight the personal nature of international educational experience and then explain some of the many individual differences that can bring about variations in the developmental trajectories of student sojourners.

Study Abroad Terminology

As the introductory chapter explained, the field of study abroad is complicated by differences in the terminology employed in different regions of the world. Several terms may represent the same concept and, in some cases, a single term may have multiple meanings. To reduce semantic ambiguity and facilitate comparisons of programmes and research findings, the Forum on Education Abroad (2011) published a glossary for study abroad professionals within and outside the United States who work with American students abroad. Coleman (2009, 2013) and Europa, the European Commission of Education, Training and Youth (European Commission 2015) review the education abroad (e.g., academic mobility) nomenclature that is prevalent in European contexts. (The definition of study abroad that I have employed in this volume was presented in the introductory chapter.)

The History of Study Abroad

Study abroad is not a new phenomenon and to understand current practices, it is helpful to have some knowledge of historical developments as well as related terminology. With this in mind, in this section I highlight some of the most significant trends, with the expectation that this will enable readers to more fully appreciate the diversity that characterises this mode of international education.

For centuries, students have bid adieu to their home country to see the world and gain international educational experience. As early as 500 BCE, historic records indicate that ancient hubs of learning (e.g., Athens, Cairo, Rome) were welcoming students from other parts of the world to study and learn. In Europe, by the eighteenth century, the 'European Grand Tour' had become popular, with elite students (e.g., the wealthy offspring of British aristocrats) travelling to Western European countries with the aspiration of acquiring greater cultural and social sophistication (Hoffa 2007; Medina 2008). The *wanderjahr* (cf. 'the Grand Tour') also emerged in Europe as an option for students from diverse backgrounds who wished to experience a cultural environment beyond their national boundaries. In this tradition, students took a year or more off from their academic studies to 'fend for themselves' with the expectation that 'real-world' experience abroad would help them to become more mature. The *wanderjahr* was the precursor to the 'gap year', a modern-day phenomenon in which secondary school graduates or university students take some extended time off from their studies to become more independent and mature through explorations in an unfamiliar environment (Hoffa 2007).

After World War II ended, the 'Junior Year Abroad' scheme became a study abroad option for American students in higher education. In this institution-sponsored programme, students could study in another country and receive credit toward a degree in their home institution. This scheme was especially popular among female undergraduates (e.g., majors in the Arts and Humanities, foreign language students) who wished to enhance their knowledge of another language and culture in the relevant host speech community (Hoffa 2007). By the 1960s, study abroad had become more accessible (e.g., feasible for people from different backgrounds and social classes), diverse (e.g., varied types of programmes), and increasingly focused on disciplinary learning, not just language and cultural enhancement. (For a detailed history of US study abroad (beginnings to 1965) see Hoffa 2007; for an account of developments in academic mobility in Europe see Coleman 2009, Murphy-Lejeune 2002, 2008; Welch 2008.)

In recent decades, partially due to accelerating globalisation, an unprecedented number of institutions of higher education across the globe have been developing implicit or explicit internationalisation policies (e.g.,

Hudzik 2015; Jones, Coelen, Beelen and de Wit 2016). In response, they are embedding an international dimension into their teaching and research, and creating many more opportunities for their students to gain some form of international educational experience, including study abroad (e.g., faculty-led tours, international exchange programmes, summer language immersion, internships).

In Europe, explicit internationalisation policies are providing direction for 'academic mobility' at institutional, national, and regional levels. In particular, the European Region Action Scheme for the Mobility of University Students (ERASMUS), which was initiated in 1987, seeks to cultivate 'European citizenship' and an international outlook (Anquetil 2006; Byram and Dervin 2008; European Commission 2015; also see http://ec.europa.eu/programmes/erasmus-plus/node_en). This European Union scheme enables higher education students in European countries to study for part of their degree in a European country that is foreign to them. The current Erasmus+ programme supports education, training, youth and sport in Europe, providing opportunities for over four million Europeans to study, train, gain experience, and volunteer abroad.

Erasmus inspired the establishment of the Bologna Process in 1999, which is now facilitating the movement of students from one country to another within the European Higher Education Area. More specifically, this scheme has made academic degree standards and quality assurance standards more comparable and compatible throughout Europe, which is facilitating the transfer of academic credits (Forum on Education Abroad 2011; Vögtle 2014; see also http://ec.europa.eu/education/policy/higher-education/bologna-process_en).

A number of regional organisations in other parts of the world are also actively promoting study abroad, including, University Mobility in Asia and the Pacific (UMAP). Founded in 1993, this voluntary association of government and nongovernmental members from the higher education sector in the Pacific Rim countries has initiated a range of programmes that are designed to increase the mobility of university students and staff (See http://umap.org/).

Variations in Contemporary Study Abroad Programming

The number of students gaining some form of international educational experience has grown tremendously in recent decades, along with the diversity of sojourn aims (e.g., language learning, exposure to other cultures, personal growth, professional enhancement, disciplinary learning). Contemporary study abroad programmes may now include a range of activities that provide students with opportunities to gain intercultural experience outside the classroom, such as internships, work placements, field research, service-learning, volunteering, directed travel linked to learning goals. Service-learning refers to:

> a specially designed experience combining reflection with structured participation in a community-based project to achieve specified learning outcomes as part of a study abroad program. The learning is given structure through the principles of experiential education to develop an integrated approach to understanding the relationship among theory, practice, ideals, values, and community.
> (Forum on Education Abroad 2011: 18)

Study abroad schemes may also offer students more opportunities to travel to 'nontraditional' settings (e.g., Argentina, Botswana, India, Jordan, Vietnam) either as a group or individually.

The actual experiences of study abroad students and their subsequent learning (e.g., intercultural, language, disciplinary) may differ substantially depending on a wide range of programme characteristics (e.g., duration; aims; focus; amount of preparation provided; setting; format; depth of reflection that is encouraged; amount of contact with locals and other international students; degree of socio-emotional support provided; re-entry preparation; and sojourn debriefings).

The duration of international educational experience can vary from a few days or weeks to more than a year. For example, study abroad students may join a micro-sojourn lasting three weeks or less, a short-term sojourn ranging from four to seven weeks, or a semester or year-long international exchange programme (Forum on Education Abroad 2011; Institute of International Education 2016; Spencer and Tuma 2008). Students at secondary and tertiary levels may choose to enhance their second language proficiency and intercultural sensitivity by taking part in a summer language immersion programme (e.g., study Chinese in Beijing or Arabic in Cairo). Postgraduates may engage in research or join courses in another country to augment their programme of studies in their home country. In addition to these short-term study abroad options, students may opt to do full undergraduate or postgraduate degrees in a country other than their home country. For example, a graduate from a Singaporean university may gain international educational experience by undertaking PhD studies in applied linguistics at a university in the UK.

Some students may venture abroad on their own to join a study abroad programme in another country; others may travel with peers from their home institution and participate in the same programme in the host country. While abroad, students may take courses in the host language at a commercial language centre or other educational institution. Some participants may study alongside international students from other countries as well as domestic students, while others remain in intact groups, taking specially-designed courses (e.g., literature, cultural studies, international business) with students from their home institution. Participants in these programmes may transfer academic credits back to the home institution. In some cases, the grades will count towards the students' grade point average, whereas in other situations they will not (e.g., only pass/fail results will be recorded). This variation, in turn, can impact the degree of investment in language and intercultural learning in the host environment, an element that will be revisited when we turn our attention to individual differences.

Secondary schools and institutions of higher education are now organising more teacher or faculty-led programmes. In this option, students typically travel in a group and remain together throughout their stay abroad. Schemes of this nature typically consist of short-term or micro-term stays in the host environment, with varying degrees of contact between the leader and students, and, possibly, between the sojourners and a partner institution (e.g., host faculty and/or students). The amount of mentoring (guided, critical reflection) and socio-emotional support offered in these programmes varies.

Following this model, a secondary school teacher of English in Kuala Lumpur, Malaysia, for example, may travel to New Zealand with her students for a 12-day intensive English language and cultural enhancement programme. The micro-sojourn may include a homestay (or residence in a dormitory), language lessons with host teachers, intercultural communication workshops, cultural site visits, and informal activities with Australian peers. Later in the year, the Malaysian students may reciprocate by hosting their New Zealand counterparts. In another example, a professor of Chinese (Putonghua) in Toronto may accompany a group of students to Beijing and teach Chinese language, literature, intercultural communication, or cultural studies courses alongside local professors. She may also supervise out-of-class activities (e.g., service-learning, work placements, ethnographic fieldwork, interview research) to encourage active participation in the host culture, and promote language and (inter)cultural development, global citizenship, and disciplinary learning. Alternatively, study abroad students may take formal classes in the mornings and be free to explore the host community on their own in afternoons with no guided, critical reflection or experiential learning activities embedded in their programme of study. There are many possibilities and variations in faculty-led study abroad programmes.

Internationalisation initiatives are also resulting in a significant increase in international exchange programmes for both students and faculty. This model generally entails reciprocal movement of participants (e.g., faculty, students, staff, or community members) between countries (Forum on Education Abroad 2011). As more educational institutions sign exchange agreements with foreign counterparts, this is creating more opportunities for secondary and tertiary-level students to join an exchange programme and stay abroad for a longer period of time (e.g., a semester, an academic year). As mentioned above, there are also growing opportunities to participate in exchange programmes in non-traditional settings. Further, students may participate in a micro-or short-term study abroad programme, which may serve as a confidence-building springboard for a longer-stay abroad (e.g., a year-long international exchange programme, postgraduate studies abroad, employment outside one's home country).

International exchange students who have an advanced level of proficiency in the host language may take courses alongside host nationals and other international students and then transfer some or all of their academic credits back to their home institution. With this arrangement, the second language participants can simultaneously enhance their language proficiency and academic knowledge in other areas of study (e.g., accounting, science). While abroad, they may also hone their professional skills (e.g., business, health care) in a second language either through coursework, service-learning, or a supervised internship. They may also take language enhancement courses in other languages.

While abroad, student sojourners may engage in a range of activities in and outside the classroom and assume various roles (familiar and new). For example, they may take language enhancement courses or enroll in subject matter courses (e.g., engineering, history) at a tertiary institution, serve as a teaching assistant, take part in a supervised internship or work placement scheme in the host community, undertake volunteer work or engage in service-learning, or perform a combination of these options. On site, they may also carry out a focused, small-scale research project (e.g., ethnographic investigation of a local cultural scene) or participate in other experiential activities that have been designed to promote more meaningful engagement with the host speech community or other international students (Jackson 2006, 2008, 2010, 2016a, 2018a; Knight and Schmidt-Rinehart 2010; Roberts, Byram, Barro, Jordan and Street 2001). Students may also take part in programmes that do not specifically aim to foster critical reflection.

Due to the emergence of English as the global language of internationalisation, advanced English as an international language (EIL) students no longer need to travel to English-speaking countries (e.g., Australia, Canada, England, the United States) to pursue further studies in English. Many non-English speaking countries now offer English-medium courses in their programmes of study (even full degrees), providing second language sojourners with exposure to local (and global) perspectives in a range of disciplines (Altbach 2016a, 2016b; Jenkins 2013; Knight 2016). Taiwanese marketing majors, for example, can now travel to Finland or the Netherlands to take English-medium courses in their area of specialisation. Through interaction with domestic and international students, they may hone their intercultural communication skills in English, their lingua franca. Some of the participants may also choose to take language enhancement courses in Finnish or Dutch and gain more exposure to the local scene on campus and the wider community. Within these exchange programmes, as in the short-term, faculty-led options, the quality and degree of interaction with the host language and culture can vary substantially.

Another programme element that can have a significant impact on the language and (inter)cultural learning of sojourners is the housing arrangement, which can take many forms (e.g., independent accommodation; living with a host family; residence in a boarding house, youth hostel, or dormitory on campus; the sharing of an off-campus apartment or house with host nationals, other international students, or co-nationals). In some cases, international students may live in close proximity to the host institution and/or urban centre and have many opportunities to engage in social activities; in other situations, newcomers may live with co-nationals in a less expensive area to save money. They may then find themselves isolated, far from the social scene on campus. Unless they have a high level of motivation, they may not make the effort to gain exposure to local communities of practice due to the inconvenience involved. Thus, some housing arrangements may be more conducive to the formation of relationships with people who have a different linguistic and cultural background. Further, when living conditions are very different from what newcomers are accustomed to it can pose an adjustment challenge that can be difficult for some to overcome.

Another element that can impact the degree of immersion in the host environment is the use of electronic tools of communication. Advances in technology and social media (e.g., the use of e-mail, Skype, Facebook, WeChat, and other electronic means) are now enabling sojourners in many parts of the world to keep in regular contact with home, if they choose. This can make the 'immersion' experience far different from previous generations (Coleman and Chafer 2010; Donatelli 2010).

As this brief review suggests, the quality and amount of pre-sojourn preparation, sojourn support, and re-entry debriefings can differ greatly in study abroad programmes, ranging from no support to credit-bearing intercultural coursework at all stages that is designed to facilitate, deepen, and extend sojourn learning. (See Chapter 7 for a review of intercultural interventions in study abroad.) It is, therefore, important to be mindful of programme elements when digesting publications that centre on interculturality in study abroad.

Other Environmental Factors

I have identified some of the many variations that exist in study abroad programmes today but this review would be incomplete without some discussion of other environmental factors that can lead to differences in the experiences and learning of student sojourners. For example, access, and power-related issues can significantly hamper or enhance sojourn learning and engagement in the host environment (Coleman 2013; Jackson 2008, 2010; Kinginger 2009, 2013).

Within the context of border crossings, Kim (2015b) defines host receptivity as 'the degree to which a given host environment is structurally and psychologically accessible and open to a particular group of strangers' (p. 440). Not surprisingly, the amount and quality of exposure study abroad students have to local communities of practice can have a profound impact on their access to the host language and social activities. If they feel welcomed and have many chances to interact with domestic students (and other host nationals) in a meaningful way, they may more quickly feel at home in the new environment; this naturally may facilitate their intercultural development, language acquisition, and emotional well-being (Kim 2012, 2015a, 2015b; Ward, Bochner and Furnham 2001). Conversely, if there is low host receptivity and the newcomers feel unwanted and disrespected, they may have few chances for social interactions with locals and little or no incentive to engage. This, in turn, can limit their language and intercultural development, personal growth, and identity expansion (e.g., broadening of their sense of self) (Kim 2015b; Ward et al. 2001). (See Chapter 3 for a more in-depth discussion of acculturation and socialisation and Chapter 4 for more on identity-related issues in study abroad.)

Issues related to power (resistance and inequality) and positioning (e.g., status) can adversely affect the quality of sojourn experience and learning. For example, a power imbalance may be present when second language speakers interact with first language speakers in the host environment. In intercultural encounters involving domestic and international students, differing levels of proficiency and variations in the degree of familiarity with prevailing sociopragmatic norms can result in newcomers feeling disadvantaged and uncomfortable, especially if their hosts are impatient and have limited intercultural communication skills (Shively and Cohen 2008). (Without international experience, their hosts may have little understanding of and empathy for international students who may be struggling with adjustment issues (e.g., a language barrier, homesickness).) Further, if the hosts in a homestay situation are unilingual, they may not fully appreciate the challenges facing second language students.

Other environmental elements may pose difficulties for study abroad students, including unfamiliar weather patterns, food/diet, pollution (e.g., air, noise, water), congestion (e.g., reduced personal space), or study atmosphere. Moving from an urban university campus to a rural area can also be confronting for some.

Individual Differences

In addition to the programme features and environmental factors described above, individual differences can affect the substance and quality of international educational experience. Generally, individual differences are described 'in terms of variable *internal* conditions, such as aptitude, learning styles and preferences, and motivation' (Benson 2012: 222). In the past decade, in particular, a number of scholars from different areas of study including psychology and applied linguistics have focused their attention on the identification and scrutiny of individual characteristics that can play an influential role in language and intercultural learning both at home and abroad (Benson 2012, Benson et al. 2013; Dörnyei 2005; Gregersen and MacIntyre 2014; Kim 2015a, 2015b). This work has led to new theoretical insights and understandings that have profound implications for study abroad educators and researchers who are concerned about the enhancement of sojourn learning.

In this section, I examine some of the many individual factors that have been identified in the literature on study abroad, namely: agency, goals and expectations, and psychological and affective dimensions (e.g., attitudes, motivation, investment, imagined selves/identities, self-confidence, self-efficacy beliefs, and anxiety or communication apprehension, willingness to communicate, patience and tolerance for ambiguity, personality traits). While not exhaustive, this review draws attention to the complexity and variability in sojourn experience.

Agency

Agency implies movement (e.g., physical, social, intellectual) (van Lier 2011). In study abroad contexts, this element can play a significant role in determining how sojourns unfold. From an ecological, poststructuralist perspective, students are individuals ('social agents') who possess their own aims, needs, desires, concerns, and attributes (e.g., personality traits) (Baxter 2016; Jackson 2008; Kirkhart and Kirkhart 2015). Their mindset (e.g., degree of empathy and openness to other cultures) and the actions they take in the host environment can significantly affect the quality of their sojourn experience as well as learning outcomes.

In the host environment, some student sojourners actively participate in social happenings (e.g., accept invitations to events organised by their hosts) and make a concerted effort to cultivate meaningful friendships with individuals who have a different cultural background (e.g., locals, other international students). With resilience and a positive frame of mind, these individuals take full advantage of linguistic and cultural affordances in the local speech community (e.g., frequently initiate conversations in the host language, make an effort to include host nationals and other international students in their social networks, try new things). By the end of their stay, they may feel very at ease and at home in the host environment and believe that they have broadened their sense of self.

By contrast, sojourners who possess a more ethnocentric mindset, have a low tolerance for ambiguity, and fear cultural difference may avoid intercultural interactions, restricting themselves to formal, academic contexts in the host environment. They may spend nearly all their free time with co-nationals and much of their conversations may focus on perceived negative elements in the host environment. When invited to participate in intercultural activities (e.g., social functions hosted by local students) they decline, preferring to remain in the company of co-nationals who provide a familiar, safe haven. With limited access to local communities of practice, they then reduce their exposure to the host language and culture. This, in turn, can hamper their language and intercultural development. These sojourners may then return home with heightened ethnocentrism and little interest in intercultural interactions.

As these examples illustrate, the developmental trajectories of individual sojourners can vary tremendously. Two students with a similar background may be in the same study abroad programme and host environment but their sojourn experiences may differ a great deal due to the choices they make. The learning situation of student sojourners is variable and complex, with agency a key factor in bringing about differing outcomes.

Sojourn Aspirations, Expectations, and Emotions

Another element that can vary among sojourners relates to aspirations, emotions, and expectations for the stay abroad. An optimistic mindset coupled with realistic expectations can facilitate positive sojourn outcomes. Some investigations of international educational experience have found that individuals who set realistic goals for their stay abroad and are positive about the challenges that lie ahead are better positioned to deal with the difficulties that they may face in the host environment (Beaven and Spencer-Oatey 2016; Jackson 2008, 2010, 2013; Savicki 2015). In contrast, individuals who possess a negative mindset and believe that they are inadequately prepared for study abroad (or who have parents who question their ability to cope in a foreign land far away from home for the first time) may be more anxious about what lies ahead. Self-doubts can heighten acculturative stress and hamper adjustment in the host environment (Kim 2015a; Savicki 2015).

In case studies of Chinese study abroad students, Benson et al. (2013) found a clear link between individual expectations (e.g., imagined self-identities) and sojourn experiences, noting that 'students tend to experience what they expect to experience' (p. 145). Drawing on their database, the researchers explained the potential impact of pre-sojourn expectations and imaginings:

> There is a pattern that runs across most of the narratives in our data set, in which students tend to experience what they expect to experience. Siri exemplifies this, although she was unusual in imagining an identity that was not conducive to positive development; she expected that English people would laugh at her English, and was resistant to the idea that the experience of study abroad would lead to change.

In most cases, however, students imagined identities that would lead to positive effects. In particular, they saw themselves as willing and enthusiastic participants in study abroad who would take advantage of every opportunity to use and develop their English. Often, the opportunities were fewer and more difficult to manage than they expected, but in general the students returned with a sense of having developed in a positive direction.

(ibid. p. 145)

The findings of Benson et al.'s (2013) study and those of other study abroad scholars (e.g., Jackson 2008, 2010) suggest that negativity can lead to a self-fulfilling prophecy. In contrast, positivity can foster resilience, that is, the ability to press on in the face of adversity and result in a stronger desire to seek out intercultural engagement. This, in turn, can provide more opportunities for student sojourners to enhance their language proficiency as well as their intercultural communication skills and understanding.

Interestingly, while expectations of success can facilitate learning in an international setting, sojourners with unrealistic imaginings may become disappointed and disillusioned when they encounter challenges in the host environment even if they started off with a positive mindset (Ting-Toomey and Chung 2012; Ward et al. 2001). Thus, study abroad researchers advise pre-sojourn orientations to include some discussion about positivity *and* the benefits of setting realistic sojourn aims (e.g., Bennett 2008, 2009; Jackson 2014).

Aspirations and expectations may also be affected by the nature of the programme. International educational experience is not necessarily voluntary. In some academic programmes (e.g., Asian studies, Global Studies, Modern Languages), students may participate in a study abroad programme to fulfill a requirement in their programme of studies in their home institution. For example, students who are majoring in Japanese studies in Hong Kong may be obliged to participate in a year-long international exchange programme in Japan at an institution that has been approved by the home institution. Modern language students in the UK and in other parts of Europe may be required to spend part of their degree programme in a country where the target language is widely spoken (Coleman 2009; McKinnon 2018). Whether international educational experience is voluntary or a programme requirement may influence the ways in which the students prepare for and act during their sojourn.

Language and Intercultural Attitudes

Language and intercultural attitudes may also influence the developmental trajectories of student sojourners. Language attitudes are the feelings that people have about their own language variety or the language varieties of others (Garrett 2010). In individuals, these learned predispositions are influenced by their linguistic and cultural experiences (e.g., intercultural, second language interactions) and socialisation within particular sociocultural and political environments. Language attitudes may vary from favourable to unfavourable. To complicate matters, within a specific context or language situation (e.g., study abroad), individuals may possess both positive and negative feelings towards a language or elements of the language (e.g., accents, scripts, sociopragmatic norms associated with the host language) (Baker 1992; Garrett 2010).

Second language acquisition specialists have found that an individual's language attitudes at a particular time and space can influence his or her motivation to learn and use the language, whether in the home environment or abroad (Yashima, Zenuk-Nishide and Shimizu 2004). In relation to study abroad, unconscious or conscious attitudes towards the host language (e.g., a particular variety of English) can enhance or inhibit an individual's level of investment in the mastery of the host language (e.g., the amount of effort expended to seek out opportunities to practice the host language in social situations) (Wanner 2009). A positive view of the host language and culture can inspire newcomers to interact with host nationals, whereas negative perceptions may hamper their willingness to use their second language and engage in intercultural interactions (Isabelli-García 2006; Jackson 2015d, 2016b, 2017a).

Closely linked to attitudes towards language is the notion of intercultural attitudes. In Byram's (1997) model of intercultural competence, the construct of 'intercultural attitudes' (*savoir être*) encompasses 'curiosity and openness, readiness to suspend disbelief about others cultures and belief about one's own intercultural attitudes' (Byram, Gribkova and Starkey 2002: 12). Deardorff's (2004, 2006, 2008) process model of intercultural competence also suggests that intercultural attitudes are foundational to the development of intercultural competence. (See Chapter 6 for more details about these models.)

When student sojourners possess a high level of curiosity about their new environment and the people they meet, they are better positioned to take advantage of affordances, especially if they make a genuine effort to push past stereotypes. As they engage in intercultural interactions with an open, optimistic mindset, they are apt to experience more growth in intercultural sensitivity than students who possess a rigid, ethnocentric mindset and avoid intercultural interactions.

Motivation and Investment

Ginsberg and Wlodkowski (2015) define motivation broadly as 'the natural human capacity to direct energy in pursuit of a goal' (p. 634). Within the context of study abroad, motivation is sometimes referred to as expectations, drives, motives, reasons, and aspirations (Isabelli-García 2006;

Kinginger 2009; Krzaklewska 2008). With regard to second language acquisition, motivation encompasses 'the attitudes and affective states that influence the degree of effort that learners make to learn an L2' (Ellis 1997: 75). This notion may also be extended to an individual's desire to enhance his or her degree of intercultural competence.

Psycholinguists maintain that motivation can play a pivotal role in language and intercultural learning, influencing the depth of investment, persistence, and, ultimately, proficiency attainment (Dörnyei, MacIntyre and Henry 2015; Ginsberg and Wlodkowski 2015; Jackson 2016c, 2017a).

Studies of language learners have identified several types of motivation, including an instrumental orientation (e.g., the learning of a language to get a high-paying job or to gain admission to a prestigious institution of higher education abroad) and an integrative orientation (e.g., the learning of a language and the enhancement of intercultural communication skills in order to become close to host nationals who speak that language) (Gardner 1985, 2010; Gregersen and MacIntyre 2014). If study abroad students are largely driven by instrumental motives with regard to their academic studies, they may be less motivated to invest a lot of time and energy in their host courses if the grades they receive will not count towards their grade point average in their home institution. Conversely, student sojourners who are keen to make the most of their academic experience abroad may continue to work hard to learn as much as possible even if their grades will not count in their grade point average. These students may appreciate the opportunities the courses provide for meaningful intercultural interactions and exposure to new ideas and approaches.

More recently, drawing on self-determination theory, personality trait psychology, social cognitive theory, and attribution theory, Dörnyei's (2009) L2 Motivational Self System has drawn attention to the impact of learner-specific elements (e.g., proficiency level, personality traits, cognitive ability, emotional state, self-identities) and learning situational factors (e.g., teacher, institutional culture, sociopolitical environment) on an individual's language (and culture) learning motivation, which can change over time. Self-determination research has categorised motivation as intrinsic (e.g., the desire to learn a language because it is enjoyable and interesting) or extrinsic (e.g., the learning of another language to benefit from certain rewards such as the fulfillment of a language requirement for admission to postgraduate studies) (Gardner 2010; Ryan and Deci 2002; Ushioda 2014).

Re-conceptualising the notion of integrativeness within the context of English as a global lingua franca, Dörnyei (2005, 2009) reframed language learning motivation in terms of 'possible/ideal selves'. Drawing on psychological theories of the self (Higgins 1987; Markus and Nurius 1986), the L2 Motivational Self System consists of the following dimensions: the 'Ideal L2 self', the 'Ought-to L2 self', and the 'L2 learning experience'. Dörnyei (2009) defines the former as 'the L2-specific facet of one's ideal self' (p. 29), whereas the 'Ought-to L2 self' encompasses 'the attributes that one believes one ought to possess (i.e., various duties, obligations, or responsibilities) in order to avoid possible negative outcomes' (p. 29). The 'L2 learning experience' refers to 'situation-specific motives related to the immediate learning environment and experience' (ibid.: 29). This framework posits that language learning motivation is driven by the desire to reduce the discrepancy between one's actual self and ideal possible selves, whether in one's home environment or abroad. This notion resonates with intercultural development (e.g., the desire to become more interculturally competent to reduce the discrepancy between one's actual and ideal intercultural selves).

As this theory suggests, there is now more recognition of the dynamic, socially situated nature of motivation, and more awareness that the degree and type of second language motivation may be self-determined or externally imposed on individuals (Dörnyei et al. 2015; Ushioda 2014). Instead of viewing motivation as a fixed construct, more and more researchers are recognising the dynamic, multifaceted nature of this complex construct. Dörnyei (2009), for example, argues that an individual learner's language learning motivation may be impacted by learner-specific elements (e.g., 'Ought-to L2 self', proficiency level, personality traits, cognitive ability, emotional state) and learning situational factors (e.g., teacher, school culture, sociopolitical environment), among others, and, thus, the degree and type of motivation may alter over time. For example, in the home environment, an individual's language learning motivation may intensify after gaining acceptance to join an exchange programme in a country where the language is widely spoken in daily life.

It is often assumed that second language students who participate in study abroad programmes will have a strong motivation to integrate into the host community (e.g., make friends with host nationals) and, through immersion, gain ample access to local communities of practice and experience significant gains in their language proficiency. For a variety of individual and environmental reasons, however, sojourners may not develop meaningful multicultural relationships and may gain less exposure to the host language than anticipated (Coleman 2013; Jackson 2015d).

Self-Efficacy and Self-Confidence

The concept of self-efficacy is defined by Bandura (1994: 71) as 'people's beliefs about their capabilities to produce designated levels of performance that exercise influence over events that affect their lives'. More simply, self-efficacy refers to 'individuals' beliefs about their capabilities to perform well' (Graham and Weiner 1995: 74). Bandura (1994) found that people with a high self-efficacy tend to approach difficulties with a positive mindset and persevere, whereas those who have a low self-efficacy may perceive challenges as too threatening and retreat, which then stymies their learning.

Linking this ability construct to motivation in second language learning and use, Ehrman (1996) observes that 'enhanced self-efficacy—that is, more expectations of good results—tends to increase motivation. It also increases willingness to take risks'. Mills (2014) concurs, observing that confidence in one's capabilities is a critical element in successful L2 learning. Based on a review of language learning motivation studies, Mercer and Williams (2014) note that 'having a positive sense of self, irrespective of how that is defined, is invaluable for successful learning in terms of reducing anxiety, enhancing motivation, developing persistence and promoting autonomy, self-regulation and an effective, flexible use of strategies' (p. 182). To develop meaningful multicultural relationships in a second language, whether in one's home environment or abroad, individuals must possess sufficient self-confidence and self-efficacy beliefs to initiate and sustain intercultural interactions in that language. Knowledge of effective learner strategies and the ability to monitor one's language use and intercultural communication strategies can build confidence in second language sojourners (Allen 2013; Mills 2014).

Willingness to Communicate (WTC)

Investigations of second language learning suggest that self-efficacy beliefs are closely tied to an individual's degree of investment in language learning as well as his or her willingness to communicate (WTC) in that language. Within the context of language learning, MacIntyre, Clément, Dörnyei, and Noels (1998) define WTC as an individual's 'readiness to enter into discourse at a particular time with a specific person or persons, using a L2' (p. 547). Newcomers may possess a high level of willingness to communicate (WTC) in the host language (MacIntyre et al. 1998) and have expectations for significant gains in their proficiency but find it difficult to initiate and sustain interactions in their second language. External variables, such as host receptivity and the amount of access to the host community, can enhance or impede an individual's WTC in the host language (or another second language).

Besides second language self-efficacy beliefs, a number of other individual differences can also influence one's WTC in an additional language, such as the desire to interact or connect with a certain individual, one's level of self-confidence and self-esteem, the degree of investment in language proficiency enhancement, and the amount of anxiety or language/intercultural communication apprehension (e.g., fear of interacting with people who have a different linguistic and cultural background) (Gregersen and MacIntyre 2014; Sampasivam and Clément 2014).

Language and Intercultural Anxiety

Language anxiety refers to 'a feeling of tension and apprehension specifically associated with L2 contexts, including speaking, listening, and learning' (MacIntyre and Gardner 1994: 284). Previous negative language learning experiences may lead to a heightened level of anxiety in intercultural situations and reduce an individual's desire to communicate in that language. Conversely, positive experiences may lessen tension and enhance an individual's WTC and desire to build constructive multicultural relationships through the use of the second language.

Individuals who have had little or no interaction with people who have a different linguistic and cultural background prior to their sojourn may experience intercultural anxiety in the host environment and, at least, initially hold back from initiating or engaging in intercultural interactions. Fearful of cultural difference, they may have some anxiety and concerns about potential intercultural misunderstandings, anticipating a language and/or cultural barrier. In contrast, other sojourners, who also have had limited intercultural contact, may express the desire to experience intercultural diversity in real life and feel confident that they will be able to cope well in intercultural situations.

While a reduced stress level and an elevated WTC have the potential to bring about more second language use and intercultural learning; Gregersen and MacIntyre (2014: 216) note that 'without the decision to act upon those behavioral intentions to communicate, learners may still not use the language, despite their ability and the opportunity to do so'.

Patience and Tolerance for Ambiguity

Interculturalists have identified a number of other behavioural characteristics that can influence how individuals interact in a new environment, including tolerance for ambiguity (or tolerance of ambiguity) and degree of patience. Deller and Stahl (2015) refer to the former as '[t]he ability to resist stressful situations and to function effectively in a new environment where the expatriate experiences ambiguity, complexity, and uncertainty' (p. 14). While this particular definition was written with expatriates in mind, it also applies to international students who find themselves in an unfamiliar linguistic and cultural environment, where '[t]here seem to be no rules or understandable patterns, even for the normal routine of daily living' (Tucker 2015: 317).

Sojourners can find it very frustrating when they discover that their usual ways of accomplishing daily tasks do not work well in the host environment. At times, they may be unsure about when and what will happen (e.g., who speaks or acts first, what responses or actions are deemed appropriate in a particular social situation). Impatient individuals who have a low tolerance for ambiguity may find adjustment more difficult than newcomers who are less stressed in situations where they do not fully understand what is going on. As Chapter 3 explained, without effective coping skills, a high level of acculturative stress and frustration with new roles and responsibilities can hamper the adjustment process.

Conversely, patient individuals who are very tolerant of ambiguity may be more relaxed and open to new ways of being. Hence, these elements can lead to differences in the way that stays abroad unfold.

Personality

Another individual difference that has been noted by study abroad researchers is the role of personality in language learning and the development of intercultural competence. Personality refers to 'the relatively enduring behavioral and cognitive characteristics of an individual' (Kirkhart and Kirkhart 2015). Associated with this construct are a number of personal traits that have been identified by psychologists, including introversion, extroversion, openness (open-mindedness), positivity, flexibility, and strength.

A number of psychologists have developed theories about personality and its influence on cross-cultural adjustment, second language learning/use, and intercultural interactions. Y.Y. Kim (2001, 2015b), for example, developed the integrative theory of communication and cross-cultural adaptation, which identifies variables that can account for differences in the ways individuals adapt to a new environment. Kim (2015b) observed that border crossers differ in their 'more or less enduring personality traits' (p. 440). Her theory posits that the following personality traits or characteristics can significantly affect an individual's 'ability to endure the experiences of adaptive stress' (ibid.: 440), namely: '1) openness ("an internal posture that is receptive to new information", 2) strength ("the quality of resilience, patience, hardiness and persistence", and 3) positivity ("an affirmative and optimistic outlook that enables the individual to better endure stressful events with a belief in the possibilities of life in general")' (Kim 2012: 238). Her model helps to raise awareness of multiple factors that can lead to differing developmental trajectories in border crossers, including student sojourners.

Implications for Intercultural Interventions

This chapter identified a wide range of external and internal elements that can influence the intercultural learning and engagement of international students. Previous experiences, sojourns goals and expectations, degree of preparedness, attitudes, behavioural characteristics, and personality traits, are just some of the many factors that influence international educational experience and result in differing outcomes.

The complexity and individual nature of study abroad pose challenges for programme providers, including intercultural educators who seek to optimise the intercultural learning and engagement of student sojourners. In addition to preparing detailed profiles of their participants, seasoned educators recognise the need to be cognisant of specific features in the study abroad programme. This is essential if they are to design pedagogical interventions that can make a positive difference in intercultural learning and engagement. Chapter 7 explores innovative ways in which study abroad educators in different parts of the world are addressing individual differences and programme variations.

Conclusion

This chapter drew attention to some of the many external or environmental elements (e.g., programme variations, power relations, host receptivity, degree of socio-emotional/intercultural support provided) and internal variables (e.g., motivation, intercultural attitudes, investment, willingness to communicate, tolerance for ambiguity, personal traits) that can profoundly influence international educational experience. A complex mix of these factors can lead to startlingly different sojourns (e.g., amount of contact with local communities of practice, degree of exposure to the host language and culture, depth of reflexivity, second language use, and intercultural engagement) and, ultimately, result in significant variations in developmental trajectories (e.g., differing degrees of language and intercultural learning and identity expansion). Therefore, it is important for researchers to pay attention to the 'whole person' development of student sojourners and recognise the potential effect of various individual and contextual elements on language and intercultural development.

As this chapter has illustrated, there is considerable diversity in international educational programmes, participants, and contexts. There is no such thing as '*the* study abroad experience'. This often-used phrase is far too reductionist and simplistic to be useful or meaningful today. Accordingly, in my view, in any presentations or publications about study abroad research or pedagogical interventions, it is incumbent on scholars to provide a thick, rich description of the participants, the programme, and context of their work.

An awareness of the many variables that can affect learning in an international context can benefit multiple stakeholders (e.g., study abroad researchers, administrators, intercultural educators, student sojourners). In particular, it is important for educators who are responsible for designing, implementing, and assessing study abroad programmes to have a solid grasp of the individual differences and external factors that can lead to variations in learning outcomes. When reading the next two chapters, which centre on assessment and pedagogy in intercultural, international education, it will be helpful to keep the content of the present chapter in mind.

Further Reading and Resources

Benson, P. (2012) 'Individual difference and context in study abroad', in W.M. Chan, K.N. Chin, S.K. Bhatt and I. Walker (eds), *Perspectives on Individual*

Characteristics and Foreign Language Education, Berlin: Mouton de Gruyter, pp. 221–38.

This chapter provides a succinct review of multiple individual and external elements that can influence the second language identity development and intercultural learning of study abroad students.

Deters, P., Gao, A., Miller, E.R. and Vitanova, G. (eds) (2015) *Theorizing and Analyzing Agency in Second Language Learning: Interdisciplinary Approaches*, Bristol: Multilingual Matters.

Drawing on diverse theoretical and methodological approaches, this edited volume illustrates how language learner agency can be investigated. It raises awareness of variations in agency, which have pedagogical implications for second language learning and teaching.

Gregersen, T. and MacIntyre, P.D. (2014) *Capitalizaing on Language Learners' Individuality: From Premise to Practice*, Bristol: Multilingual Matters.

This book identifies and examines learner characteristics (e.g., anxiety, beliefs, cognitive abilities, motivation, strategies, styles and willingness to communicate) that can influence language learning.

Muñoz, C. (ed.) (2012) *Intensive Exposure Experiences in Second Language Learning*, Bristol: Multilingual Matters.

This edited collection showcases the role of intensive exposure as a critical characteristic in the comparison of language learning processes and outcomes from diverse learning contexts, including study abroad.

6 Assessment and Evaluation

Introduction

In past decades it was often assumed that tertiary students who gained some form of international educational experience would become more global-minded and interculturally competent, and also hone their second language proficiency simply by being present in an environment where the language was spoken in daily life. Times are changing. The dramatic rise in the number of study abroad participants has been accompanied by an increase in empirical research that has scrutinised the language and intercultural learning of student sojourners. As explained in preceding chapters, the findings have raised awareness of variability in sojourn outcomes. While some participants meet the linguistic and intercultural goals of their programme, others return home with a higher level of ethnocentricism and little interest in engaging in intercultural interactions in their second language, raising doubts about the benefits of their stay abroad. The developmental trajectories of student sojourners are idiosyncratic and far from straightforward.

In international education, assessment is becoming commonplace for multiple reasons. Along with growing recognition of inconsistent sojourn outcomes, more broadly, institutions of higher education are facing mounting pressure to become more accountable for the funds that are expended on all facets of education, including study abroad. A significant amount of time, energy, and resources are required to develop and administer study abroad programmes, and questions are increasingly being posed about the benefits accrued. Further, the shift in higher education towards learner-centeredness has led to a focus on what students actually gain from educational initiatives, including study and residence abroad. An emphasis on outcomes-based assessment (OBA) in institutions of higher education has resulted in a surge in documentation and assessment of student learning, including language and intercultural development through study abroad (Bolen 2007a; Deardorff 2015a; Savicki and Brewer 2015a).

In many educational contexts, international officers with no background in assessment are being pressed to measure the learning of study abroad participants and furnish evidence of the intercultural learning of second language sojourners. They may also be called on to evaluate various types of study abroad programmes (e.g., faculty-led sojourns, fieldwork placements, international exchange programmes, intercultural interventions). Accordingly, due to multiple 'push and pull' factors, in many institutions of higher education, the 'culture of assessment' is taking hold, with the intercultural dimension a central element.

This chapter begins by discussing the complex nature of interculturality and the components commonly associated with intercultural competence. I also describe several models of intercultural competence development that are influencing the ways in which intercultural assessment plans are conceived and implemented. I then offer definitions of terms and concepts that dominate the literature on assessment and evaluation, and review assessment tools, methods, and strategies that are currently being employed to assess the intercultural learning and engagement of sojourners in a range of study abroad programmes and contexts. In this chapter I also explain the importance of systematically evaluating study abroad programmes and their components (e.g., intercultural interventions).

Conceptions of Interculturality and Intercultural Competence

As I pointed out in Chapter 1, the construct of interculturality is complicated and scholars from different disciplines and backgrounds have divergent ideas about what it entails and how or even whether it should be assessed. Some critical interculturalists argue that it is too difficult and problematic to accurately and reliably measure an individual's degree of interculturality. In their estimation, most forms of assessment do not fit with contemporary, critical notions of intercultural learning as a continuous non-linear process, with both progress and regression throughout one's life (Dervin 2016, 2017; Kennedy, Díaz and Dasli 2017). Consequently, they shy away from any form of assessment of intercultural development and question the ethics of current assessment practices.

Within the broader context of international education, educators, researchers and administrators often refer to the construct of 'intercultural competence' in relation to the assessment of the intercultural learning of student sojourners. To complicate matters, many other terms are employed such as cultural or intercultural sensitivity, cultural intelligence, global-mindedness, global perspectives, global citizenship, global competence, international competence, and so on (Bolen 2007b; Deardorff 2010, 2015a; Fantini 2009, 2012b; Jackson 2014). In this chapter I will primarily refer to the measurement of intercultural competence, especially in relation to study abroad.

Before engaging in the assessment of intercultural competence, assessment scholars maintain that it is important to begin by defining this construct as one's conception will or should provide direction for the ways in which intercultural learning is perceived and measured. As noted earlier, this is not a simple task. For many decades scholars from different disciplines have put forward numerous definitions (Griffith, Wolfeld, Armon, Rios and Liu 2016; Sinicrope, Norris and Watanabe 2007).

Deardorff (2009a) edited a comprehensive volume in which scholars from a variety of disciplines and cultural backgrounds offered their understandings of intercultural competence (e.g., Deardorff 2009b; Spitzberg and Changnon 2009). A review of the chapters revealed that cross-cultural psychologists, anthropologists, international educators, and social psychologists have tended to focus on the traits, skills, and behaviours of interculturally competent individuals who reside temporarily or permanently in a new environment. Consequently, many notions of intercultural competence centre on adaptability and effectiveness in unfamiliar cultural contexts (e.g., the adaptation of immigrants, the mindset and behaviours that facilitate the intercultural adjustment of student sojourners) (see Chapter 3). Broader conceptions of intercultural competence generally refer to intercultural traits, knowledge, and behaviours associated with intercultural interactions whether in one's home environment or abroad.

A number of communication specialists have offered their views about the traits and behaviours associated with intercultural competence. 'Interculturally competent persons', according to Chen and Starosta (2006: 357), 'know how to elicit a desired response in interactions and to fulfill their own communication goals by respecting and affirming the worldview and cultural identities of the interactants.' For these scholars, intercultural communication competence refers to 'the ability to acknowledge, respect, tolerate, and integrate cultural differences that qualifies one for enlightened global citizenship' (ibid.: 357). In Jandt's (2016: 53) estimation, effective intercultural communicators possess personality strength (with a strong sense of self and are socially relaxed), well-developed communication skills (verbal and nonverbal), psychological adjustment (ability to adapt to new situations), and cultural awareness (understanding of how people of different cultures think and behave). For this communication specialist, intercultural communication competence requires 'understanding dominant cultural values and understanding how our own cultural values affect the way we perceive ourselves and others' (Jandt 2007: 184).

In the field of education, Dervin and Gross (2016) suggest that the following aspects be borne in mind when discussing intercultural competence. They argue that any model of intercultural competence is first and foremost ideological and political and should thus be considered as a product of a given ideology. They add that intercultural competence should pay attention to the principle of 'diverse diversities', or the idea that a given individual has several characteristics and identities which intersect when they negotiate encounters with others (see Chapter 4). Finally, they remind us that many models of intercultural competence concentrate on the success of intercultural encounters and ignore the potential learning benefits of communication breakdowns, noting that we should include recognition and experience of failure (e.g., miscommunication, misunderstandings) in intercultural training (see Chapter 7).

Definitions of intercultural competence have also been put forward by applied linguists who have focused on second language speakers. For example, in his definition of what he terms 'intercultural communicative competence', Byram (1997) focuses on the ability to nurture meaningful intercultural relationships through the use of a second language. The close connection between language, culture, and intercultural competence is also conveyed in the notion of the 'intercultural speaker', which Byram and Zarate (1997) proposed to describe foreign language/culture learners who are able to successfully establish intercultural relationships through the use of their second language. Byram, Gribkova and Starkey (2002) depict intercultural speakers as competent, flexible communicators who 'engage with complexity and multiple identities' and 'avoid stereotyping which accompanies perceiving someone through a single identity' (p. 5). The de-centring of the native speaker as an ideal model for language learners and the concept of the intercultural speaker have drawn attention to the knowledge, attitudes, and skills needed to engage in constructive, meaningful intercultural dialogue in a second language (Byram 2009; Dasli and Díaz 2017a).

For critical applied linguists Dervin and Dirba (2006), second language speakers possess intercultural competence 'when they are able/ willing to communicate effectively with others, accept their position as "strangers" when meeting others, and realise that all individuals, including themselves, are multicultural and complex (sex, age, religion, status in society, etc.)' (p. 257). Further, Guilherme (2004) suggests that *critical* intercultural speakers are able to 'negotiate between their own cultural, social and political identifications and representations with those of the other' (p. 298), and, in the process, become mindful of 'the multiple, ambivalent, resourceful, and elastic nature of cultural identities in an intercultural encounter' (ibid.: 125). A high level of proficiency in a second language does not ensure a high level of sociopragmatic awareness or intercultural competence (Bennett and Bennett 2004; Byram 2012; Fantini 2012a; Jackson forthcoming b). As noted by Jackson (2012) in relation to second language study abroad students, '[a]dvanced knowledge of the grammar and vocabulary of the host language [does] not ensure intercultural competence or satisfactory social intercultural interaction' (p. 455). (Revisit Chapter 4 for more discussion about the close connection between language, culture, and identity.)

Through a survey of more than 20 prominent intercultural communication experts from various backgrounds and disciplines (e.g., Michael

Byram, Janet Bennett, Guo-Ming Chen), Deardorff (2004) sought to arrive at a common conception of intercultural competence. The top three elements that the scholars associated with this construct were: 'awareness, valuing, and understanding of cultural differences; experiencing other cultures; and self-awareness of one's own culture' (ibid.: 247). After reviewing nine definitions of intercultural competence, the participants in this research selected one proposed by Byram (1997: 34) as most pertinent to their institution's internationalisation strategies: 'Knowledge of others, knowledge of self; skills to interpret and relate; skills to discover and/ or to interact; valuing others' values, beliefs, and behaviors; and relativising one's self. Linguistic competence plays a key role' (Deardorff 2006: 247). Interestingly, even though the majority of the experts surveyed were not language specialists, their selection suggests that they recognised the importance of the linguistic dimension in intercultural interactions.

Drawing on her study and work in international education, Deardorff (2015c) defines intercultural competence broadly as 'communication and behavior that are both effective and appropriate in intercultural interactions, with *effective* referring to the degree to which the individual's goals are achieved and *appropriateness* referring to the manner and context in which those goals are achieved' (p. 218). Although scholars continue to debate what constitutes intercultural competence and stress the complexity of this construct, her definition is often cited in study abroad research publications and the literature on assessment practices in international education.

Models of Intercultural Competence Development

In Deardorff's (2009a) *SAGE Handbook of Intercultural Competence* multiple conceptions and models of intercultural competence are presented and examined in relation to applications in various contexts (e.g., study abroad, intercultural research and education) (e.g., see Spitzberg and Changnon 2009; Deardorff 2006, 2009b) with the explicit aim of providing readers with 'practical guidance on researching and assessing this elusive construct' (Deardorff 2009d: xi). While most of the chapters in this comprehensive volume centre on Western perspectives, the editor made an effort to include the contributions of scholars from various disciplines in other parts of the world (e.g., Africa, China, the Arab World, India, Latin America). Even so, it is important to acknowledge that our field is still dominated by European and North American conceptions, theories, and models of intercultural competence and this, in turn, impacts the ways in which this construct is defined and measured.

In this section, we take a look at some of the frameworks that have influenced the assessment of intercultural dimensions in study abroad: Byram's (1997) model of intercultural communicative competence,

Fantini's (2009) intercultural competencies dimensions model, M.J. Bennett's (1993) developmental model of Intercultural sensitivity (DMIS), Hammer's (2012) intercultural development continuum (IDC), and Deardorff's (2004, 2006) process model of intercultural competence.

Byram's Model of Intercultural Communicative Competence

In Europe particularly, Byram's (1997) model of intercultural communicative competence has profoundly affected intercultural pedagogy and assessment, including work in study abroad contexts. The framework he proposed built on notions of communicative competence put forward by applied linguists in relation to the teaching and learning of foreign languages (e.g., Hymes 1966, 1972; Canale and Swain 1980). Communicative competence refers to 'what a speaker needs to know, and what a child needs to learn, to be able to use language appropriately in specific social/cultural settings' (Swann, Deumert, Lillis and Mesthrie 2004: 42).

In the first part of his model, Byram (1997) cites the following *linguistic* elements as characteristic of an interculturally competent second language speaker (intercultural speaker):

- Linguistic competence: the ability to apply knowledge of the rules of a standard version of the language to produce and interpret spoken and written language.
- Sociolinguistic competence: the ability to give to the language produced by an interlocutor—whether native speaker or not—meanings which are taken for granted by the interlocutor or which are negotiated and made explicit with the interlocutor.
- Discourse competence: the ability to use, discover and negotiate strategies for the production and interpretation of monologue or dialogue texts which follow the conventions of the culture of an interlocutor or are negotiated as intercultural texts for particular purposes.

(Byram 1997: 48)

The second part of Byram's framework identifies five *savoirs* or components that are linked to the *cultural* dimension of the intercultural speaker's competence. The first two are considered prerequisites for successful intercultural/ interlingual communication:

- Intercultural attitudes (*savoir être*)—curiosity and openness, readiness to suspend disbelief about others' cultures and belief about one's own intercultural attitudes.
- Knowledge (*savoirs*)—of social groups and their products and practices in one's own and interlocutor's country.

108 *Assessment and Evaluation*

Finally, the next three components feature the skills deemed necessary for successful communication across cultures and languages:

- Skills of interpreting and relating (*savoir comprendre*): ability to interpret a document or event from another culture, to explain it and relate it to documents or events from one's own.
- Skills of discovery and interaction (*savoir apprendre/faire*): ability to acquire new knowledge of a culture and to operate this knowledge in real-time communication.
- Critical cultural awareness (*savoir s'engager*): an ability to evaluate critically and on the basis of explicit criteria, perspectives, practices and products in one's own and other cultures and countries.

(Byram et al. 2002: 12–13)

For Byram (2009), critical cultural awareness is the most crucial element that should be promoted in second or foreign language education.

Byram's *saviours* were incorporated into the *Council of Europe's Common European Framework of Reference for Languages: Learning, Teaching Assessment* (CEFR) (2001), which serves as a guide for the teaching and assessment of intercultural competence in European nations (Byram and Parmenter 2012). The European Centre for Modern Languages (ECML) also drew on Byram's framework to develop an intercultural assessment guide for language teachers, which is employed in study abroad contexts (Lázár, Huber-Kriegler, Lussier, Matel and Peck 2007). More recently, a number of interculturalists have been assisting the Council of Europe with the development of a Reference Framework of Competences for Democratic Culture to be adapted for use in primary and secondary schools and higher education and vocational training institutions throughout Europe as well as national curricula and teaching programmes, which include both mobile and non-mobile students. (See www.coe.int/en/web/education/competences-for-democratic-culture.)

Byram's work and the subsequent publications of the Council of Europe have raised awareness of the need to enhance the intercultural awareness, skills, and attitudes of language learners, including those who study abroad. Familiarity with the grammar rules and vocabulary in another language does not necessarily mean that someone is interculturally competent. Byram's model of intercultural communicative competence, however, is not without limitations. For example, some scholars have criticised it for not providing specific, concrete guidelines for intercultural teaching and assessment. The development of the CEFR (2001), which is currently being revised, was an attempt to bridge the gap between theory and practice.

In the past decade, a number of critical interculturalists (e.g., Boye 2016; Dasli and Díaz 2017a; Dervin 2016, 2017; Díaz 2013; Houghton

2012; Risager 2007) have cited additional reservations about Byram's model and its use by educators who aim to teach and measure the intercultural communicative competence of language learners, including student sojourners. Drawing on the work of Risager (2007), for example, Díaz (2013) maintains that the connection between language and culture lacks clarity in Byram's framework.

> While Byram's model stresses the inseparable relationship between language and culture, it ultimately lacks a systematic view of this relationship (Risager 2007) in a way that can be mapped onto the mechanics of everyday practice. This is highly problematic.
> (Díaz 2013: 6)

In Díaz's (2013) view, concerns about 'internal conceptual discrepancies' in Byram's model raise further questions about its applications in intercultural teaching and assessment.

> In Byram's ICC [intercultural communicative competence] model, IC is conceptualised as including *cognitive, behavioral, and affective* dimensions . . . however this conceptualisation of 'competence' that underlies the rest of ICC's sub-components: linguistic, sociolinguistic, and discourse competences. Indeed, although Byram and Zarate developed their model specifically in the context of foreign language teaching, its influential notion of 'intercultural competence' does not specifically deal with the interrelationship of these *saviours* and the linguistically oriented sub-components of the CC model they aimed to complement. These sub-components were conceived within predominantly cognitive and psycholinguistic dimensions.
> (Díaz 2013: 8)

While Byrams's model is still very influential in Europe, critics question its applicability in non-Western contexts, noting that this 'individual-oriented list type model' has been conceived in relation to individualistic cultures (e.g., Houghton and Yamada 2012; Matsuo 2012). In some quarters, intercultural language education and assessment that draws on this model is viewed as 'an organized and carefully structured mechanism through which individuals are activated as critical social agents who are encouraged to act towards particular social and political ends' (Houghton 2012: 183; also see Dervin and Gross 2016). This observation raises further ethical concerns about the appropriateness of Western models of intercultural competence for intercultural interventions and assessment in other regions of the world. It also points to the need for more indigenous perspectives and models of intercultural competence that have been developed by scholars from diverse linguistic, cultural and disciplinary backgrounds.

Fantini's Intercultural Competencies Dimensions Model

Drawing on his own research findings and a review of conceptions of intercultural competence put forward by other interculturalists, Fantini devised the intercultural competencies dimensions model, which, as the name suggests, incorporates multiple elements associated with this construct (Fantini 2009, 2012a; Fantini and Tirmizi 2006). Underpinning this framework are Fantini's perceptions of cultural competence and intercultural competence, and the differences between these constructs. The former denotes 'the ability that enables us to be members within our own society'; it entails the 'gradual process of enculturation beginning at birth' (Fantini 2012a: 270). Thus, in this model, cultural competence refers to the mastery of one's 'native language-culture (linguacultural) system' (Fantini 2012a: 270), whereas intercultural competence encompasses 'a complex of abilities needed to perform "effectively" and "appropriately" when interacting with others who are linguistically and culturally different from oneself' (Fantini and Tirmizi 2006: 12). The notion of 'effectiveness' relates to an individual's perception of his or her own intercultural competence (an 'etic' or outsider's perspective), while 'appropriateness' refers to how this performance is viewed by the hosts (an 'emic' or insider's perspective).

Fantini (2012a) posits that interactions with individuals who have been socialised in a different linguistic and cultural environment, whether at home or abroad, open up the possibility of entering 'a new language-culture' (p. 271). As individuals gain more experience with unfamiliar ways of being (e.g., divergent worldviews and communication styles), they may gradually become interculturally competent if they embrace the attributes and behaviours in his model. While the development of a 'second linguaculture' can be challenging for individuals (e.g., study abroad students and other border crossers), Fantini (2009, 2012a, 2012b) argues that it can potentially be transformative or life-changing.

Both Byram's (1997) and Fantini's (2009) models may be referred to as co-orientation frameworks as they both seek to conceptualise the ways in which individuals achieve intercultural understanding through communicative mutuality and shared understandings (Boye 2016; Reid 2013). Successful intercultural communication entails the effective and appropriate use of language and the other dimensions that these applied linguists associate with linguistic and intercultural competence.

Fantini's (2009) holistic framework encompasses four dimensions (attitudes, awareness, knowledge, skills), eight attributes or personal characteristics (curiosity, openness, empathy, patience, tolerance for ambiguity, humour, suspended judgment, flexibility), three interrelated areas (cooperation for mutual benefit, communication without disorientation, formation, maintenance of relationships), as well as a developmental process and target language proficiency. Fantini (2009, 2012a) asserts that, through the process of deep reflection and introspection, the dimensions of knowledge, (positive) attitudes, and skills (e.g., communication) can bring about enhanced intercultural awareness, which, in turn, can foster the development of the other dimensions in his model and result in a higher degree of intercultural competence.

Many theories of intercultural competence overlook language proficiency; however, similar to Byram's (1997) model, it is a core element in Fantini's framework. For this applied linguist, '[p]roficiency in a second language at any level enhances all other aspects of intercultural competence in quantitative and qualitative ways' (Fantini 2009: 459); further, he maintains that 'the lack of second language proficiency, even minimally, constrains us to think about the world and act within it entirely in our native system, a decidedly ethnocentric approach' (p. 459). This scholar also emphasises that linguistic and intercultural competence are interrelated but not equal.

For Fantini (2009, 2012b), intercultural competence development involves a longitudinal, ongoing process, which is impacted by such aspects as the amount and quality of intercultural contact and an individual's motivation (instrumental, integrative) to master the host language and learn about the host culture (Fantini 2009: 459). He calls on educators to consider all of the components in his model when designing second language programmes and intercultural interventions for mobile or non-mobile students. More than a decade after it was formulated, Fantini's framework is still guiding intercultural interventions and assessment schemes in study abroad programmes and language courses in many parts of the world (e.g., see Deardorff and Arasaratnam-Smith's volume (2017)).

The Developmental Model of Intercultural Sensitivity (DMIS)

A number of intercultural theorists have proposed conceptual models that aim to depict the process of becoming interculturally competent. Within the context of study abroad, one of the most influential frameworks is the developmental model of intercultural sensitivity (DMIS), a six-stage model that was first proposed by Milton Bennett in the late 1970s (Bennett 1993, 2012). In relation to this linear model, Bennett and Bennett (2004) regard intercultural competence as 'the ability to communicate effectively in cross-cultural situations and to relate appropriately in a variety of cultural contexts' (p. 149), whereas intercultural sensitivity refers to the developmental process that impacts an individual's psychological ability to deal with cultural differences.

Phenomenological in nature, this theoretical framework seeks to account for the observed and reported experiences of individuals in intercultural encounters. 'The underlying assumption of the model is that as one's *experiences of cultural difference* becomes more sophisticated, one's competence in intercultural relations increases' (Bennett and Bennett 2004: 152). The DMIS centres on the constructs of ethnocentricism and ethnorelativism (Bennett 2009). In the former, 'the worldview of one's own culture is central to all reality' (Bennett 1993: 30), whereas the latter is linked to 'being comfortable with many standards and customs and to having an ability to adapt behavior and judgments to a variety of interpersonal settings' (ibid.: 26).

In this theory, intercultural sensitivity is viewed as a progressive, scalar phenomenon, which is associated with personal growth and the development of an intercultural orientation, that is, 'a mindset capable of understanding from within and from without both one's own culture and other cultures' (Bennett, Bennett and Allen 2003: 252). M.J. Bennett (1993, 2012) posits that the development of intercultural sensitivity occurs as the constructs and experiences of cultural differences evolve toward heightened awareness and acceptance of those differences. Specifically, the DMIS theorises that individuals move from ethnocentric stages where one's culture is experienced as 'central to reality' (denial, defence, minimisation), through ethnorelative stages of greater recognition and acceptance of difference (acceptance, adaptation, and integration) (Paige and Bennett 2015) (see Figure 6.1). People do not necessarily follow a linear progression (e.g., advancing to the next phase in sequence), however.

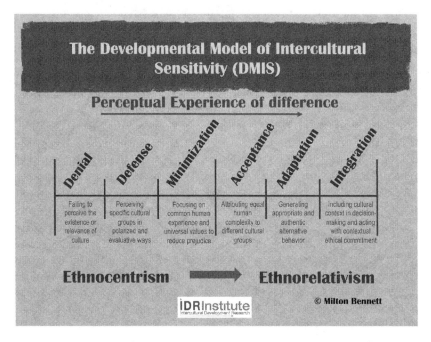

Figure 6.1 The Developmental Model of Intercultural Sensitivity (DMIS)

Due to severe acculturative stress or unpleasant intercultural experiences, for example, they may temporarily retreat to a lower level of sensitivity in the continuum of development (e.g., view the world around them through a more ethnocentric lens).

Denial of difference measures a worldview that ignores or simplifies cultural difference. In this stage, one's own culture is experienced as the only real one. *Polarisation: defence/reversal* measures a judgmental orientation that views cultural differences in terms of 'us' and 'them', whereby one's own culture (or an adopted one) is experienced as the best way of doing things. In *defence of difference*, 'us' is uncritically viewed as superior over 'them' (people who have a different cultural background), whereas in *reversal* (R), the opposite bias prevails. *Minimisation* (M) measures a worldview that emphasises cultural commonality and universal values. With limited cultural self-awareness, individuals in this phase are still viewed as ethnocentric; they may not pay sufficient attention to cultural differences, assuming that other cultures are similar to their own. *Acceptance of difference* measures a worldview that can comprehend and appreciate complex cultural differences, whereas *adaptation to difference* identifies the capacity to alter one's cultural perspective and adapt one's behaviour so that it is appropriate in a particular cultural context. *Integration*, the sixth and final stage in the DMIS, encompasses two forms: *contextual evaluation* and *constructive marginality*. Paige and Bennett (2015) explain that the former refers to 'the process of evaluating multiple cultural perspectives in making choices' about how to best proceed in intercultural situations, whereas the latter refers to the ability to cross cultural boundaries with ease (p. 524). Constructive marginals are depicted as 'cultural bridge builders' who 'draw strength from their multiple cultures and often apply their expanded cultural knowledge and skills to help others work more effectively in culturally diverse environments' (Paige and Bennett 2015: 524). The DMIS posits that ethnorelative worldviews (*Acceptance, Adaptation, Integration*) have more potential to generate the attitudes, knowledge, and behaviour that constitute intercultural competence and facilitate adjustment in a new milieu.

Linked to the DMIS, the intercultural development inventory (IDI) was developed by Hammer and Bennett to assess the intercultural competence of individuals and groups. This psychometric instrument has been subjected to cross-cultural validity testing (e.g., Hammer 2011, 2012, 2015; Hammer, Bennett and Wiseman 2003). The DMIS and IDI are not without critics, however. Concerns have been expressed about the conception of culture underpinning the model (e.g., Boye 2016) and a number of applied linguists (e.g., Liddicoat 2011; Liddicoat, Papademetre, Scarino and Kohler 2003) criticise the DMIS for not paying attention to the language dimension in relation to intercultural development. These scholars also question the model's usefulness to measure progression in short-term sojourns.

> Bennett et al. (1999) propose a model of development that is presented at a very high level of abstraction and the linearity they present ranges across very high-level elements of intercultural competence developed over a quite extensive period of time. However, at a lower level of abstraction and over a shorter period of time, it appears unlikely that the development of intercultural competence is a linear, scalar phenomenon. Moreover, there is little overt linking between interculturality and language in this model and the place of language and of language teaching in the model is not readily apparent.
> (Liddicoat 2011: 848)

Similarly, when comparing Byram's and Bennett's models, Garrett-Rucks (2012) suggests that the latter is 'more suitable for an immersion context or to measure long-term changes in an immersion environment' (p. 26).

The IDI is still widely used in international education; however, due to the constraints cited above, some applied linguists avoid using the DMIS and IDI altogether. Alternatively, others may choose to use the IDI in concert with the collection and analysis of qualitative data (e.g., reflective journals, portfolios) and other measures of second language proficiency to gain insight into the intercultural competence of second language sojourners in research projects or intercultural pedagogical interventions in study abroad programmes.

The Intercultural Development Continuum (IDC)

Following further empirical investigations of the IDI, a revised version of the DMIS was put forward by Hammer (2012, 2015), along with a modified, third version of the IDI, which reflects changes in the model. Instead of six stages, as in the DMIS, the intercultural development continuum (IDC) is a five-stage model, with minimisation depicted as a transitional phase between ethnocentric (denial and polarisation) and ethnorelative (acceptance and adaptation) stages. Hammer (2012) posits that denial and polarisation reflect a monocultural mindset, whereas acceptance and adaptation are indicative of an intercultural or global (more open) mindset.

Hammer (2012) maintains that 'integration, as described in the DMIS, is concerned with the construction of an intercultural identity rather than the development of intercultural competence' (p. 119). For this reason, he eliminated it from the IDC. instead of providing a measure of integration, the third version of the IDI assesses 'cultural disengagement', that is 'the degree to which an individual or group exercises a sense of disconnection from a primary cultural community' (Hammer 2012: 119).

Assessment and Evaluation 115

When comparing the DMIS and IDC, Vande Berg (2015a) observes that both view intercultural development as an 'intentional process through which learners come to construct their experience of cultural difference and similarity in increasing complex and creative ways' (p. 230).

The Process Model of Intercultural Competence

Drawing on the input of 23 leading interculturalists, Deardorff (2004, 2006) devised a process model that has also significantly influenced study abroad research and assessment. As indicated in Figure 6.2, her graphic

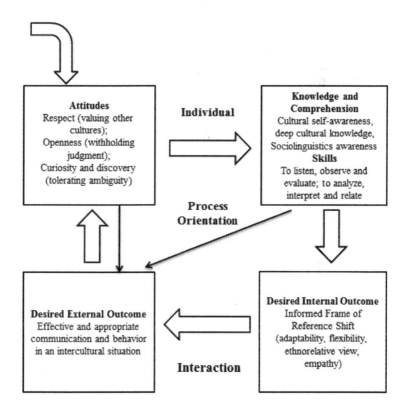

NOTES:
- Begin with attitudes, move from individual level (attitudes) to interaction level (outcomes)
- Degree of intercultural competence depends on degree of attitudes, knowledge/comprehension and skills achieved.

Figure 6.2 The Process Model of Intercultural Competence

representation of intercultural competence depicts movement from 'the individual level of attitudes/personal attributes to the interactive cultural level in regard to the outcomes' (p. 194). Her framework draws attention to the internal shift in frame of reference that is essential for effective and appropriate behaviour in intercultural encounters.

Deardorff's (2004, 2006) process model recognises the *ongoing* complexity of the development of intercultural competence and the importance of reflection in the lifelong journey towards interculturality. Similar to Byram's (1997, 2006) models, her conceptual framework accentuates the central role that attitude plays in intercultural development. In descriptions of this framework, Deardorff (2004) notes that the intercultural experts she surveyed stressed that 'the attitudes of openness, respect (valuing all cultures), curiosity and discovery (tolerating ambiguity)' are essential for individuals to become interculturally competent (p. 193). In accord with Byram's (1997) 'savoirs', her model indicates that intercultural competence necessitates knowledge and understanding of 'one's own cultural norms and sensitivity to those of other cultures' (Deardorff 2008: 37).

Deardorff's process model (2004, 2006, 2008, 2015a, 2015b; Deardorff and Jones 2012) identifies key internal outcomes that may occur as a consequence of 'an informed frame of reference shift', namely, adaptability, an ethnorelative perspective, empathy, and a flexible mindset. Her graphic also specifies desired external outcomes that can be assessed (e.g., 'behaving and communicating appropriately and effectively' in intercultural situations). In Deardorff's (2008) words, her model provides 'a holistic framework for intercultural competence development and assessment' (p. 42).

International educators and organisations concerned with higher education have made use of Deardorff's (2006) research-based consensus model of intercultural competence to develop rubrics to guide the assessment of the intercultural competence of students, including participants in study abroad programmes (e.g., the Association of American Colleges and Universities (AAC&U)). Essentially, a rubric is an evaluation tool or set of guidelines that is created with the aim of promoting the consistent application of learning objectives or standards in a programme or pedagogical intervention, or to measure learners' degree of attainment against a consistent set of criteria (e.g., traits and behaviours associated with intercultural competence) (Stevens and Levi 2013). It is important to note that the AAC&U rubric is meant to serve as an example for institutions and not to be used as is unless the six elements it illustrates align with the selected learning outcomes. 'There must be alignment between stated learning outcomes and the measures or the results will be invalid, no matter how valid and reliable the measure is' (Deardorff, personal communication, 1 May 2017).

Criticality and Notions of Intercultural Competence

A growing number of critical interculturalists argue that the way in which intercultural competence has been conceived and assessed has serious limitations.

> Assessment raises another concern about how ICC [intercultural communicative competence] is conceptualized. Use of the term 'competence' evokes positivist, assessment-driven agendas underlining communicative competence models and associated iterations.
> (Díaz 2013: 8)

Further, critics maintain that there should be much more of an emphasis on criticality in intercultural competence models and applications (Dervin 2016; Dasli and Díaz 2017b; Houghton and Yamada 2012; Piller 2017). Criticality is defined by Díaz (2013) as 'critical thinking, critical self-reflection and critical action' (p. xviii).

Critical intercultural scholars point to the need for creative, interdisciplinary approaches in intercultural assessment and underscore the importance of incorporating ideas from the 'periphery' (outside Europe and America) in conceptions of intercultural competence and interculturality (Dasli and Díaz 2017a, 2017b; Holliday 2011; Jackson 2017b). They also argue that more attention should be placed on criticality when investigating the intercultural development of participants in study abroad programmes (Jackson 2017b; Jackson and Oguro 2018b).

Fundamental Elements and Terminology in Assessment

Before examining some of the approaches and tools used to assess intercultural competence in study abroad contexts, it is helpful to have an understanding of some of the basic terminology and concepts commonly associated with assessment and evaluation. Similar to intercultural competence and interculturality, there are many terms and definitions in the assessment literature.

Assessment and Outcomes-Based Assessment (OBA)

In higher education, assessment is concerned with learning, teaching, and outcomes. One of the most frequently quoted definitions for assessment was put forward by Angelo (1995), a testing specialist in the United States, who describes the assessment of student learning in this way:

> Assessment is an ongoing process aimed at understanding and improving student learning. It involves making our expectations explicit and public; setting appropriate criteria and high standards

for learning quality; systematically gathering, analyzing, and interpreting evidence to determine how well performance matches those expectations and standards; and using the resulting information to document, explain, and improve performance. When it is embedded effectively within larger institutional systems, assessment can help us focus our collective attention, examine our assumptions, and create a shared academic culture dedicated to assuring and improving the quality of higher education.

(Angelo 1995: 7)

In relation to study abroad, the Forum on Education Abroad (2011) defines assessment as '[t]he process of measuring effectiveness, usually through the articulation of goals, the development of associated measures and the identification of observable outcomes, used to inform whether the initial goals were achieved' (p. 21). Within the wider context of education, this conception fits with the definition of outcomes-based assessment (OBA) provided by Driscoll and Wood (2007), which is also relevant to this discussion:

We describe OBA as an educational model in which curriculum and pedagogy and assessment are all focused on student learning outcomes. It's an educational process that fosters continuous attention to student learning and promotes institutional accountability based on student learning.

(Driscoll and Wood 2007: 4)

An OBA approach to assessment, which is becoming increasingly common in higher education and international education, stems from a shift in emphasis on 'inputs' (e.g., teaching, content knowledge) to 'outcomes' (e.g., learning, understanding of core constructs and issues). OBA requires desired outcomes to be identified before a programme and assessment scheme are implemented. Within this orientation, a learning outcome refers to a stated, explicit expectation for student learning (e.g., intercultural development) (Banta and Palomba 2015; Driscoll and Wood 2007). Thus, an OBA approach begins with a clear indication of what learners should be able to do by the end of an intervention and then focuses on the organisation of the curriculum, instruction, and assessment that will facilitate the learning process (e.g., the development of intercultural competence of student sojourners). Crucially, the modes of assessment that are employed must be closely aligned with the stated learning outcomes for the results to be useful and valid (Angelo 1995; Angelo and Cross 1993; Deardorff 2015a).

Assessment and Evaluation

Assessment is closely linked to the notion of 'evaluation'. While the terms are sometimes used interchangeably, testing experts generally refer to evaluation as 'the process of critical examination involving interpretation and judgment related to effectiveness and quality' (Forum on Education Abroad 2011: 22). Within the context of pedagogical interventions in study abroad (e.g., intercultural communication courses), evaluation is product-oriented and typically focuses on grades (e.g., IDI scores, language proficiency scores) (Zukroff, Ferst, Hirsch, Slawson and Wiedenhoeft 2005).

Formative and Summative Assessment

Assessment may also be categorised as formative or summative. Formative assessments are employed to gather information about how study abroad students are performing to provide guidance for changes within the programme (e.g., intercultural interventions) (Angelo and Cross 1993; Deardorff 2015a; Suskie 2009). Summative assessments are implemented to evaluate the final outcomes of a programme or intercultural intervention (e.g., grades in an intercultural communication course, a comparison of pre- and post-intercultural sensitivity scores for research/evaluation purposes) (Angelo 1995; Deardorff 2015a). Assessment scholars maintain that it is vital for study abroad professionals to include both forms of assessment (e.g., formative, summative) in their assessment plan.

Motives for Assessment

It is also important to be mindful of differences in the motives or driving force for assessment. As I explained in the introduction, in study abroad contexts, an assessment plan may be implemented for multiple reasons, such as to enhance student learning and engagement or for accountability. In the former, the emphasis is on gaining information from the assessment of student learning to provide direction for constructive changes in the design and delivery of a programme or course (e.g., a pedagogical intervention that aims to enhance intercultural development and engagement). (This aspect is discussed further in Chapter 7.) Accountability, on the other hand, refers to the provision of concrete evidence of learning that affirms the quality of a programme or pedagogical intervention (e.g., a comparison of pre- and post-study abroad measures of intercultural competence to furnish administrators with an indication of the quality of the programme) (Zukroff et al. 2005).

Assessment Processes

By unpacking Angelo's (1995) definition of assessment that was presented earlier in this chapter, we gain a sense of the core elements that should feature in the assessment process. Firstly, it is important for educators to begin by making learning expectations 'explicit and public'. In other words, learning goals for a study abroad programme (or intercultural intervention) should be clearly articulated and made available to all stakeholders (e.g., administrators, faculty, students) before the programme gets underway. Measurable objectives and performance benchmarks for study abroad courses or programmes should be identified and used to guide the assessment process (Engberg and Davidson 2015). Angelo (1995) maintains that standards of excellence are vital when setting learning expectations and the criteria for evaluating learning outcomes.

Further, the continuous improvement of the quality of intercultural development in study abroad programmes should be a key aim in the assessment process. To this end, it is incumbent on educators to use valid and reliable ways to assess the intercultural development of students. In this way, they can gauge to what degree the learning objectives have been met. For this to happen, the instrument must measure what it purports to measure (possess content validity) and produce stable, consistent results (be reliable). Testing experts maintain that it is imperative for educators to employ multiple measures at strategic intervals and not rely on a single instrument administered before and after study abroad (Deardorff 2015b, 2016; Deardorff and Arasaratnam-Smith 2017).

A number of intercultural educators suggest that the results generated through a well-thought-out assessment scheme can provide evidence to document and support explanations of student performance (e.g., intercultural development in a study abroad programme with reflective elements). Drawing on these results, as Chapter 7 explains, educators can then re-examine programme objectives, methods, and assessment measures linked to an intercultural intervention and make changes to deepen intercultural learning. In addition to providing useful feedback to study abroad participants about their learning, the data can help guide the design and delivery of intercultural interventions (current and future offerings) (see Chapter 7).

Technology and Assessment

With advances in technology, study abroad professionals now have more options related to the assessment of intercultural competence. Some instruments (e.g., self-report surveys, psychometric tools) may be administered and scored entirely online, with reports generated by computer programmes (e.g., IDI profiles). In addition to the administration of online questionnaires, mixed-mode or fully online intercultural communication courses for study abroad students may also generate material that can be assessed with the help of rubrics (e.g., forum posts, fieldwork posts, reflective essays). Software also enables student sojourners to produce eportfolios (digital portfolios) to showcase their work and provide evidence of growth in intercultural awareness and sensitivity (Deardorff 2015b; Zubizarreta 2009).

Intercultural Competence Assessment Tools

Over the years, more than 100+ tools have been developed to measure intercultural competence and many have been employed in study abroad contexts (Deardorff 2015a; Fantini 2009, 2012b; Paige and Stallman 2007; Stemler and Sorkin 2015). Some focus solely on the assessment of intercultural competence or sensitivity and are directly linked to specific conceptual frameworks or models of intercultural development, whereas others have a broader scope, with intercultural aspects as only one of the dimensions. Instruments may differ with regard to the number of constituent constructs and dimensions they aim to measure, and whether or not they are linked to a particular theory or model. The amount of research that has been invested in their development and testing also varies, leading to significant differences in their degree of validity and reliability.

While some intercultural assessment instruments have been developed in-house/locally, others are commercial and may require training and accreditation before they can be used (e.g., the IDI, IES). Nowadays, many commercial tools are delivered through an online format, though some are also available in a paper and pencil format. I will describe a few of the most commonly used assessment tools that feature in study abroad research and education.

- The *AAC&U Intercultural Knowledge and Competence Value Rubric* was developed by faculty representing colleges and universities in various parts of the United States who were affiliated with the Association of American Colleges and Universities (AAC&U). Drawing on the DMIS (Bennett 1993) and Deardorff's (2006) intercultural framework, this instrument identifies learning outcomes and fundamental criteria for the following outcomes: cultural awareness, verbal and nonverbal communication strategies, and attitudes of curiosity, openness, and empathy. The rubric is intended as an example for institutions to use to evaluate student learning (formative assessment) rather than for grading purposes. Institutions are expected to modify the AAC&U rubric according to the specific learning objectives they have set for their student population.
  (See www.aacu.org/value/rubrics/intercultural-knowledge)

- The *Cross-Cultural Adaptability Inventory* (CCAI), which was developed by Kelley and Meyers (1995, 1999), is a self-scoring instrument that aims to facilitate intercultural transitions. This commercial tool takes 25–30 minutes to complete. The developers maintain that it facilitates the identification of an individual or group's strengths and weaknesses in four skill areas that are fundamental to effective intercultural communication and interaction: emotional resilience (the ability to handle acculturative stress), flexibility/openness (degree of receptivity to new ideas and ways of being), perceptual acuity (the ability to recognise and interpret cultural cues), and personal autonomy (strength and confidence in one's identities, values, and beliefs). Among other applications, the CCAI is administered to assess readiness for study abroad and facilitate the intercultural mentorship of student sojourners.

(See http://ccaiassess.com/)

- The *Global Perspectives Inventory* (GPI) aims to measure an individual's global learning and development in relation to cognitive, intrapersonal, and interpersonal dimensions. It also aims to gather the respondent's perception of the community and level of involvement in selected curricular and co-curricular activities. This web-based tool assesses three dimensions associated with global learning and development, and each dimension has two scales. GPI data provides an indication of how students think (cognitive), how they perceive themselves (intrapersonal), and how they relate to people who have a different cultural background (interpersonal). According to the GPI website, approximately 200 educational institutions in the United States and abroad have used this instrument to assess intercultural competence, global learning, and study abroad experiences. The developers maintain that the results can be used to steer conversations about student development, programme enhancement, and institutional effectiveness.

(See www.gpi.hs.iastate.edu/dimensions.php)

- The *Intercultural Development Inventory* (IDI) is a statistically reliable, cross-culturally valid measure of intercultural competence (Hammer 2012). Version 3 of the IDI is linked to the IDC (Hammer 2011, 2012, 2015), a model that has been adapted from the DMIS (Bennett 1993, 2012). This 50-item questionnaire, which can be completed in 15–20 minutes, is available online in many languages. The analysis of IDI results enables the development of a graphic profile of an individual's or group's actual and perceived levels of intercultural competence, along with textual interpretation of intercultural development and related transitional issues. Individuals who complete the IDI are provided with an individual developmental plan (IDP), which offers suggestions for further enhancement of intercultural competence. The IDI must be administered by a qualified IDI administrator and the results are processed and presented by the IDI, LLC in the United States. The IDI results are used for intercultural research, teaching, and assessment in study abroad contexts.

(See https://idiinventory.com/products/the-intercultural-development-inventory-idi/)

- The *Intercultural Effectiveness Scale* (IES), which was developed by the Kozai Group in the United States, aims to evaluate skills

considered essential for effective communication with people who have a different cultural background. The instrument is used by educational institutions to assess pre- and post-levels of intercultural competencies (e.g., pre- and post-study abroad measures of intercultural effectiveness). Data may be used to provide direction for intercultural competence development in intercultural communication courses and other diversity training initiatives. Similar to the IDI, respondents are provided with a detailed individual feedback report to guide future intercultural learning and administrators must receive training to become qualified administrators.
(See www.kozaigroup.com/intercultural-effectiveness-scale-ies/)

- The *Global Competence Aptitude Assessment* (GCAA) measures the components of global competence that are presented in Hunter's (2004) global competence model, which centres on the knowledge, skills, and attitudes that are thought to be necessary for global competence including 'intercultural capability', 'global awareness', 'open-mindedness', among others (see also Deardorff and Hunter 2006). The questions in the instrument are based on diverse regions around the world, with particular emphasis placed on countries that make significant contributions to the world's population and economy. In addition to business contexts and non-profit organisations, the instrument is used in education to assess learning outcomes in study abroad (e.g., pre- and post-measures of global competence).
(See www.globallycompetent.com/aboutGCAA/about.html)

For a more comprehensive list of instruments that are employed to assess intercultural competence in study abroad (as well as other contexts), see Fantini (2009, 2012b) and Paige (2004). The Intercultural Communication Institute also offers a comprehensive list of intercultural training and assessment tools on their website (see http://intercultural.org/training-and-assessment-tools.html). In addition to categorising various conceptual models of intercultural competence, Griffith et al. (2016) summarise the merits and weaknesses of a number of intercultural assessment tools and review empirical studies that have employed these instruments to measure intercultural development. An earlier report by Sinicrope et al. (2007) describes and reviews tools that are being used to measure intercultural competence. Roy, Wandschneider and Steglitz (2014) provide a more focused review of three instruments: the BEVI (beliefs, events, values inventory), IDI, and GPI.

Diverse Assessment Techniques and Strategies

A variety of means and strategies are used to track and measure the intercultural development of study abroad students, including both direct and indirect measures. Indirect evidence of intercultural learning is 'a *perception* of learning that occurred or data providing a basis for inference' (Deardorff 2015b: 18). In addition to the instruments mentioned above, which include self-report questionnaires, other forms of indirect assessment are study abroad programme satisfaction forms, interviews, focus groups, student evaluations, inventories, and document analysis (e.g., analysis of intercultural course syllabi, programme files) (Bolen 2007b; Deardorff 2015a, 2015b).

Direct methods of assessment provide evidence of 'actual learning or performance' (Deardorff 2015b: 18). Examples include a review of the written coursework of study abroad students (e.g., intercultural reflective essays, papers, project reports), portfolios, eportfolios, the analysis of oral performance (e.g., videotaped or audiotapes of students engaged in intercultural interactions), and observations of study abroad educators (Deardorff 2015a). Portfolio assessment refers to a collection of selected materials produced either by an individual over time or scores from various assessments or both (Griffith et al. 2016; Zubizarreta 2009). There is no standard approach to portfolio assessment and the content (material) assembled, the platform (paper vs. digital), and scoring method employed (e.g., use of rubrics) vary among study abroad contexts. A systematic review of portfolios or eportfolios, which may contain reflective diary entries, sojourn essays, and/or online forum posts, can open a window into the intercultural development of student sojourners. Material of this nature can capture context-specific intercultural communication skills and the refinement of those skills over time. Intercultural competence may be assessed periodically through a review of material that is submitted before, during, and after study abroad (Salisbury 2015; Zubizarreta 2009).

Assessment Challenges and Constraints

Measuring the intercultural learning of students who take part in study abroad programmes is challenging for many reasons. Griffith et al. (2016) observes that the assessment of intercultural competence (ICC) is constrained by multiple conceptual and methodological issues.

> First, little consensus seems to exist regarding the requisite skills and abilities that contribute to ICC. Second, the measurement of ICC has overrelied on self-report methods that do not adequately cover the entire spectrum of the construct. Specifically, existing measures often tap self-referent cognitions without adequately capturing the affective and behavioral aspects that are inherent in intercultural interactions. Finally, the psychometric properties of existing measures leave much room for improvement.
>
> (Griffith et al. 2016: 36)

The conceptualisation of intercultural competence is complicated and the lack of a consistent definition of what constitutes this construct makes it difficult to ascertain the most effective and appropriate ways to measure it (Deardorff 2009c, 2015a; Fantini 2012b). Scholars use different definitions of core constructs and, to complicate matters, they may also operationalise the same concepts in different ways. There are divergent views about what constitutes the basic components of intercultural competence and differing ideas about how they are enacted in real-world intercultural interactions (Roy et al. 2014; Van de Vijver and Leung 2009). There may also be a lack of clarity and understanding about the conception of intercultural competence that underpins a particular approach to assessment.

A review of the literature on study abroad assessment shows that there is considerable variability in the tools and approaches employed to assess the intercultural development of student sojourners. This means that comparing the outcomes of study abroad programmes that have used different conceptions of intercultural competence and assessment methods may be problematic and misleading.

In many studies, self-reports (e.g., survey questionnaires, interviews) are employed to offer insight into the intercultural mindset of student sojourners. While data of this nature can capture attitudes and declarative knowledge (e.g., awareness of culture-related facts), measurement concerns such as 'respondent faking' or inflation responses can limit the usefulness of these measures. Respondents may provide inaccurate responses or offer self-descriptions that make them appear more open, flexible, and interculturally competent than they actually are, or vice versa. Future-oriented optimism may compel individuals to respond to items in terms of their idealistic self rather than provide answers that more accurately reflect their current ideas, attitudes, and actions. Accordingly, in agreement with Merino and Tileag (2011: 91), I underscore the need to be aware of the limitations of self-reports when reading personal accounts of international experience and discourses on interculturality in study abroad.

Reliance on self-report data (indirect assessment) as the sole means of assessing intercultural competence is ill-advised for many reasons. In addition to the limitations mentioned above, the biases of assessors may influence reports on intercultural competence development (e.g., the ways study abroad data is gathered and interpreted, how interview excerpts are selected to illustrate developmental trajectories). Individuals who collect and process data of this nature possess differing degrees of understanding about interculturality and also have variable assessment skills and knowledge. These variables can significantly influence the ways in which the intercultural development of student sojourners is tracked, measured, and reported. I draw attention to this element as more and more study abroad personnel who have little or no background in assessment or intercultural education are being pressed to measure the intercultural competence of student sojourners (e.g., provide evidence of the benefits of international educational experience). It is therefore important to be mindful of expertise and quality issues when digesting study abroad presentations and publications.

Other measurement issues may plague the use of some of the intercultural instruments that are used to assess the intercultural competence of study abroad students, especially in-house tools that have not been adequately researched. For example, their reliability and validity may be inadequate, resulting in the collection of data that is not reflective of the intercultural competence of respondents.

Another challenge of intercultural assessment in study abroad relates to the timing of the data collection. Many studies gather measures of intercultural sensitivity or competence before and immediately after the sojourn. This only provides a snapshot of student learning at these points in time. Due to many of the concerns cited above, intercultural assessment experts recommend that both indirect and direct measures be collected and analysed on an ongoing basis throughout a study abroad programme to develop a holistic, more complete picture of intercultural learning (e.g., the developmental trajectories of students). As Deardorff (2015a: 65-6) explains:

> Utilizing both direct and indirect evidence is crucial in international education in order to provide a more complete view of student learning. Thus, a mixed-methods assessment approach should mean direct and indirect evidence, not just multiple measures under one or the other categories.

As intercultural development is a lifelong endeavour it is also important to bear in mind that the impact of study abroad may not be realised until long after students have returned home. For this reason, Zarate and Gohard-Radenkovic (2004) prefer to speak about 'the recognition' of intercultural competences rather than assessment. Dervin and Gross (2016) also remind us that intercultural competence may never be 'acquired', as it is—and should be—a lifelong learning process.

Evaluation of Study Abroad Programmes and Intercultural Interventions

Most of this chapter has centred on individual assessment and intercultural competence development in relation to study abroad. In particular, I have discussed the use of assessment to determine whether the learning goals in a study abroad programme have been achieved (summative assessment). I also reviewed the collection and processing of assessment data with the aim of providing direction for the enhancement of student learning and engagement (formative assessment).

In addition to individual assessment, systematic programme reviews and institutional assessment are also important in relation to the intercultural dimension of study abroad. A programme review refers to 'the comprehensive evaluation of a program based on a critical examination of its component parts' (Forum on Education Abroad 2011: 22). A review of this nature may be carried out by study abroad personnel who are associated with the programme (an internal review) or by an outside agency (external review). This process may focus on a study abroad programme or a specific element (e.g., intercultural course for student sojourners).

An institution-wide review of internationalisation initiatives, including study abroad programmes, may also be conducted at an institution. The assessment of various elements, including intercultural interventions, may be carried out by a campus or programme institutional review board (internal assessment) or by external reviewers. The results of programme evaluations can provide direction for the refinement of study abroad policies and practices, and lead to the design and implementation of creative intercultural interventions. The next chapter explores some of the many ways in which educators are intervening in study abroad programmes to enhance the intercultural learning and engagement of student sojourners.

Conclusion

Assessment and evaluation in international education are here to stay! With the push for quality assurance and accountability in higher education, international officers, study abroad professionals, and interculturalists are increasingly being called on to assess the language and intercultural learning of study abroad participants. Accordingly, study abroad programmes, including intercultural pedagogical interventions, are being monitored more than in past years. In many parts of the world, a culture of assessment is taking root and influencing study abroad practice. Many programmes now have well-developed intercultural assessment plans and the results are being used to enhance the quality of future offerings. Study abroad researchers may also incorporate the assessment of intercultural competence into their studies and this, too, is contributing to advances in international education.

In light of these developments and imperatives, I have devoted a full chapter to intercultural assessment and evaluation, drawing attention to core elements in the assessment process in relation to the intercultural development of study abroad students. In addition to highlighting numerous benefits of assessing intercultural competence, I have identified multiple limitations of current assessment practices and offered suggestions for the enhancement of future efforts. The next chapter focuses on intercultural interventions in study abroad programmes and the role of assessment is revisited as it is a core element in OBA approaches to curriculum design and development.

Further Reading and Resources

Bolen, M. (ed.) (2007) *A Guide to Outcomes Assessment in Study Abroad*, Carlisle, PA: Forum on Education Abroad.

This edited collection provides a rationale for outcomes assessment in education abroad and includes chapters that review various instruments and approaches that are being used to measure intercultural development and other learning outcomes in relation to international educational experience.

Deardorff, D.K. (2015) *Demystifying Outcomes Assessment for International Educators: A Practical Approach*, Sterling, VA: Stylus Publishing.

Designed for international educators and administrators who do not have a background in assessment, this book provides an accessible introduction to learner-centred, outcomes-based assessment in study abroad.

Deardorff, D.K. (2016) 'How to assess intercultural competence', in H. Zhu (ed.), *Research Methods in Intercultural Communication*, Chichester: John Wiley and Sons, pp. 120–34.

In this chapter, the author reviews core elements and issues in relation to the assessment of intercultural competence.

Fantini, A.E. (2012b) 'Multiple strategies for assessing intercultural communicative competence', in J. Jackson (ed.), *Routledge Handbook of Language and Intercultural Communication*, Abingdon, UK: Routledge, pp. 390–405.

In this chapter, the author explains why the lack of clarity about what constitutes intercultural communicative competence makes it difficult to assess. After stressing the need for multiple assessment modes and strategies, Fantini reviews various assessment instruments, providing details about their purpose and source.

Savicki, V. and Brewer, E. (eds) (2015) *Assessing Study Abroad: Theory, Tools, and Practice*, Sterling, VA: Stylus Publishing.

Intended for study abroad advisors, administrators, and educators, this edited collection provides case studies of the assessment of study abroad programmes, drawing attention to the limitations and benefits of various assessment tools and strategies.

7 Intercultural Interventions

Introduction

It is not unusual for students to expect to become more interculturally competent and global-minded through international educational experience. Second language learners may also assume that they will become fluent speakers of that language if they reside and study in an environment where it is widely spoken. Expectations of language and cultural immersion in the host environment are often shared by students, parents, educators, and administrators in higher education. As explained in previous chapters, however, international education researchers have discovered that a complex mix of internal and external factors can lead to very different learning paths and outcomes. Deep intercultural learning and substantial gains in language proficiency may not occur without a pedagogical intervention.

In study abroad programmes that do not have any form of intercultural mediation, some students may develop meaningful multicultural relationships and simultaneously enhance their intercultural competence and language skills while in the host environment. These individuals may also become much more attuned to global affairs and acquire a more cosmopolitan, global identity. In sharp contrast, however, many others may spend nearly all of their free time conversing in their first language with co-nationals and, contrary to their expectations, end up having a 'bubble experience' abroad. Avoiding intercultural interactions and second language use, they may return home with little or no interest in language learning or multicultural friendships. In some cases, ethnocentric, xenophobic, or racist tendencies may even become further entrenched.

As the previous chapters have explained, recent study abroad research indicates that simply being present in the host environment does not ensure an immersion experience, advances in intercultural competence, host language learning, or the development of multicultural friendships and global perspectives. The attributes and actions commonly associated with global citizenship (e.g., empathy, interculturality sensitivity, adaptability) are not necessarily cultivated through international experience (Jackson 2014; Olson and Kroeger 2001). Consequently, more and more scholars advocate research-driven intercultural interventions in study abroad programmes at all stages: pre-sojourn, sojourn, and re-entry (Baumgratz-Gangl 1992; Jackson 2012; Jackson and Oguro 2018b; Plews and Misfeldt 2018; Vande Berg et al. 2012a).

This chapter begins with a review of shifts in understandings of how adults learn best and implications for the design and delivery of intercultural training and education programmes. Advances in conceptions of culture, theory-building, research, pedagogy, and technology are bringing about significant changes in the ways in which educators intervene to deepen the intercultural learning and engagement of both mobile and non-mobile students. As the measurement of student learning is a core element in the curriculum design process, I briefly discuss the application of some of the assessment tools and methods that were featured in Chapter 6 and underscore the vital role that programme evaluation should play to provide quality assurance and direction for subsequent revisions. Finally, I describe diverse forms of intercultural mediation that are carried out during various phases of the study abroad cycle in different parts of the world, including innovative online interventions. Examples of comprehensive intercultural interventions that extend from the pre-sojourn phase to re-entry are also provided.

Shifting Pedagogies and Perspectives

As Chapters 1 and 2 have explained, ideas about what constitutes culture, interculturality, and global citizenship have evolved over time. Even today, scholars do not fully agree on definitions of these constructs (Deardorff 2006, 2008, 2009b, 2015c; Spencer-Oatey 2012), although contemporary intercultural theorists are increasingly embracing critical perspectives that challenge static, unitary notions of culture (e.g., Abdallah-Pretceille 2003; Dasli and Díaz 2017b; Díaz 2013; Dervin 2016; Dervin and Gross 2016; Holliday 2011; Piller 2010, 2017). Naturally, shifts in understandings of these core elements have resulted in differing ideas about the most appropriate and effective ways to propel students to higher levels of intercultural awareness and competence both in the home environment and abroad. Within the field of education, there have been significant changes in understandings about how students best acquire knowledge and skills; this has resulted in changes in ideas about the most effective ways to teach (Groen and Kawalilak 2014; Merriam and Bierema 2014). This, too, has affected intercultural pedagogy in international education. Let us examine some of these developments.

Advances in Pedagogy

Traditional didactic or teacher-focused forms of education centre on the transfer of information from the teacher to the student. In this orientation, the teacher is positioned as a source of knowledge (e.g., the expert or source of wisdom), while the learner tends to be viewed as a passive recipient. In teacher-centred approaches, the emphasis is on the quality, quantity, structure, and transmission of content; the onus is on individual students to process and master the material presented (Light, Cox and Calkins 2009).

Through systematic research on teaching and learning, education scholars have been developing more insight into how students, including adults, actually learn (Groen and Kawalilak 2014; Merriam and Bierema 2014). By the 1980s, enriched understandings about the learning process brought about shifts in the roles and responsibilities of teachers and students. Moving away from didactic forms of education, institutions of education in Western countries, in particular, began to adopt more learner-centred forms of teaching, which transferred the focus of instruction from the teacher to the student, to varying degrees. In learning-focused conceptions of teaching, instructional approaches and techniques aim to foster student autonomy and self-responsibility for learning. Students are deemed active 'agents' engaged in the process of lifelong learning rather than passive vessels or recipients of knowledge (Light et al. 2009; Weimer 2012). This orientation has been informed by constructivist learning theory, which emphasises the crucial role that learners play in constructing meaning from new information and prior experience (Barkley 2010; Pritchard and Woollard 2010). In this approach, '[l]earning is much more than information transfer or habit formation; It is a developmental, experiential, and holistic process wherein learners individually construct, and with members of their various groups co-construct, the meaning that they experience in the world' (Vande Berg 2015a: 229). Constructivist, student-centred pedagogy embraces the notion that students can learn through social interactions with peers (Cavana 2009).

The field of intercultural training (formerly referred to as cross-cultural training), which emerged in the 1960s, has been profoundly affected by the move towards more learner-centred, theory-driven education. Initially, intercultural trainers with a background in anthropology, applied linguistics, and/or intercultural communication were pressed to meet the expectations of employers who were sending staff abroad (e.g., a government body, an educational institution, a business corporation). In the United States, for example, early intercultural training focused on helping military personnel, diplomats, volunteers (e.g., Peace Corps workers), business people, and other expatriates deal more effectively and appropriately with a language barrier and cultural difference in the country where they would be posted (Kohls with Brussow 1995; Kohls and Knight 1994; Mikk 2015; Pusch 2004; Sorrells 2012; Storti 2009). Most of the material used in these training sessions drew on examples from 'the field' rather than intercultural communication theories and systematic research (Martin et al. 2012).

As the number of students joining study abroad programmes began to swell, scholars in various disciplines (e.g., applied linguistics, cross-cultural psychology) began to pay closer attention to the adjustment challenges of student sojourners (e.g., language and intercultural transitions) (Bochner 2006; Cushner and Karim 2004; Furnham 2010, 2015; Furnham and Bochner 1986; Gullahorn and Gullahorn 1963; Oberg 1960; Paige 2015a; see Chapter 3, this volume). Their research findings and conceptual models helped to inform the content, curricula, and approaches in intercultural interventions that seek to prepare students for international educational experience (Jackson 2012; Paige 2015b; Paige and Vande Berg 2012).

With the shift to more learner-centred teaching, intercultural communication instructors began to assume the role of mentor rather than 'sage on the stage' or expert who transmits knowledge to students. Basically, cultural mentoring is 'an intercultural pedagogy in which the mentor provides ongoing support for and facilitation of intercultural learning and development' (Paige 2013: 6). As a reflective mindset is crucial in the mentoring process, the facilitator continuously encourages students to think more deeply and critically about their intercultural attitudes and actions, and prompts them to set realistic goals for future intercultural interactions. In this approach, the facilitator tries to 'help them learn to reflect on themselves as cultural beings, and to become aware of the ways that they characteristically respond to and make meaning within different cultural contexts' (Lou, Vande Berg and Paige 2012: 415).

Contemporary intercultural educators maintain that it is possible for students to develop a more open, intercultural mindset through experiential learning (Kolb 1984; Passarelli and Kolb 2012; Smolic and Martin 2018) and, more specifically, structured, critical reflection on 'real world' intercultural experience (Giovangeli, Oguro and Harbon 2018; Hoult 2018; Jackson and Oguro 2018b; Moon 2000, 2004; Paige 2013). Consequently, guided critical reflection lies at the heart of many contemporary pedagogical interventions that are now being designed to enhance and extend the intercultural learning of student sojourners.

Advances in technology and social media are also facilitating changes in the way intercultural education is being conceived and implemented in study abroad contexts. For example, eLearning platforms (e.g., Blackboard, Moodle) are enabling online or blended intercultural interventions throughout the study abroad cycle Later in the chapter, we look at some examples of technology-enhanced schemes.

Broadening the Scope: Internationalising the Campus

In recognition of the diversity in the United States and other countries with large immigrant populations, in the 1970s, it is also important to note that intercultural training began to encompass non-mobile individuals (e.g., students, educators, staff) who would not venture abroad. For a variety of reasons, higher education administrators began to pay more attention to internationalisation, including intercultural initiatives designed to further the intercultural development of staff and students who remain on campus as well as study abroad students (e.g., pre-departure students, returnees) (Egron-Polak and Marmolejo 2017; Knight 2008, 2015, 2016). Publications and presentations related to this work further enriched the field, in terms of both theory-building and pedagogy.

The term 'internationalisation at home' (IaH), which was coined in Europe, refers to 'the embedding of international/intercultural perspectives into local educational settings' (Turner and Robson 2008: 15). Concerned that internationalisation efforts were concentrating on the small percentage of students who were able to study abroad, IaH was created with the explicit aim of raising the global awareness and intercultural understanding of 'non-mobile' students and faculty. More recently, Beelen and Jones (2015: 8) define IaH more precisely and inclusively as 'the purposeful integration of international and intercultural dimensions into the formal and informal curriculum for all students, within domestic learning environments'. This broader conception includes intercultural interventions for students who will not study abroad, outbound exchange students, inbound study abroad students, and returning study abroad sojourners (e.g., credit-bearing intercultural transition courses, workshops, schemes that seek to integrate domestic and non-local students).

A related development is the desire to integrate more international, intercultural perspectives into the curriculum in higher education to benefit *all* students and the wider society, not just individuals who gain study abroad experience. Leask, Green and Whitsed (2015) explain that the 'internationalisation of the curriculum' (IoC) movement entails 'the process of incorporating international, intercultural and global dimensions into the content of the curriculum as well as the learning outcomes, assessment tasks, teaching methods and support services of a program of study' (p. 34). Intended for both study abroad and 'non-mobile' students, innovative IoC practices are changing the ways in which institutions of higher education promote interculturality and this, too, is affecting the design and delivery of study abroad programming.

Evolving Conceptions of Culture

In the early days of intercultural training, instructors generally drew on definitions of culture that emphasise different layers or dimensions of this construct (e.g., values, observable artefacts, basic underlying assumptions), its impact on behaviour (e.g., patterns of communication in cultural groups), and the transmission of certain elements from one generation to another (e.g., norms of behaviour, worldviews, traditions) (Komisarof and Zhu 2016; Spencer-Oatey 2012). An often quoted definition that guided much of the early work in our field was put forward by Kroeber and Kluckhohn (1952: 181):

> Culture consists of patterns, explicit and implicit, of and for behaviour acquired and transmitted by symbols, constituting the distinctive achievements of human groups, including their embodiment in artifacts; the essential core of culture consists of traditional (i.e., historically derived and selected) ideas and especially their attached values; culture systems may, on the one hand, be considered as products of action, on the other, as conditional elements of future action.

While some early intercultural interventions were culture-specific (e.g., orientations for American military personnel who would be based in Japan or diplomats/support staff who would serve in Iraq), others were culture-general, focusing more broadly on the development of language and (inter)cultural awareness and sensitivity (e.g., knowledge about the influence of culture on communication and the dimensions on which cultures may differ) (Pusch 2004; Martin et al. 2012).

Among contemporary intercultural educators, there is now much more recognition of the need to explicitly define what is meant by culture and intercultural competence before designing an intercultural intervention. Further, as research in recent years has focused attention on the individual, developmental nature of intercultural learning, intercultural educators are paying more attention to the affective (e.g., emotional), cognitive (e.g., critical thinking) and behavioural (e.g., verbal) dimensions of intercultural learning (Dervin 2016; Jackson 2015b, 2015c; Marginson and Sawir 2011). As in other areas of education, this has led to a shift away from a focus on the transmission of cultural knowledge to more learner-centred, holistic approaches that promote critical reflection (deep thinking about past, present, and future actions) and intercultural engagement (Dervin 2016; Jackson and Oguro 2018a, 2018b; Holliday 2011). This, in turn, has resulted in more emphasis on autonomous, lifelong learning within the context of study abroad. The ultimate aim is to empower participants to assume more responsibility for their own language and intercultural learning.

In addition to drawing attention to the attributes and skills that facilitate multicultural relationship-building, critical intercultural researchers are raising awareness of external or environmental elements (e.g., host receptivity, power imbalances, colonial privilege) that may hinder or facilitate the learning and engagement of student sojourners (e.g., Dervin and Layne 2013; Díaz 2013; Hoult 2018; Jackson 2012; Sorrells 2012, 2013) (see Chapter 5). Committed to the promotion of deep reflection and learning, critical scholars now advocate a move away from a focus solely on the development of intercultural competence to the promotion of criticality. Through intercultural interventions, educators who embrace this orientation may strive to help their students hone the capacity to engage in critical evaluation of intercultural experience (Dasli and Díaz 2017b; Díaz 2013; Dervin 2017; Liddicoat 2017). This mode of inquiry is associated with the following philosophy:

> [A] reflective, exploratory, dialogic and active stance towards cultural knowledge and life that allows for dissonance, contradiction and conflict as well as consensus, concurrence, and transformation. It is a cognitive and emotional endeavor that aims at individual and collective emancipation, social justice, and political commitment.
> (Guilherme 2002: 219)

The current emphasis on criticality in both language and intercultural communication pedagogy is now influencing the design and delivery of intercultural education in a growing number of study abroad programmes and contexts. For example, Sorrells (n.d.) employs what she terms 'ethical intercultural praxis' to encourage students to actively engage in 'self-other dialogue, reflection and action that is grounded in social justice'. Interventions of this nature are helping students to acquire many of the attributes and dimensions associated with global citizenship (e.g., a deeper understanding of social justice, empathy, interculturality).

Theoretical Underpinnings

Over the years, numerous theories have influenced the design and delivery of intercultural interventions (e.g., value orientation frameworks, cross-cultural adjustment models, experiential learning theory, transformative learning theory, models of intercultural competence, critical theory (Byram 1997; Bennett 2015; Deardorff 2006; Jackson 2018a; Landis, Bennett and Bennett 2004; Mikk 2015). Initially, value orientation frameworks for understanding cultural difference (e.g., Hall 1976; Hampden-Turner and Trompenaars 1998; Hofstede 1980; Kluckhohn and Strodtbeck 1961) and cross-cultural comparisons guided most interventions that aimed to enhance the intercultural competence of students, including study abroad students (Cushner and Karim 2004; Jackson 2012).

Hofstede's work, in particular, continues to influence intercultural training, especially the preparation of business students for international internships and study abroad. It is important to bear in mind, however, that Holliday (2012) and Holmes (2012), and many other critical interculturalists criticise Hofstede's model for promoting essentialist representations of Otherness, whereby culture is viewed as synonymous with nation (the 'culture as nation' orientation) and diversity within cultures is largely ignored.

Since the mid-1960s, the curves of adjustment models, which were described in Chapter 3, have been widely used in study abroad interventions, especially pre-sojourn orientations, which aim to help students deal with culture shock and quickly adjust to the new environment. These models, however, are not derived from empirical research and contemporary researchers have discovered that student sojourners may not experience the phases that they depict. La Brack (2010: 2) argues that the curve models cannot accurately predict 'the depth, length, or even occurrence of culture shock'. In light of recent investigations, more study abroad educators tend to use these models simply to raise awareness of *potential* issues associated with cultural adjustment rather than as a depiction of a fixed sequence of stages that most student sojourners experience (Forum on Education Abroad 2011). Many other educators are choosing not to use the curve models at all.

In another important development, more intercultural educators and study abroad professionals recognise that acculturative stress and the resulting disequilibrium can stimulate intercultural learning and personal growth (e.g., self-confidence, self-efficacy), especially if guided by a competent mentor (Giovanangeli et al. 2018; Kim 2001, 2012; Jackson 2014, 2017b, 2017c, 2018a, in preparation; Paige 2013). As noted by J.M. Bennett (2008: 17), '[t]he resulting teachable moment, or trigger events, are often the stimuli for developing intercultural competence. Well facilitated, such events can turn culture shock into culture learning.' As noted in Chapter 6, 'failures' (e.g., unsatisfactory intercultural interactions) are teachable moments and a valuable part of the learning process.

Kolb's experiential learning cycle (Kolb 1984; Passarelli and Kolb 2012) and Mezirow's transformative learning theory (Mezirow 1994, 2009; Taylor 2015) have underpinned the design of many intercultural interventions. In the former, learning refers to 'the process whereby knowledge is created through the transformation of experience' (Kolb 1984: 41); knowledge is thought to emerge from 'the combination of grasping and transformative experience' (p. 41). Passarelli and Kolb (2012) maintain that if learners are to gain from international experience, they must begin with their own intercultural interactions, engage in reflective observation, advance to a stage of abstract conceptualisation, and then actively experiment with their new ideas and understandings of intercultural communication. In keeping with learner-centred approaches to education, teachers who follow this model assume the role of facilitator rather than that of an expert who transmits knowledge.

The experiential learning cycle resonates with Mezirow's (1994, 2009) transformative learning theory, which posits that individuals who engage in critical self-analysis may experience transformation in response to significant events in their lives (e.g., studying abroad, culture shock). In this adult learning theory, intercultural competence development involves a continuous learning process with 'new or revised interpretations of the meaning of one's experience' (Mezirow 1994: 222). By engaging in critical reflection, individuals may acquire the knowledge and skills that will help them to recognise and accommodate cultural difference. Further, Mezirow (1996) argues that this process has the potential to result in 'contextual relativism', a life-altering transformation, which encompasses the restructuring or broadening of one's sense of self. His theory has inspired many educators to place critical reflection at the heart of intercultural mediations for student sojourners.

Several models or theories of intercultural competence have also significantly influenced the design, implementation, and assessment of intercultural interventions in study abroad contexts. Byram's (1997) model of intercultural communicative competence, Deardorff's (2008) process model of intercultural competence, and Hammer's (2011, 2012, 2015) intercultural development continuum, a modified version of the developmental model of intercultural sensitivity (M.J. Bennett 1998, 2012), are some of the most widely used models in study abroad practice today (see Chapter 6). Although each model has unique elements and characteristics, all of them recognise the developmental nature of intercultural competence. Furthermore, the theorists who have devised these frameworks call on educators to bridge the theory–practice divide and create learner-centred study abroad programmes that address the specific attitudes, knowledge, and skills that bolster intercultural awareness and engagement in the host environment.

As mentioned in the previous section, critical theorists (e.g., Dasli and Díaz 2017b; Dervin 2016, 2017; Guilherme 2002; Holliday 2011, 2012; Komisarof and Zhu 2016; Piller 2017) are also affecting change in the ways in which intercultural interventions are designed, delivered, and measured. Stressing the need to move away from reductionist notions of 'culture as nation', they criticise simplistic intercultural training schemes that focus solely on cultural difference, present static images of culture, and provide students with a list of do's and don'ts to guide their behaviour in the host environment.

Critical theorists, postcolonialists, and many contemporary study abroad scholars call on intercultural educators to design programmes and activities that can help student sojourners grasp the complexity of interculturality, recognise the harmful consequences of stereotyping and colonial privilege, engage in reflexivity, and acquire a more critical, deeper understanding of the Self and Others (Dervin 2012, 2016; Jackson 2018a; Jackson and Oguro 2018b). Using various techniques, materials, and approaches, intercultural educators are now taking up this challenge and devising innovative interventions that encourage study abroad students to resist 'large culture', essentialist perspectives of Othering (Borghetti and Beaven 2018; Hepple 2018; Holliday 2011, 2012, 2018). Through research-inspired interventions, across the globe, more and more intercultural educators are encouraging students to push past romanticised notions of the host country and study abroad to set realistic, meaningful goals for their sojourn (Dervin and Härkönen 2018; Holmes, Bavieri and

Ganassin 2015; Hoult 2018). Jackson and Oguro (2018b) describe 11 innovative pedagogical interventions that have been implemented in various study abroad programmes to foster critical intercultural learning and engagement in different parts of the world. In an edited collection, Plews and Misfeldt (2018) present 12 chapters that describe study abroad programmes and pedagogy that aim to promote second language learning in the host environment.

Assessment and Evaluation in Study Abroad Contexts

Assessment is also a core element in intercultural education, including interventions that target study abroad students (Deardorff 2015a; Fantini 2012b; Saunders, Hogan and Olson 2015; Savicki and Brewer 2015a). As Chapter 6 explained, assessment can furnish valuable information about the intercultural awareness and learning of individual students, offer direction for intercultural interventions, determine the effectiveness of intercultural activities, and also guide data collection, interpretation, and use (Miller and Leskes 2005; Salisbury 2015). In effect, assessment can play a vital role in all phases of the curriculum design cycle: needs analysis, the setting of learning goals, the preparation of a syllabus or plan for the intervention, materials development, the shaping of teaching and learning activities, instructional and assessment strategies, and curriculum reform or revision (Fink 2013; Ornstein and Hunkins 2017; Savicki and Brewer 2015b). The assessment of student learning (e.g., measurement of intercultural learning) and the internal or external evaluation of the intervention itself (e.g., programme evaluation) both merit attention and are increasingly apt to be required in institutions where study abroad interventions are implemented.

As the previous chapter has illustrated, in the past two decades there has been a dramatic increase in the number of intercultural competence assessment tools available for study abroad educators (e.g., the Global Mindedness Scale, the Intercultural Development Inventory, the Intercultural Sensitivity Scale, to name a few). (See Fantini 2009, 2012b and the website of the Intercultural Communication Institute (http://intercultural.org/training-and-assessment-tools.html) for a list of instruments; also, Chapter 6 this volume.) Today, in part due to the influence of critical theorists, there is much more awareness of the importance of understanding the conceptions of culture and intercultural competence that underpin these instruments to determine if they are in line with the philosophy behind the intervention and a good fit with the desired learning outcomes. Educators are also becoming more mindful of the need for professionals to validate instruments through rigorous studies in various cultural contexts (e.g., measure both content and construct validity and reliability) (Bolen 2007b; Deardorff 2015a; Salisbury 2015; Savicki and Brewer 2015a).

As well as a dramatic increase in the number and variety of instruments available (e.g., psychometric tests, questionnaires, protocols), there is more recognition of the need to clearly define learning aims before implementing a programme and assessment scheme (Angelo 1995; Deardorff 2015a; Suskie 2009). Also, more educators now recognise the need to employ a variety of means (e.g., the analysis of intercultural reflections journals, portfolio assessment) to track and assess the intercultural learning of student sojourners at various stages of the study abroad cycle rather than rely on a single measure or only collect pre- and post-intervention data (Deardorff 2015a; Saunders et al. 2015). While quantitative measures (e.g., statistics) are still strongly emphasised in many quarters, qualitative data is becoming more accepted and valued as study abroad professionals and administrators better understand how data of this nature can offer useful insight into the learning situation and impact of an intervention (Bleistein and Wong 2015; Jackson 2015b).

With more emphasis on quality assurance and learning outcomes in institutions of higher education, administrators are requiring thorough, systematic investigations of all elements of study abroad programmes, including intercultural interventions, to determine what is working (and what is not) (Gozik 2015; Zukroff, Ferst, Hirsch, Slawson, and Wiedenhoeft 2005). A well-planned and executed programme review can identify which elements are meeting programme objectives and suggest areas that need improvement. Educators who implement an intercultural intervention may carry out an internal review or, alternatively, external evaluators may periodically be tasked with providing an impartial evaluation of a programme or specific components. Whatever the approach, intercultural educators need to be mindful of assessment and evaluation issues when designing and implementing intercultural interventions in study abroad programmes, especially in this age of accreditation, accountability, and quality assurance. (Revisit Chapter 6 for a fuller discussion of assessment and evaluation issues.)

Intercultural Interventions Throughout the Study Abroad Cycle

As more and more educators and administrators recognise the need for intercultural mediation in study abroad programmes, we are witnessing tremendous growth in the range and diversity of interventions that seek to bolster intercultural learning and engagement in many parts of the world (Jackson and Oguro 2018a; Lou et al. 2012; Plews and Misfeldt 2018). Some schemes focus on pre-sojourn preparation, whereas others take place while the students are in the host country (e.g., face-to-face, online, blended learning). A smaller number of re-entry schemes or programmes seek to enhance and extend the intercultural learning of study abroad returnees. The field is also being enriched by a number of comprehensive intercultural education programmes that encompass all stages of the study abroad cycle, such as the use of PluriMobil materials in Europe (Cuenat 2018) and the Bosley/Lou intentional targeted intervention (ITI) model in the United States (Lou and Bosley 2012; Bosley 2018). Advances in research, theory-building, pedagogy, assessment, programme evaluation, and communications technology are all impacting the work of intercultural educators in study abroad contexts. Let us take a look at some of these interventions.

Pre-Sojourn Preparation

Much has been written about the challenges study abroad students may face in an unfamiliar international environment, and the strategies that can help them deal with the natural ups and downs of adjustment (e.g., Jackson 2014; Kim 2001, 2012; Ward, Bochner and Furnham 2001; Chapter 3 this volume). Accordingly, international educators have designed a variety of pre-sojourn interventions to prepare students for possible adjustment challenges and help them optimise the potential of study abroad (e.g., Bennett 2009; Hepple 2018; Vande Berg et al. 2012a).

Despite more awareness of the need for interventions, however, many study abroad programmes still provide no pre-sojourn preparation or only a few hours of orientation before the students travel to the host country. Moreover, these brief sessions generally focus on logistics (e.g., security issues, the transfer of credits, travel arrangements) with little attention paid to the setting of sojourn goals, language and culture-learning strategies, and the benefits of diversifying one's social network in the host environment. Recent research suggests that these orientations are inadequate for many students, and increasingly intercultural educators argue that more attention should be paid to the affective, behavioural, cognitive, and linguistic dimensions of educational sojourns in the pre-sojourn phase (Jackson 2012; Jackson and Oguro 2018a; Vande Berg, Paige and Lou 2012b).

Scaffolding Study Abroad Experience

A well-designed, carefully sequenced, intercultural education course or series of workshops during the pre-sojourn stage can provide students with a frame of reference to help them make sense of their intercultural experience and more easily adjust to the new environment. Pre-sojourn interventions (e.g., workshops, courses) can stress the benefits of setting realistic sojourn goals, raise awareness of common adjustment issues, and prompt discussion of diverse language and culture learning strategies that can help newcomers feel at home in the host environment and optimise their stay abroad (Bathurst and La Brack 2012; Thebodo and Marx 2005).

Whenever possible, in line with the tenets of experiential learning, seasoned intercultural educators advise intercultural educators to build on the participants' existing (inter)cultural knowledge and previous international experience in the pre-sojourn phase when designing intercultural communication courses or workshops for outbound study abroad students (Jackson 2008, 2010, 2017b, 2018a; Passarelli and Kolb 2012). To this end, the preparation of detailed profiles of the participants, including a diagnostic assessment of interculturality, is essential to refine the curriculum or intervention plan (Almarza, Martinez and Llavador 2015; Harsch and Poehner 2016). In particular, it can be very helpful to have an understanding of such aspects as their language and intercultural attitudes, motivation, language proficiency, readiness for intercultural learning, and sojourn goals when designing and sequencing activities that will be used in the intervention. For educators who assume the role of cultural mentor, this groundwork is essential (Jackson 2017b, 2017c, 2018a; Paige 2013, 2015b).

Salient programme characteristics (e.g., goals, duration, housing, language component, activities) should also be taken into account when designing pre-sojourn schemes (Jackson 2012; Selby 2008). Experienced intercultural educators maintain that this groundwork is essential to develop meaningful learner-centred interventions that can help propel students to higher levels of intercultural learning and engagement. As noted in Chapter 6, it is also important to consider learning objectives when designing and selecting modes of assessment for intercultural interventions.

Intercultural educators also recommend that this phase address pre-departure assumptions and concerns, including myths about study abroad (e.g., automatic personal transformation) (Holmes et al. 2015). This phase should also help students develop a reflective, more critical mindset to facilitate the processing of intercultural experience in a metacognitive way (by 'thinking about thinking') (Jackson 2011; Penman and Ratz 2015). As noted by Zull (2012: 183):

> Preparation for the study abroad experience should include developing the habit of intentional introspection by the student, followed by actions that test new ideas and awareness of the process, both by students and by faculty advisors.

The systematic scaffolding of international educational experience has the potential to bring about more positive sojourn outcomes.

Demystifying the Adjustment Process

Student sojourners who have never travelled outside their home country may be especially anxious about living and studying abroad, far from friends and family. Even students with travel experience may benefit from developing more awareness and understanding of common elements that newcomers may experience in an unfamiliar environment (e.g., differences in verbal and nonverbal communication styles and cultural values, language and culture shock, heightened racial awareness, identity confusion) (Thebodo and Marx 2005; Ward et al. 2001). In view of that, many contemporary study abroad orientations review the natural ebbs and flows of cross-cultural adjustment in pre-departure orientations and encourage discussion of a range of coping mechanisms or strategies. While facilitators may present the W-curve model of adjustment (Gullahorn and Gullahorn 1963) to raise awareness of *potential* adjustment challenges; as noted in Chapter 3, it is important to be mindful of the lack of empirical evidence to support this framework; sojourners may have very different development trajectories than what is depicted in these models. This aspect should be conveyed to students in pre-departure sessions that use this model.

Although culture shock was originally viewed as a 'disease' and phenomenon to be avoided (Oberg 1960), nowadays more intercultural educators recognise the potential benefits of experiencing some of the discomforts of culture shock as it can prompt deeper reflection on Self and Other, which, in turn, can lead to enhanced language and intercultural awareness and personal growth (e.g., more self-reliance, advances in maturity and problem-solving ability) (Jackson 2014; Kim 2012). It is important for students to recognise that they can learn a great deal from disappointing intercultural experiences if they take the time to 'unpack' them. In the pre-departure phase, when discussing common adjustment issues, facilitators may also point to the use of constructive language and culture learning strategies and coping mechanisms that can promote resilience, the constructive management of acculturative stress, and active involvement in the host environment.

Encouraging the Setting of Realistic Goals and Expectations

Since unrealistic, unmet expectations can lead to disappointment and disillusionment on stays abroad, intercultural educators may encourage the participants to access current, accurate information about the host environment while they are still in the home country. If the pre-sojourn orientation is targeted at a group that will study in the same host country, facilitators may opt to explore culture-specific information (e.g., sociopragmatic norms of politeness, local vocabulary) with the participants (Shively 2010). Students may be encouraged to develop a basic understanding of the history, geography, and religion(s) of the host country, as well as the linguistic and sociopolitical context. In situations like this it is incumbent on facilitators to raise awareness of diversity *within* cultures and draw attention to the potentially harmful effects of stereotyping,

Otherisation, and reductionism or essentialism (Dervin 2012; Dervin and Gross 2016; Holliday 2011, 2012; Jackson 2017d; Jackson and Oguro 2018b; Sorrells 2015; Sorrells and Sekimoto 2016). In an essentialist orientation, 'social groups are assumed to share universal and homogeneous characteristics without consideration for variation across cultures, within groups, or over time' (Sorrells 2015: 298) and this can hamper the cultivation of constructive, respectful multicultural relationships.

To stimulate student interest and involvement, facilitators who will have a series of pre-departure meetings with a cohort of outbound students may encourage small groups to gather information about specific aspects of the host environment (e.g., surf the web, visit cultural centres/trade offices, do library research, interview international exchange students from the host country) and report back to the larger group (Jackson 2008, 2010). In student-led sharing sessions, facilitators may encourage the students to learn more about the host environment prior to departure (e.g., review the website of the host institution). At this stage, in accord with the tenants of learner-centred education, intercultural educators can prompt students to assume more responsibility for their own sojourn learning.

Researchers have discovered that student sojourners who are unfocused or unrealistic about what they can accomplish during their stay abroad may become easily discouraged and overwhelmed in the new environment, and return home without fully benefiting from their sojourn (Jackson 2014; Holmes et al. 2015; Ward et al. 2001). Therefore, intercultural educators also recommend that students be prompted to set specific, realistic goals for their impending sojourn in various domains (e.g., academic, linguistic, intercultural, personal, social). After adequate information has been provided about the study abroad programme (e.g., duration, housing, curriculum, setting) and the students have researched current information on the host environment, intercultural educators may encourage participants to set specific learning targets for their sojourn and also consider how their stay abroad will fit into their long-term plans. Facilitators at this stage may also encourage students to periodically revisit their goals and objectives once they are abroad, and then make adjustments, if necessary, to make the most of their stay in the host environment (Hepple 2018; McKinnon 2018).

Promoting Awareness of Self and Other

Increasingly, interculturalists have discovered that building up knowledge of the host language and culture is insufficient preparation for stays abroad. Prior to a sojourn, more intercultural educators are making an effort to raise students' awareness of the influence of their primary language and cultural socialisation on their behaviour, values, intercultural attitudes, and identities. With enhanced self-awareness, participants are better positioned to consider the potential effect of their attitudes, perceptions, and communication styles on intercultural encounters. This process can also bring to light stereotypes and negative emotions that should be addressed in the pre-departure orientation.

The pre-departure phase may also address language-related issues, particularly if the students will reside in an environment where they will study or take courses in another language, and/or need to function in a second language on a daily basis. An awareness of the appropriate use of the host language in social situations could help newcomers become more attuned to norms of politeness and communication styles that are prevalent in the host environment. Intercultural educators maintain that an intervention of this nature can be helpful for students who have never used the host language in informal, social situations. Heightened sociopragmatic awareness (e.g., familiarity with polite forms of language use in certain social situations) can facilitate relationship-building with hosts (Devlin 2014; Shively and Cohen 2008; Thomas 1983). This is especially important for advanced foreign language learners, as their hosts are apt to expect them to employ verbal expressions and nonverbal codes that are deemed polite in that context. As mentioned earlier, it is also incumbent on educators to encourage students to become attentive observers in the host environment to see if what they have learned fits with their 'real-world' experience.

To develop sociopragmatic awareness, students who will travel to the same country may also work through dialogues and discourse completion exercises that centre on common speech acts in the host environment (e.g., discourse expressions and sequences frequently used for requests, apologies, and refusals) (LoCastro 2003; Shively 2010; Taguchi 2015; Timpe 2014). In some interventions, students are presented with reality-based scenarios to analyse, first on their own and then in groups. The facilitator then prompts them to consider how they might react in similar situations in the host environment. Some intercultural educators maintain that this activity affords students the opportunity to confront issues and raise questions in the safety of the classroom before travelling to the host country. Intercultural educators who facilitate these activities maintain that they can bolster self-confidence, reduce anxiety, foster a positive mindset, and enhance the willingness of the students to communicate with host nationals and other individuals who have a different linguistic and cultural background.

Underpinning many pre-sojourn intercultural interventions is the belief that familiarity with a range of language and culture-learning strategies can help students to manage intercultural transitions more effectively and maximise their learning in the host environment. To this end, intercultural educators have developed a number of innovative techniques and resources (e.g., see Bennett 2015; Berardo and Deardorff 2012; Deardorff and Arasaratnam-Smith 2017; Hammer 2015; Jackson 2018a, 2018b; Mikk et al. 2009). A range of experiential learning activities (e.g., role plays, simulations, ethnographic interviews with individuals who have a different cultural background) are now being used in different parts of the world to provide students with the opportunity to experience and/ or reflect on the challenges of intercultural communication before they cross borders (Berardo and Deardorff 2012; Bosley 2018; Passarelli and Kolb 2012). In pre-sojourn interventions, students may also be prompted to discuss and analyse sojourner accounts (e.g., excerpts from interview transcripts, blog entries, diary excerpts, study abroad essays), critical incidents (e.g., brief scenarios that illustrate intercultural miscommunication), or cases (e.g., longer, problem-based narratives that depict intercultural situations) (Jackson 2008, 2012, 2014, 2017b).

Ethnographic Approaches to Language and Culture Learning: Making the Familiar Strange

In some study abroad programmes, an ethnographic approach to language and cultural learning may be used in the pre-sojourn phase to help student sojourners become better prepared for life in the host speech community (Roberts, Byram, Barro, Jordan and Street 2001). Carefully designed and sequenced ethnographic education can encourage short-term sojourners to become more focused and engaged in the host culture (Jackson 2006, 2008, 2011, 2016a). Prior to going abroad, they can be introduced to the methods and issues of ethnographic exploration: research ethics, participant observation, the recording of detailed field notes, interviewing techniques (including the facilitation of informal ethnographic conversations), and the use of visuals (e.g., digital photographs, graphics). Through weekly tasks, students can hone the skills and confidence necessary to undertake a small-scale ethnographic project in their home environment; with adequate support and preparation, they can gradually move from descriptions of cultural scenes to more sophisticated interpretation and analysis. Jackson (2006, 2008, 2011, 2016a) has found that the process of 'making the familiar strange' can heighten students' awareness of linguistic and/or cultural elements or practices in their home environment and encourage them to become more observant and independent after they arrive in the host country.

Learning From Returnees

Students with international experience can be a valuable resource in the pre-sojourn phase. In particular, study abroad returnees who experienced gains in intercultural/second language competence and developed constructive multicultural relationships during their sojourn may inspire their peers who have yet to venture abroad. With enthusiasm and a positive tone, returnees (or inbound international exchange students) can offer encouragement and practical advice to optimise study abroad. Drawing on their own experience, they might discuss strategies that they have found helpful to deal with acculturative stress and build relationships with their hosts. They could also encourage the setting of realistic goals and inspire newcomers to take steps to influence the ways in which their own sojourn unfolds. As these comments suggest, it is important for intercultural educators to give some thought to the selection of students who will share their experiences (e.g., intercultural attitudes, optimistic mindset).

Preparing for the Housing Situation

The housing arrangements for student sojourners can vary a great deal (e.g., campus dormitory, homestay, off-campus apartment), and, when appropriate, intercultural educators can take this element into account when designing pre-sojourn interventions. If the students will live with host families, for example, some attention can be devoted to homestay life in the pre-departure phase. While it is often assumed that this type of housing will automatically lead to meaningful multicultural relationships and ample access to the host culture and language, study abroad researchers have found that this is not always the case (e.g., Benson 2017; Diao, Freed and Smith 2011; Jackson 2008, 2010; Rodriguez and Chornet-Roses 2014; Wilkinson 1998). To help student sojourners make the most of their homestay situation, intercultural educators generally recommend that the following topics and issues be addressed in the pre-sojourn phase: ways to break the ice and build relationships (e.g., sharing photos of one's family with hosts), variations in self-disclosure, roles and responsibilities of hosts and students, and sociopragmatic norms of politeness or conventions in the host family and wider community.

Pre-sojourn intercultural education could also benefit host families. For example, prior to the arrival of the students, some institutions hold an orientation session for host families which typically includes an overview of the study abroad programme (e.g., aims, schedule), background information on the sojourners and their home country, insight into the dangers of stereotyping and Otherisation, and a list of common symptoms of language and culture shock (Hansel 2007; Jackson 2008, 2010). Roles and responsibilities of hosts and sojourners may be clarified in this orientation, emphasising the need for hosts to explain and negotiate 'family rules' early on to avoid misunderstandings. The opportunity for hosts and guests to learn from each other may be emphasised as well. Discussion may also include practical strategies to help the newcomers adjust and more fully participate in host family life, with experienced hosts sharing their experiences.

The Sojourn

The amount of support provided to students while they are in the host country varies significantly, depending, in part, on the nature, format, and duration of the programme, available funding, and staff expertise and interest. Many study abroad programmes have little or no intercultural interventions during the sojourn and students are expected to quickly adjust and fit into the new environment. As educators and programme administrators become more familiar with research findings that point to the need for some form of mediation to promote intercultural learning, the number and variety of sojourn interventions is on the rise (Brewer, Shively, Gozik, Doyle and Savicki 2015; Jackson 2012; Jackson and Oguro 2018b; Mikk 2015; Paige 2015b; Paige and Vande Berg 2012).

Promoting Intercultural Learning and Engagement in the Host Environment

In faculty-led initiatives, intercultural education may be incorporated into the curriculum in the host environment; in some cases, facilitators from both home and host institutions may work together to promote intercultural learning and engagement. Compulsory or elective intercultural education courses may be offered to newcomers, which may include both local and international students, with the aim of facilitating social and academic integration on campus. Students who have joined an international exchange programme may enroll in intercultural communication courses in the host environment, participate in an online intercultural transitions course hosted by their home institution (e.g., Jackson 2017c, 2017d, 2018a, forthcoming c, in preparation), seek help from counsellors who have been trained to offer support and guidance to international students (Arthur 2004), join orientations and intercultural activities organised by their host institution, participate in a 'buddy' programme (interact with a local student mentor), or they may simply fend for themselves.

'Unpacking' International Experience Through Critical Reflection

Increasingly, intercultural educators are incorporating activities into their sojourn interventions that promote critical reflection, dialogue, and self-analysis, such as the writing of a diary, journal, or blog (Jackson 2010; Passarelli and Kolb 2012). The process of writing about one's sojourn experiences can be cathartic (Ochs and Capps 2001) and intercultural educators who include this in their interventions maintain that it can help students deal with the psychological strains of living and studying in an unfamiliar linguistic and cultural environment (Brewer and Moore 2015; Jackson 2008; Savicki 2015). Through the act of writing and reflecting on their stories, sojourners can become more aware of their positioning in the new environment, their reactions to cultural difference, and the ways in which they interact with individuals who have a different linguistic and cultural background. In this way, they can learn from disappointing intercultural interactions as well as ones that they deem more successful. This process may also help to further raise their metacognitive awareness and facilitate self-regulation (encourage reflection on their intercultural actions).

Throughout the sojourn, intercultural educators may prompt students to periodically review their diaries, blogs, or other accounts of their sojourn learning as the process of revisiting lived experiences (e.g., critical incidents, successful intercultural interactions, communication breakdowns) may deepen language and intercultural awareness and lead to new insights. With some distance from the emotional impact of the events, students may then be in a better position to reconsider what led to miscommunication or intercultural conflict situations (e.g., the absence of discourse markers of politeness that are expected in the host environment, the use of a direct style of communication in a situation where indirectness is more common). In this approach, as recommended by Kolb (1984); Mezirow (1994, 2009); and Moon (2000, 2004) and scholars who advocate critical reflection and criticality in education (e.g., Dasli and Díaz 2017b; Dervin 2017; Jackson and Oguro 2018a) facilitators or cultural mentors may continuously encourage students to 'unpack' their international experience and become more 'mindful' in current and future intercultural encounters.

Providing Socio-Emotional Support and Guidance Through Debriefings

Study abroad researchers have discovered that many student sojourners need socio-emotional support to deal with adjustment issues in a constructive way and become more independent and engaged in the host environment (Jackson 2008, 2010; Paige 2015a, 2015b; Ward et al. 2001; Ward 2015). With this finding in view, intercultural educators may facilitate regular debriefings to help students make sense of unfamiliar practices in their new environment. In these sessions, the sojourners can also be encouraged to initiate interactions with host nationals and other international students. Intercultural educators have found that sharing experiences with other newcomers may foster camaraderie, reduce stress, and encourage newcomers to become more active in the host environment. Facilitators may encourage sojourners to share experiences and raise questions about confusing or troubling intercultural encounters in face-to-face meetings or online (or a mixture of both) (Jackson 2008, 2010, 2012, 2017c, 2017d, 2018a). An additional benefit of these sharing sessions is that sojourners may become aware of elements in the host culture that they might have overlooked or misunderstood. Intercultural educators have also discovered that group discussions can help students learn about the language and culture-learning and relationship strategies that their peers are finding useful. In this way, the students can gain inspiration and learn from each other.

In debriefing sessions during the sojourn, intercultural educators may also take this opportunity to deal with issues related to discriminatory practices, racism, privilege, social injustice, ethnicity, positioning, and identity misalignments, etc. As these topics are of a sensitive nature, it requires well-developed interpersonal communication skills, empathy, patience, and mindfulness on the part of the facilitator. Sojourners can draw strength from sessions of this nature if the intercultural educator is non-judgmental, engages in active listening, and encourages the open expression of ideas and experiences. In debriefing sessions, students may be prompted to take stock of their learning, reflect on their pre-sojourn goals, and consider what they can realistically accomplish in the remainder of their stay.

As well as facilitating full-group sharing sessions while students are abroad, some intercultural educators are ensuring there are opportunities for individualised problem solving so that issues may be dealt with before they become major obstacles to intercultural adjustment. For students who are reluctant to share their views in an open forum, some intercultural educators are administering short questionnaire surveys with open-ended questions to stimulate reflection on a variety of issues and concerns (e.g., intercultural adjustment, host-sojourner relationships, positioning in the new environment, personal goals, language development, cultural knowledge, intercultural communicative competence, attitudes toward the host culture and language, social justice). While safeguarding the identities of the students, facilitators may then incorporate these issues into full-group debriefing sessions, drawing attention to common themes as well as aspects that have been overlooked.

Leading an Ethnographic Life

With adequate pre-sojourn preparation, sojourners in some study abroad programmes (e.g., faculty-led) may conduct small-scale ethnographic projects in the host environment. Through sustained contact in a cultural scene of their choice, sojourners can gain exposure to different worldviews and authentic communication styles and speech genres (e.g., humour) (Jackson 2006, 2008, 2016a). For example, students may explore cultural scenes (e.g., nursing homes for the elderly, charity shops) or practices in the host environment (e.g., pet-keeping, hobbies) and, in the process, build closer ties with their hosts, and practice using the host language in informal, social situations. Some students may also venture into the community to immerse themselves in a cultural scene, such as a charity shop or senior citizens centre.

As they carry out their research, student sojourners can learn to systematically observe, listen, interpret, and analyse the behaviour and discourse of their 'informants'. Ethnographic projects can provide students with a purpose for intercultural interactions and inspire more in-depth and meaningful dialogue. With adequate preparation and the support of regular research advising sessions, students can assume ownership of their projects and take on more responsibility for their language and intercultural learning (Jackson 2008, 2016a, 2018b; Roberts et al. 2001). Regular advising sessions and discussions can raise the group's awareness of a broader range of cultural aspects and help foster a supportive community of explorers, who are more engaged in the world around them. Advocates of this approach maintain that projects of this nature have the potential to deepen students' awareness of social and cultural elements in the host environment and, ultimately, enhance their linguistic and intercultural competence. Projects of this nature have the potential to be very empowering for student sojourners, including second language learners.

Promoting Meaningful Intercultural Dialogue Through Other Forms of Experiential Learning

Besides ethnography, intercultural educators can employ other forms of experiential learning (e.g., small-scale, weekly tasks that require intercultural interactions) to encourage students to take fuller advantage of affordances in the host environment (Jackson 2017c, 2017d, 2018a; Passarelli and Kolb 2012). To meet the needs, abilities (e.g., proficiency level, intercultural sensitivity level), and situations of particular groups of sojourners, intercultural educators in many parts of the world are devising innovative intercultural activities or projects (Jackson and Oguro 2018a). A growing number of study abroad researchers have discovered that, without these interventions, one cannot assume that language and intercultural learning will occur simply because the students are residing in the host culture. Instead of engaging in meaningful intercultural dialogue with their hosts, they may use avoidance strategies and limit their exposure to the host language and culture (e.g., only engage in brief service encounters, avoid extended conversations with hosts). Pedagogical interventions that promote language and intercultural engagement are critical for many study abroad participants.

Preparing for Re-Entry

Many intercultural educators also recognise the need to encourage students to prepare for re-entry near the end of their sojourn, even if the stay in the host culture has not been very long (Kartoshkina 2015; La Brack 2015; Niesen 2010). In some innovative programmes, learner-centred debriefing sessions, either face-to-face or online, prompt sojourners to revisit their pre-sojourn goals and take stock of their language and (inter) cultural learning and personal expansion shortly before their return home. The participants may also be prompted to reflect on their feelings about leaving their hosts/the host culture and to think about appropriate ways to say goodbye. Facilitators may encourage students to reflect on their expectations for re-entry and to consider ways that they might sustain their language and intercultural learning once they are back on home soil. Many intercultural educators have found that debriefing sessions provide an excellent opportunity for students to assess their sojourn learning and set goals for further intercultural learning.

Post-Sojourn

While most intercultural interventions in study abroad programmes focus on the pre-sojourn and sojourn phases, research is drawing attention to re-adjustment issues that can arise when students return home (e.g., identity misalignments, reverse culture shock) (Bathurst and La Brack 2012; La Brack 2015; Patron 2007; Szkudlarek 2010; Chapter 3 this volume). As a consequence, there is now more awareness of the benefits of devising re-entry schemes (e.g., workshops, intercultural transition courses) to enrich and extend the intercultural learning of study abroad returnees (Jackson 2015b, 2015c; Jackson and Oguro 2018b; Lee 2018; Martin and Harrell 2004; Meyer-Lee 2005; Thebodo and Marx 2005).

Even after only a short stay abroad, students may experience symptoms of reverse (re-entry) culture shock when they return home, especially if they have been very open to cultural differences and changed in ways that they did not anticipate (e.g., developed a broader worldview, acquired a more intercultural, global persona, became more invested in second language learning and use) (Furnham 2015; Jackson 2014, 2015a; Savicki 2015; Ward et al. 2001; Ward 2015). As explained in Chapter 3, some returnees are surprised to discover that their re-entry is more turbulent than their adjustment to the host environment and they are ill-equipped to deal with the identity confusion and malaise that can occur in this phase of study abroad.

With these findings in mind, intercultural educators are developing innovative programmes that provide a safe place for returnees to critically reflect on sojourn and re-entry experience. In these interventions, facilitators may raise awareness of identity-related issues and encourage participants to discuss their new understandings of their place in the world and the role of language in expressing their expanded sense of self. Activities (e.g., group discussions, reflective writing tasks) may be incorporated into the intervention to encourage returnees to reflect on concrete ways to apply their developing intercultural skills and knowledge in the academic arena as well as in their social life and future career. The returnees may also be encouraged to take fuller advantage of affordances in their home environment to use their second language and initiate intercultural interactions (either face-to-face or online). The continuous lifelong nature of intercultural competence development can be re-emphasised in this phase.

Intercultural education in the post-sojourn phase can consolidate sojourn learning and also encourage returnees to set realistic goals for further language and intercultural enhancement, personal growth, and international experience. It can provide the impetus and support some returnees need to keep their 'global self' alive once they return home, and, in the process, encourage the further cultivation of meaningful multicultural relationships, which is in line with common internationalisation goals of contemporary institutions of higher education.

In re-entry programmes, intercultural educators typically encourage participants to share their experiences with future sojourners so that their peers who are not yet mobile can benefit from what they have gained from living and studying abroad. Critical intercultural education can also help returnees become better equipped to serve as buddies or partners for inbound international exchange students.

Not all interventions in this phase require students to meet face-to-face with other returnees and an intercultural educator. In some contexts, institutions may encourage study abroad participants to access an eLearning platform to discuss their international experience and re-entry. Alternatively, as the following section explains, they may be directed to study abroad websites that have been designed to encourage critical reflection on sojourn experiences and the setting of goals for further personal expansion.

Online Intercultural Interventions

Advances in information and communications technology (e.g., the Internet, social media, Skype or QQ, WeChat), have significantly impacted the nature of study abroad (Coleman and Chafer 2010; Donatelli 2010; Jackson in preparation; Lee 2018) and opened up exciting possibilities for intercultural interventions at all stages of the study abroad cycle (Jackson and Oguro 2018b). While most study abroad interventions involve face-to-face meetings, tech-savvy scholars are now offering blended courses (e.g., hosting online forums) or designing intercultural interventions that can be fully implemented online (e.g., Jackson 2018a; in preparation). Some interventions are on a small scale (e.g., targeting students in a single course or programme), whereas others are intended to be widely accessed by study abroad students in many institutions or regions (MOOCs—massive open online courses). While some schemes make use of eLearning platforms (e.g., Blackboard, Moodle), others involve the creation of sophisticated websites that seek to promote and support the intercultural development of study abroad students in a particular region or even a much broader audience.

Telecollaboration or online intercultural exchange refers to class-to-class interactions via virtual intercultural contact that are designed to promote language and intercultural learning (Guth and Helm 2010). In the United States, Lee (2018) created a telecollaborative exchange project to encourage American study abroad returnees (from a programme in Spain) to interact with first language (L1) speakers of Spanish in Spain so that both groups would further develop their language awareness and intercultural communication skills. Over the course of a semester, they took part in task-based activities that encouraged them to discuss cross-cultural issues and share intercultural experiences and perspectives.

At a university in Hong Kong, Jackson (2017c, 2017d, 2018a, in preparation) developed a fully online intercultural transitions course to deepen the intercultural learning and engagement of international exchange students while they are in the host environment. This intervention integrates multiple theories and constructs: notions of 'small' and 'large cultures' (Holliday 2012), the developmental nature of intercultural learning (Hammer 2012, 2015), and poststructuralist notions of identity change and personal transformation (Block 2007; Mezirow 1994; Taylor 2015). Cultural mentoring or guided critical reflection (Giovanangeli et al. 2018; Hammer 2012; Jackson 2018a; Paige 2013, 2015a; Paige and Goode 2009; Vande Berg 2015b) underpins this approach.

While some online interventions employ an eLearning platform and target a small number of study abroad participants, others involve the development of websites which aim to reach a much larger number of student sojourners. For example, supported by a grant from the US Department of Education and the IFSA Foundation, the Project for Learning Abroad, Training, and Outreach (PLATO) created the *Global Scholar: Online Learning for Study Abroad* (http://globalscholar.us/) (Rhodes 2011). This site integrates new activities with material from the *What's Up With Culture?* website (La Brack 2003) (www2.pacific.edu/sis/culture/) and *Maximizing Study Abroad: A Students' Guide to Strategies for Language and Culture Learning and Use* (Paige, Cohen, Kappler, Chi and Lassegard 2006).

The *Global Scholar* online courses, which are freely available on the internet, introduce students to the opportunities and challenges of studying abroad. Modules explore strategies to prepare for the sojourn, review possible adjustment issues, suggest ways to make the most of study abroad experience, and identify issues that may arise after the return home. The courses aim to promote the refinement of skills in intercultural observation, adaptation, and communication that can be used throughout the study abroad cycle. As the *Global Scholar* courses were created with American students in mind, the developers decided to create *iStudent 101: Online learning for international students* to provide comparable resources for international students at all phases of study abroad: pre-sojourn, sojourn, post-sojourn) (http://istudent101.com) (Rhodes 2011).

Systematic research is needed to fully grasp the impact and usefulness of these online websites and courses.

Interventions That Target All Phases of Study Abroad: From Entry to Re-Entry

Most of the intercultural interventions that I have reviewed so far specifically target a particular phase of international education; however, as research underscores the need for intercultural interventions throughout the study abroad cycle, a number of schemes now encompass all phases: pre-sojourn, sojourn, and re-entry. Some are small scale and have been specially designed for a small group of students in the same discipline at the same home institution who sojourn in the same host setting (e.g., Jackson 2008, 2010). Other initiatives are on a much broader scale (e.g., institution-wide, nation-wide, regional). For example, some collaborative, inter-institutional ventures are driven and supported by governments with the aim of bolstering the intercultural learning and engagement and global citizenship attributes of large numbers of study abroad students in many states or countries. In this section, we will take a look at a few of these holistic schemes.

In her 2006 book entitled *Mobilité Erasmus et communication interculturelle* (Erasmus mobility and intercultural communication), Anquetil introduced a holistic approach that aimed to help students develop observation skills and a profound understanding of the other, while becoming more self-reflective, unlocking their self-identities and questioning ethnocentrism (ibid.: 224). The main goal of the proposed interventions was to train students to learn to be *a stranger* (ibid.: 227). Both inbound and outbound students were able to take part in different forms of training: intercultural workshops, meetings with former Erasmus students, explorations of travel narratives, discussions of strangeness, critiques of various theories of intercultural communication, and the study of specific sociocultural relations between countries; workshops helped inbound students to develop sociocultural and intercultural competences (e.g., learn how to live in a foreign city/town, study at a new university, reflect on the position of strangers in a society).

In the United States, the Center for Advanced Research on Language Acquisition (CARLA) at the University of Minnesota developed the *Maximizing Study Abroad* guidebooks for students, programme professionals, and language instructors to promote the effective use of language and culture learning strategies and optimise study abroad development (Mikk et al. 2009; http://carla.umn.edu/maxsa/). Since their publication, these research-based materials have been employed by various institutions of higher education in the United States to enhance the language and intercultural learning of students throughout the study abroad cycle. The use of the *Maximizing Study Abroad* guides by study abroad programme professionals and language instructors and the effectiveness of the materials in improving students' strategies for language and culture learning and use has been documented in a mixed-methods study (see Cohen, Paige, Shively, Emert and Hoff 2005).

In Europe, a number of collaborative projects have also been developed to deepen the intercultural learning of mobile students. The European Centre for Modern Languages, for example, developed PluriMobil, a pedagogical tool that offers activities and materials to support the plurilingual and intercultural development of students before, during and after study abroad (e.g., through the promotion of language and culture learning strategies) (http://plurimobil.ecml.at/; Cuenat 2018). The developers maintain that the tool can be adapted for diverse mobility projects across all educational levels, including teacher education.

The Intercultural Educational Resources for Erasmus Students and their Teachers (IEREST) project is another example of a multilateral, intercultural education scheme that has been designed to promote mobility and intercultural learning on a large scale from the pre-sojourn to post-sojourn phase. Drawing on critical notions of interculturality and intercultural competence development, IEREST established a European network of higher education institutions which resulted in the design and piloting of intercultural teaching modules that aim to enhance the intercultural awareness and personal growth of students before, during, and after their stay abroad (Beaven and Borghetti 2016; Borghetti 2016; Borghetti and Beaven 2018; Holmes et al. 2015; Holmes, Bavieri, Ganassin and Murphy 2016). The modules include materials for face-to-face interactions as well as online learning. (See www.ierest-project.eu/.)

Conclusion

This chapter reviewed shifts in intercultural training or education, and briefly discussed the use of a variety of assessment tools and methods to document and measure the intercultural learning of both mobile and non-mobile students. I explained the rationale for the growing emphasis on criticality in language and intercultural pedagogy in study abroad contexts and provided examples of intercultural interventions that are being implemented in different parts of the world at various phases of the study abroad cycle, including online initiatives. I also described several large-scale, system-wide interventions that have been designed to foster deep intercultural learning from the pre-sojourn phase until re-entry. This chapter underscores the importance of strengthening the connection between research and practice to facilitate the work of international education professionals and enhance the language and intercultural learning and global citizenship development of study abroad participants.

In the next and final chapter, I draw together key strands in the book and summarise what I believe are the most important implications for contemporary intercultural research and pedagogy in international education. I then offer an exhilarating agenda for current and future study abroad scholars who wish to make a constructive and meaningful difference in intercultural research, theory-building, and/or practice in study abroad.

Further Reading and Resources

Jackson, J. and Oguro, S. (eds) (2018) *Intercultural Interventions in Study Abroad*, London and New York: Routledge.

    This edited volume explains the rationale for pedagogical interventions in study abroad programmes and emphasises the need for critical perspectives to promote interculturality. Theory-based, innovative examples from different parts of the globe are presented.

Landis, D., Bennett, J.M. and Bennett, M.J. (eds) (2004) *Handbook of Intercultural Training*, 3rd edn, Thousand Oaks, CA: Sage Publications.

    This collection reviews the historical development of intercultural training and includes a chapter dedicated to interventions in study abroad contexts.

Lewin, R. (ed.) (2009) *The Handbook of Practice and Research in Study Abroad: Higher Education and the Quest for Global Citizenship*, New York: Routledge.

    This handbook provides examples of pedagogical strategies and programme interventions that have been employed in diverse study abroad contexts to foster global citizenship and intercultural sensitivity.

Plews, J.L. and Misfeldt, K. (eds) (2018) Second Language Study Abroad: Programming, Pedagogy, and Participant Engagement, New York: Springer International Publishing.

    This edited volume provides examples of interventions in study abroad programmes that have been designed to enhance the language learning and intercultural engagement of student sojourners.

Savicki, V. (ed.) (2008) *Developing Intercultural Competence and Transformation: Theory, Research, and Application in International Education*, Sterling, VA: Stylus Publishing.

    This edited collection delves into notions of intercultural competence and draws on the transformative learning theory to offer ideas and strategies that study abroad professionals can employ to enhance the intercultural development of student sojourners.

Vande Berg, M., Paige, R.M. and Lou, K.H. (eds) (2012) *Student Learning Abroad: What our Students Are Learning, What They're Not and What We Can Do about It*, Sterling, VA: Stylus Publishing.

    This edited volume reviews the dominant paradigms of study abroad and provides examples of study abroad courses or programmes that apply theories related to human learning and intercultural development.

8 Taking Stock and Looking Ahead

Introduction

When I began to write this book, my primary aim was to provide a critical review of recent developments in international education research and practice, with a special emphasis on the intercultural learning and engagement of second language sojourners in study abroad contexts. In addition to raising awareness of core themes, trends, and advances in this important field of study, in this volume I sought to draw attention to limitations in current research and practice and, when feasible, suggest ways to remedy them. In my writing, I have explained the merits of narrowing the gap between theory, research, and practice and also underscored the benefits of embracing critical perspectives in all facets of work in international education. I have highlighted exciting, cutting-edge contributions that are re-shaping our field. While I have cited the work of many study abroad scholars and interculturalists in different parts of the world, due to space limitations I have had to be selective and concentrate on key research findings and contemporary developments in study abroad pedagogy. In the introduction, I also pointed out that I am increasingly embracing criticality and reflexivity in my own work. Thus, while I have sought to present diverse views in this volume, this bias is apt to be evident, especially when critiquing past practices and offering suggestions for future international education theory-building, research, and practice.

In this concluding chapter I pull together the main points in the book and use them as a springboard to offer my views about the future of interculturality research in international education. I also consider the potential of innovative, research-inspired intercultural pedagogical interventions to enhance the critical language awareness and intercultural engagement of participants at all stages of the study abroad cycle. As is evident throughout the book, in this chapter I stress that intercultural development and the cultivation of global citizenship entails a lifelong process and should involve both mobile and non-mobile students and faculty.

Evolving Understandings of Study Abroad and Interculturality

In Chapter 1, I noted that various definitions of study abroad have emerged in different regions of the world. When reviewing the literature on international educational experience, it is important to be mindful of divergent ideas about what constitutes study abroad. In particular, when digesting related publications and presentations, it is essential to pay close attention to the details provided about the attributes and features in the study abroad programme (e.g., aims, duration, format, pedagogy, type of housing) and/or intercultural intervention (e.g., philosophy, aims, duration, methodology, activities) that is being discussed. Along with programme characteristics, critical consumers of the literature on study abroad should scrutinise the information provided about the participants in a study or pedagogical intervention (e.g., language proficiency, previous intercultural/international experience, degree of intercultural sensitivity, gender).

When preparing publications and presentations, it is good practice to develop the habit of offering detailed information about the participants and programme so that the audience more fully understands the nature of the intervention or programme under study. Further, it is incumbent on scholars to clearly express their conceptions of core constructs (e.g., provide definitions of key terms) in all forms of research output. In this way, consumers can determine if the study or pedagogical approach is a good fit with their study abroad context; they are then better positioned to consider potential applications or adjustments for their own situation.

Throughout this volume, in line with the critical stance of a growing number of contemporary intercultural scholars (e.g., Dasli and Díaz 2017b; Dervin 2016, 2017; Holliday 2011, 2012, 2018; Jackson and Oguro 2018a; Komisarof and Zhu 2016; Piller 2017), I have emphasised the need for study abroad professionals to adopt a reflexive, critical mindset in their work. Periodic critical reflection on one's evolving understandings of such core constructs as culture, interculturality, and global citizenship are essential for today's intercultural education scholars as these ideas naturally influence all aspects of study abroad research and practice.

Our degree of openness towards technological advances, shifts in pedagogy, internationalisation policies, and other developments in international education (or higher education, more broadly) also impact the quality of our professional endeavours. Both our mindset and conceptual understanding influence how we interpret and evaluate work in our field (e.g., respond to novel ideas presented in conference presentations, publications, study abroad programme reports, thesis advising sessions, etc.). Whether we are aware of it or not, our beliefs and attitudes also provide direction for our own practice (e.g., how we communicate with students who are preparing to study abroad, the approach we adopt as we mentor postgraduate students and future study abroad scholars, the ways we interact with participants in an investigation of sojourn learning). Accordingly, when we reflect on interculturality, criticality, and other related constructs, it is incumbent on us to consider our own personal biases and limitations. To advance the field, it is vital for both novice and seasoned educators (and administrators) to strive towards a more open, intercultural mindset to be better prepared to incorporate new ideas and understandings into research, policies, and/or practice.

In Chapter 2 I stated that divergent conceptions of culture can influence the way one designs and conducts research. As explained in Chapter 7, it also affects how one plans and implements intercultural interventions in study abroad programmes. Citing numerous studies and publications, throughout this volume, I have raised awareness of the limitations of static, unitary notions of culture and the potential dangers of essentialism and reductionism that can ensue when individuals are constrained by monocultural or ethnocentric perspectives (Dervin 2012; Holliday 2011; Komisarof and Zhu 2016). As Holliday (2018) observes, 'there is no such thing as neutral concepts of culture (Hall 1991)'; he cautions that 'talking about cultural difference is simply a "nice" way of talking about race (Delanty, Wodak and Jones 2008)'. I am in agreement with other critical interculturalists who argue that an understanding of the dynamic, multifaceted dimensions of culture and interculturality, coupled with an open, reflexive mindset are essential to foster constructive, ethical intercultural study abroad research and practice (Dasli and Díaz 2017a; Díaz 2013; Dervin 2016; Holliday 2018; Jackson and Oguro 2018b).

Looking ahead, as more institutions of higher education embrace internationalisation and actively promote global citizenship, I believe that critical elements (e.g., critical reflection, critical thinking) will become embedded in more investigations of language and intercultural learning in study abroad contexts. I expect that critical dimensions will also become much more common in intercultural practice in study abroad programmes. Further, I predict that conceptions and understandings of reflexivity and criticality will continue to evolve in the next decade with more insights from scholars from diverse disciplines in different regions of the world. I hope that this volume contributes to this development.

Research on Interculturality in Study Abroad: Historical Trends

In Chapter 2, I surveyed some of the most influential paradigms or worldviews that have guided and continue to steer investigations of interculturality in study abroad contexts, namely (post-)positivism, interpretivism, constructivism, critical theory, and pragmatism. I also briefly discussed the impact of culturalism on the development of study abroad interventions so that readers would have a better sense of historical developments in this field of research and be better equipped to review related presentations and publications, and plan future studies. Not surprisingly, in this multidisciplinary field, diverse approaches to research have emerged over time, due, in part, to differing objectives, conceptual frameworks, emphases, definitions of core constructs (e.g., culture, interculturality), and methodological expertise.

Nowadays, fresh perspectives, new or revised conceptual models, and innovative methodologies, are bringing about exciting changes in our field. With regard to research designs and methodology, as noted in Chapter 2 and illustrated in numerous examples throughout the book, the 'social turn' in applied linguistics and intercultural communication research (Block 2003; Kinginger 2013) has led to a move away from large-scale product-oriented studies towards more in-depth qualitative studies (e.g., narrativised accounts of the journeys of individual sojourners, ethnographies, multiple case studies) or mixed-methods research that systematically incorporates both quantitative and qualitative data to develop a more comprehensive picture of the subject under study. Additionally, more scholars are taking advantage of advances in technology and social media to conduct innovative empirical research.

The ethical dimension of research has also become more important within the field of international education. Nowadays, institutions of higher education generally have a code of ethics for researchers (including student researchers) and a list of procedures that must be followed to safeguard the well-being of participants and the reputation of the institution. It is incumbent on study abroad researchers to be familiar with and comply with professional and institutional guidelines for conducting research with human participants. In particular, there is more awareness today of the need to inform individuals of their right to not participate in a study; they must be offered the opportunity to withdraw at any time while the study is underway. Further, researchers must ensure confidentiality and safeguard the well-being of the participants (Deardorff 2015a; Phipps 2013; Woodin 2016).

As the field of international education has become more mature, expectations regarding the quality of research output have increased. At minimum, it is essential for contemporary study abroad researchers to have a solid understanding of the theoretical framework that underpins their work. Further, scholars need to strive for coherence in their research so that there is a clear, logical connection between the theoretical framework, methodology, and interpretation of findings. It is also imperative for consumers to carefully review publications and presentations to discern the conception of culture and paradigm that underpins the work being described as these elements influence the ways in which study abroad issues are identified, analysed, and discussed. I recognise that this is not a simple task as paradigms are infrequently specified in publications.

Emergent Themes, Gaps, and Future Directions in Study Abroad Research and Practice

When preparing the previous chapters, a review of the literature raised my awareness of a myriad of issues related to the intercultural dimension in study abroad theories, research, and practice, including: adjustment challenges associated with acculturation/socialisation and translanguaging; the complex connection between language, culture, and identity; cross-cultural transitions and the development of interculturality; and multiple internal and external factors that can influence the developmental trajectories of student sojourners and result in divergent learning outcomes (e.g., varying degrees of intercultural sensitivity, sociopragmatic competence, intercultural engagement, diversity in social networks).

This review underscored the multifarious and idiosyncratic nature of study abroad and challenged naïve assumptions about immersion and the language and intercultural learning of student sojourners. As this volume has indicated, a number of individual elements (e.g., sojourn aims, agency, degree of intercultural sensitivity, motivation) and external or environmental factors (e.g., the degree of host receptivity, efforts made by host institutions to mix local and international students) can lead to disparate outcomes. (Also see Chapter 5.) While some student sojourners may fully benefit from their stay abroad (e.g., develop a higher level of language and intercultural awareness, make meaningful multicultural friendships, enhance their language proficiency, diversify their social network, hone the attributes associated with global citizenship) without a pedagogical intervention, many others may have limited intercultural experience, gain little or no exposure to local communities of practice, and not enhance their language proficiency or intercultural competence. Contrary to expectations, they may acquire few of the attributes or characteristics associated with global citizenship.

The chapters in this volume also drew attention to the diversity of study abroad programmes with regard to a wide range of factors including duration, goals, location, language used, housing, intercultural practice (e.g., ranging from no intervention to comprehensive intercultural education at all stages of the study abroad cycle). Some study abroad programmes are faculty-led whereas, in other situations, student sojourners venture abroad on their own to study in an environment where they are the sole exchange student from their home institution. In sharp contrast, groups may venture abroad and study the host language in classes together. Hence, there is no such thing as '*the* study abroad context'.

Further, despite encouraging advances in our field, there is ample room for improvement in the ways in which study abroad research is conceived and carried out. In particular, my survey of contemporary research in study abroad contexts brought to light the limitations of some of the methodologies and tools that are being employed to document and assess intercultural learning. For example, I found that researchers in some studies did not employ assessment measures that fit with the conception of interculturality or intercultural competence that they claim underpinned their investigation. Consequently, the results were not congruent with the researcher's worldview or the methodology employed. In some research publications, the rationale for the approach that was adopted was not adequately explained and insufficient evidence (e.g., data excerpts and analysis) was presented to support the claims that were made. Conclusions did not stem from the data presented. In Chapter 2, I raised a number of issues that are of concern among intercultural researchers in international education (e.g., theory-building, quality assurance, methodologies, ethics, and social responsibility). These observations have implications for research methods courses for postgraduate students who plan to go out into the field to carry out their own study abroad investigations. This review also raises awareness of ethical and methodological issues that merit the attention of experienced researchers.

While we have witnessed tremendous growth in study abroad research, especially in the last decade, my review also uncovered multiple issues and domains that have received scant attention. For example, there are noticeable gaps in research that systematically examines the promotion of interculturality and global citizenship in study abroad interventions. Some scholars share innovative practices in conferences but never publish their findings so that a wider audience could benefit. This is regrettable and I hope that this book will encourage intercultural educators to share their pedagogical insights in some of the publication outlets that are cited in Chapter 1 or in other venues.

Few investigations in study abroad contexts have employed a critical lens to investigate the selection process (e.g., the identification of factors that determine which students are offered a place in competitive international exchange programmes). I also note that the sojourn and re-entry experiences of under-represented populations (e.g., minority members) have only been examined by a small number of researchers and much of the work has been carried out by scholars in North America and Europe. Hence, the field would benefit from more studies of this nature in diverse geographical locations. Better understanding barriers to participation could provide direction for practical measures that could be adopted to make study abroad more attractive and meaningful for minority students.

Some scholars (e.g., Devlin 2014; Shively 2010; Taguchi 2015, 2018 Timpe 2014) have been investigating the interactional and sociopragmatic development of students who take part in study abroad programmes. More investigations of this nature in diverse settings are needed. It would also be helpful for more attention to be focused on the complex relationship between language proficiency and intercultural competence, including, the connection between sociopragmatic competence and intercultural competence (Jackson forthcoming b)

A few scholars have examined the identities and intercultural learning of heritage students (e.g., Parra 2016; Shively 2016), that is, students who join a study abroad programme in their ancestral homeland (e.g., Chinese Americans taking part in a study abroad programme in Mainland China), our field could benefit from more studies that document and systematically analyse the intercultural development and identity negotiations of this unique population.

Service learning and participation in study abroad programmes in non-traditional destinations (e.g., Botswana, Cambodia, Chile, India) is now actively promoted by institutions of higher education in some parts of the world. Our field could be further enriched by empirical research that centres on interculturality and global citizenship development in relation to the learning of participants who study in non-traditional locations.

Research that brings together scholars from home and host institutions (or members of the sending and receiving nations) would be welcomed as it could potentially lead to a deeper understanding of some of the issues that have been highlighted in this volume and also uncover factors that have been overlooked. Studies of this nature could strengthen international ties and enrich study abroad programming.

Additionally, I hope that we will see more interdisciplinary research projects that bring together scholars from different disciplinary backgrounds (e.g., applied linguistics, cross-cultural psychology, sociology, pragmatics, speech communication) to investigate interculturality in study abroad contexts. In addition to enriching theory-building, collaborations of this nature could lead to innovative research methodologies and intercultural interventions.

The field of international education could also benefit from more studies that involve collaboration between study abroad administrators, staff in international offices, and faculty members (or PhD students) who conduct study abroad research. Staff who work on the front lines (e.g., advise students about international education opportunities, facilitate pre-sojourn orientations, host welcome sessions for inbound international exchange students, offer support for students who are abroad) could provide direction for many interesting studies (e.g., identify under-researched issues or concerns). It is also essential for administrators in institutions of higher education to recognise that staff in international offices can benefit from more exposure to the findings of study abroad research. Regrettably, staff who attend the international education conferences that were mentioned in Chapter 1 may be so busy signing international exchange agreements and meeting with current international partners that they do not have time to attend academic sessions (e.g., presentations that focus on study abroad research). Consequently, valuable opportunities for professional development and dialogue are lost.

At present, only a small number of studies are truly longitudinal, with data collected at least six months after the sojourners have returned home. Most studies cease gathering data very soon after a sojourn has ended (in the immediate post-sojourn phase). While challenging to implement (e.g., participant attrition), the field would be enhanced with more research that tracks the language and intercultural development of students for several years after international educational experience. Studies of this nature could track second language use, career choices, the degree of intercultural engagement, diversity in social networks, and international experience, and many other issues that could help us to better understand the long-term benefits of international education. The data could also provide direction for refinements in existing study abroad programmes and intercultural interventions.

The Need for Diverse Voices and Perspectives

The majority of studies that have focused on second language students centre on those who sojourned in English language contexts (e.g., Western countries) or perhaps taking English-medium courses in non-English-speaking countries (e.g., Indonesian learners of English enrolled in a study abroad programme in the Netherlands). While some scholars have also investigated the language and intercultural learning of study abroad students who are studying a European language (e.g., Kinginger's (2008, 2010, 2011) case studies of American learners of French in France), only a small number of studies centre on the language and intercultural learning of speakers of non-European languages (e.g., investigations of American learners of Arabic in the Middle East, such as Bown, Dewey and Belnap's (2015) and Trentman's (2013, 2015) work).

In my estimation, there is a need for much more research that explores the intercultural development and experiences of study abroad students who are studying second languages other than English (e.g., Portuguese language learners from North America in Brazil, Arabic language learners from China in Jordan; Canadian learners of Putonghua in Taiwan). We also need more studies that investigate the intercultural development of second language speakers of English who are studying in this language in other non-English speaking countries (e.g., Japanese or Malaysian students taking English-medium courses in Hong Kong universities, where they are using English as a lingua franca on campus). More insights into lingua franca situations would be timely. With the rise in populism and anti-immigration (anti-foreigners) sentiments in some nations, more international students many prefer to study in destinations closer to home where they perceive the environment to be more welcoming.

The field would surely benefit from the infusion of indigenous voices and perspectives, including the views of postgraduate students and scholars from diverse ethnic backgrounds in different regions of the world. Presently, the majority of study abroad researchers are from Western nations, although the number of scholars from Greater China is on the rise. In keeping with the emphasis on critical reflection and criticality, I also hope and expect that more scholars from diverse backgrounds will document and critically examine their own research practices in study abroad contexts. Hopefully, for example, we will see the publication of auto-ethnographies that centre on the study abroad learning of postgraduate students from non-Western countries.

Intercultural Interventions in Study Abroad: Pedagogy and Assessment

The preceding chapters have explained that contemporary international education researchers have found that simply being present in the host environment does not ensure an immersion experience, advances in interculturality, host language learning, the development of meaningful multicultural friendships, the emergence of a more global mindset or the cultivation of the attributes and behaviours associated with global citizenship (Jackson 2012; Paige and Vande Berg 2012; Vande Berg, Paige and Lou 2012a). Consequently, more and more institutions are calling for evidence of language and intercultural learning to justify the amount of funds, energy, and resources that are devoted to the selection and support of study abroad students. As noted by Deardorff (2015a) in reference to international education, '[t]he trend in measuring learning outcomes in education is here to say' (p. 108). While many study abroad students are still being sent abroad with little or no preparation or support, this is changing, albeit slowly in some regions.

In the previous chapter, I described diverse forms of intercultural mediation that are now being implemented at various phases of the study abroad cycle in different parts of the world and also offered examples of innovative online interventions that are taking advantage of developments in communications technology. I hope that this volume has illustrated the importance of strengthening the connection between theories, research, and practice to facilitate the work of intercultural educators and enhance the language and intercultural learning of study abroad participants. In my view, this is beneficial for all stakeholders (e.g., administrators, educators, students, receiving institutions).

Chapters 6 and 7 explained how shifts in understandings of how adults learn best have led to significant changes in how contemporary intercultural training and education programmes are being shaped, implemented, and assessed. In particular, more research-based, learner-centred approaches are helping students optimise their international educational experience; innovative pedagogy is empowering study abroad students and nurturing higher levels of language awareness, intercultural sensitivity, and engagement. Many models and theories (e.g., experiential learning theory, transformative learning theory, the developmental model of intercultural sensitivity) are influencing the design and assessment of these interventions, which are enriching the developmental trajectories of a growing number of participants in different parts of the world (see Chapters 6 and 7).

In the years ahead, with more systematic study abroad research (e.g., evaluative case studies of pedagogical interventions, mixed-methods studies) and the inclusion of diverse voices (e.g., PhD researchers and practitioners from different parts of the world), no doubt we will benefit from more innovative theory-building and novel intercultural interventions in international education. I also expect and hope that study abroad educators in different parts of the world will continue to take advantage of advances in technology to develop innovative fully online or blended pedagogical interventions to enhance sojourn learning and reflexivity. At present, most of the well-known websites for study abroad students have been created in the United States with Americans in mind. Looking to the future, I envisage the development of more websites which draw on relevant theories and research to scaffold and deepen the intercultural learning of student sojourners in other geographic regions. Hopefully, inter-institutional collaboration projects will bring together tech-savvy interculturalists from different continents to develop study abroad sites that appeal to a wider audience. With more advances in technology and social media, the field will continue to evolve in ways that are difficult to predict. In the future, I anticipate more empirical studies that will examine the ways in which these developments impact intercultural learning and engagement in study abroad contexts.

The measurement of student learning in international education is also gaining more attention as institutions of higher education increasingly adopt approaches to curriculum design and development that include assessment as a core element (e.g., OBA). Accordingly, in this volume I discussed the application of some of the many intercultural competence assessment tools and methods that are now crowding the field. It is important to understand the conceptions of culture and interculturality that underpin these instruments as any tool that is employed in an intercultural intervention should fit with the aims, philosophy, and methodology or pedagogy of the particular study abroad programme or research project.

While this volume has identified exciting developments in intercultural pedagogy in study abroad, there is tremendous scope for the enhancement of these interventions. In particular, there is a pressing need for more innovations that draw on research findings and advances in conceptual frameworks and pedagogy (e.g., critical perspectives). Moreover, while many of the interventions are implemented prior to international education or during the sojourn, there is a need for more innovative pedagogical interventions to enhance and extend the intercultural learning of returnees.

While well-meaning, many study abroad programmes unintentionally promote Otherisation and essentialism. Instead of propelling students to a higher level of intercultural awareness and sensitivity, they focus too much on culture difference, largely ignoring commonalities among people from different cultural backgrounds, and the participants may end up reinforcing preexisting stereotypes. For example, intercultural interventions that employ Hofstede's (2001) value orientations framework typically encourage study abroad students to identify and compare the key values in their own culture with those of the host culture. Underpinning this approach is the belief that if students learn about the values and patterns of behaviour that are associated with the host culture or nation they will then be better positioned to communicate effectively when abroad. Even if well intentioned, studying culture differences in this manner can lead to the objectifying and essentialising of host nationals. In other words, students may presume 'universal essence, homogeneity and unity in a particular culture . . . [and] reduce cultural behavior down to a simple causal factor' (Holliday, Hyde and Kullman 2004: 2). Another potential consequence is Otherisation, that is 'imagining someone as alien and different to "us" in such a way that "they" are excluded from "our" "normal", "superior", and "civilised" group' (Holliday et al. 2004: 3). This ethnocentric stance is not conducive to the developmental of mutually satisfying multicultural relationships. Instead, the 'dark' sides if identity that were discussed in Chapter 4 (e.g., stereotyping, racism) may ensue.

Critical interculturalists are increasingly calling for a shift away from a focus solely on perceived national cultural differences towards an awareness of multiple identities and pluriculturalism in intercultural research, including work in study abroad contexts (e.g., Dervin 2016; Komisarof and Zhu 2016; Jackson and Oguro 2018a). The move towards more interpretive and critical approaches in intercultural research has significant implications for pedagogy. In accord with other critical theorists, I maintain that the materials and curricula that are employed in pedagogical interventions in study abroad contexts should transcend traditional conceptions of culture bounded by the nation-state (Holliday 2010, 2018). Intercultural educators have a vital role to play in international education as they can encourage students to push past 'us vs. them' discourse and behaviours to develop a more critical awareness of themselves and the complex nature of the globalised world in which they live.

A review of the literature on intercultural interventions in international educational contexts also drew attention to the need for adequate preparation for educators who aim to foster the intercultural learning of students. In addition to having a solid understanding of pedagogy and the most effective ways to learn, it is imperative for contemporary intercultural educators to possess an open, intercultural mindset and a willingness to embrace new ideas and perspectives. Moreover, the complexity of interculturality means that reflexivity is essential for intercultural practitioners as well as researchers. Ideally, this should be a lifelong endeavor.

Concluding Thoughts

With reference to interculturality, as this volume attests, we have come a long way in terms of theory-building, research, and practice in international education, but still have further to go to more fully grasp the complexity of study abroad experience and provide meaningful direction for pedagogical interventions. In this concluding chapter, I identified a number of research gaps and presented a rather long 'wish list' for future research and practice in international education. In particular, the infusion of reflexivity and criticality into intercultural research and practice has the potential to enhance the design, delivery, and assessment of pedagogical interventions. Accordingly, in this chapter and throughout this volume, I have urged study abroad scholars to embrace these notions in current and future endeavours.

Undeniably, international education can play a significant role in the enhancement of the attributes, skills, and actions associated with global citizenship. To more fully achieve the intercultural aims of internationalisation, much remains to be done, however. Fostering intercultural sensitivity, empathy, and global-mindedness (and other attributes and skills associated with global citizenship) may be challenging goals, but they are worthy and imperative in today's interconnected world. When setting the agenda for future research and practice in international education, it is essential to draw on diverse voices and visions. Just as quality research should inform practice, it is also important for systematic intercultural assessment and programme reviews to provide direction for the refinement of intercultural interventions.

Global citizenship and the development of global competencies are vital for everyone. To this end, efforts should be made to promote interculturality among *all* students, faculty, and staff in institutions of higher education, not just those who gain some form of international experience. For this reason, I advocate advances in IaH (Internationalisation at Home) and IoC (Internationalisation of the curriculum) initiatives to foster interculturality on campus (and in the wider community) and encourage meaningful intercultural engagement.

When I began this volume, I aimed to help readers better understand the core constructs and historical dimension of work in this field, especially developments related to interculturality in study abroad contexts. I sincerely hope that my review and suggestions will inspire other intercultural innovations in theory-building, research, and practice in international education so that future study abroad students will more fully benefit from their stay in the host country.

References

Abdallah-Pretceille, M. (1986) *Vers une Pedagogic interculturelle*, Paris: Publications de la Sorbonne.
Abdallah-Pretceille, M. (1999) *L'éducation interculturelle*, Paris: PUF (Que sais-je?).
Abdallah-Pretceille, M. (2003) *Former en Contexte Hétérogène: pour un Humanisme du Divers*, Paris: Anthropos.
Adler, P. (1975) 'The transitional experience: An alternative view of culture shock', *Journal of Humanistic Psychology*, 15: 13–23. doi: 10.1177/002216787501500403.
Allen, H.W. (2013) 'Self-regulatory strategies of foreign language learners: From the classroom to study abroad and beyond', in C. Kinginger (ed.) *Social and Cultural Aspects of Language Learning in Study Abroad*, Amsterdam and Philadelphia: John Benjamins Publishing Company, pp. 47–72.
Almarza, G.G., Martinez, R.D. and Llavador, F.B. (2015) 'Identifying students' intercultural communicative competence at the beginning of their placement: Towards the enhancement of study abroad programmes', *Intercultural Education*, 26(1): 73–85. doi: 10.1080/14675986.2015.997004.
Altbach, P. (2016a) 'The emergence and reality of contemporary internationalization', in P. Altbach (ed.) *Global Perspectives on Higher Education*, Baltimore: Johns Hopkins University, pp. 3–14.
Altbach, P. (2016b) 'The imperial tongue: English as the dominating academic language', in P. Altbach (ed.) *Global Perspectives on Higher Education*, Baltimore: Johns Hopkins University, pp. 140–8.
Althusser, L. (1971) *Lenin and Philosophy and Other Essays*, New York: Monthly Review Press.
Amelina, A., Devrimsel, D.N., Faist, T. and Schiller, N.G. (2012) *Beyond Methodological Nationalism: Research Methodologies for Cross-Border Studies*, New York: Routledge.
Amselle, J.-L. (2010) *Rétrovolutions*, Paris: Stock.
Angelo, T.A. (1995) 'Reassessing (and defining) assessment', *The AAHE Bulletin*, 48(2): 7–9.
Angelo, T.A. and Cross, K.P. (1993) *Classroom Assessment Techniques: A Handbook for College Teachers*, San Francisco: Jossey-Bass.
Anquetil, M. (2006) *Mobilité Erasmus et communication interculturelle* (Erasmus Mobility and Intercultural Communication), Collection Transversales, Berlin: Peter Lang.

Appadurai, A. (1996) *Modernity at Large: Cultural Dimensions of Globalization*, Minneapolis, MN: University of Minnesota Press.

Appadurai, A. (2006) *Fear of Small Numbers: An Essay on the Geography of Anger*, Durham: Duke University Press.

Arthur, N. (2004) *Counseling International Students: Clients from around the World*, New York: Springer.

Audi, R. (2011) *Epistemology: A Contemporary Introduction to the Theory of Knowledge*, New York and Abingdon: Routledge.

Austin, J.L. (1962) *How to Do Things with Words*, Oxford: Oxford University Press.

Baker, C. (1992) *Attitudes and Languages*, Clevedon: Multilingual Matters.

Bandura, A. (1994) 'Self-efficacy', in V.S. Ramachaudran (ed.) *Encyclopedia of Human Behavior, Volume 4*, New York: Academic Press, pp. 71–81.

Banta, T.W. and Palomba, C.A. (2015) *Assessment Essentials: Planning, Implementing, and Improving Assessment in Higher Education*, San Francisco: Jossey-Bass.

Barkley, E.F. (2010) *Student Engagement Techniques: A Handbook for College Faculty*, San Francisco: Jossey-Bass.

Bathurst, L. and La Brack, B. (2012) 'Shifting the locus of intercultural learning: Intervening prior to and after student experiences abroad', in M. Vande Berg, R.M. Paige and K.H. Lou (eds) *Student Learning Abroad: What Our Students Are Learning, What They're Not, and What We Can Do about It*, Sterling, VA: Stylus Publishing, pp. 261–83.

Bauman, Z. (2004) *Identity*, Cambridge: Polity.

Baumgratz-Gangl, G. (1992) *Compétence Transculturelle et Echanges Educatifs*, Paris: Hachette.

Baxter, J. (2016) 'Positioning language and identity: Poststructuralist perspectives', in S. Preece (ed.) *The Routledge Handbook of Language and Identity*, London and New York: Routledge, pp. 34–49.

Beaven, A. and Borghetti, C. (2016) 'Interculturality in study abroad', *Language and Intercultural Communication*, 16(3): 313–17. doi: 10.1080/14708 477.2016.1173893.

Beaven, A. and Spencer-Oatey, H. (2016) 'Cultural adaptation in different facets of life and the impact of language: A case study of personal adjustment patterns during study abroad', *Language and Intercultural Communication*, 16(3): 349–67. doi: 10.1080/14708477.2016.1168048.

Beelen, J. and Jones, E. (2015) 'Redefining internationalization at home', in A. Curaj, L. Matei, R. Pricopie, J. Salmi and P. Scott (eds) *The European Higher Education Area: Between Critical Reflections and Future Policies*, New York: Springer, pp. 59–72.

Behrent, S. (2007) *La Communication Alloglotte* (Communication in a Non-Local Language), Paris: L'Harmattan.

Benjamin, S. and Dervin, F. (2015) *Migration, Diversity and Education: Beyond Third Culture Kids*, London, UK: Palgrave MacMillan.

Bennett, J.M. (1998) 'Transition shock: Putting culture shock in perspective', in M.J. Bennett (ed.) *Basic Concepts of Intercultural Communication*, Yarmouth, ME, USA: Intercultural Press, pp. 215–24.

Bennett, J.M. (2008) 'On becoming a global soul: A path to engagement during study abroad', in V. Savicki (ed.) *Developing Intercultural Competence and*

Transformation: Theory, Research, and Application in International Education, Sterling, VA: Stylus Publishing, pp. 13–31.
Bennett, J.M. (2009) 'Cultivating intercultural competence: A process perspective', in D. Deardorff (ed.) *The Sage Handbook of Intercultural Competence*, Thousand Oaks, CA: Sage Publications, pp. 121–40.
Bennett, J.M. (2015) 'Essential principles for intercultural training', in J.M. Bennett (ed.) *The Sage Handbook of Intercultural Competence, Volume 1*, Los Angeles: Sage Publications, pp. 293–7.
Bennett, J.M. and Bennett, M.J. (2004) 'Developing intercultural sensitivity: An integrative approach to global and domestic diversity', in D. Landis, J.M. Bennett and M.J. Bennett (eds) *Handbook of Intercultural Training*, 3rd edn, Thousand Oaks, CA: Sage Publications, pp. 147–65.
Bennett, J.M., Bennett, M.J. and Allen, W. (1999) 'Developing intercultural competence in the language classroom', in R.M. Paige, D.L. Lange and Y.A. Yershova (eds) *Culture as the Core: Integrating Culture into the Language Curriculum*, Minneapolis: CARLA, University of Minnesota, pp. 13–46.
Bennett, J.M., Bennett, M.J. and Allen, W. (2003) 'Developing intercultural competence in the language classroom', in D.L. Lange and R.M. Paige (eds) *Culture as the Core: Perspectives on Culture in Second Language Learning*, Greenwich, CT: Information Age Publishing, pp. 237–70.
Bennett, M.J. (1993) 'Towards ethnorelativism: A developmental model of intercultural sensitivity', in R.M. Paige (ed.) *Education for the Intercultural Experience*, 2nd edn, Yarmouth, ME: Intercultural Press, pp. 21–71.
Bennett, M.J. (1998) 'Intercultural communication: A current perspective', in M.J. Bennett (ed.) *Basic Concepts of Intercultural Communication: Selected Readings*, Yarmouth, ME: Intercultural Press, pp. 1–34.
Bennett, M.J. (2012) 'Paradigmatic assumptions and a developmental approach to intercultural learning', in M. Vande Berg, R.M. Paige and K.H. Lou (eds) *Student Learning Abroad: What Our Students Are Learning, What They're Not, and What We Can Do about It*, Sterling, VA: Stylus Publishing, pp. 90–114.
Benson, P. (2012) 'Individual difference and context in study abroad', in W.M. Chan, K.N. Chin, S.K. Bhatt and I. Walker (eds) *Perspectives on Individual Characteristics and Foreign Language Education*, Berlin: Mouton de Gruyter, pp. 221–38.
Benson, P. (2017) 'Sleeping with strangers: Dreams and nightmares in experiences of homestay', *Study Abroad Research in Second Language Acquisition and International Education*, 2(1): 1–20.
Benson, P., Barkhuizen, G., Bodycott, P. and Brown, J. (2013) *Second Language Identity in Narratives of Study Abroad*, Basingstoke: Palgrave.
Berardo, K. (2006) 'The U-curve of adjustment: A study in the evolution and evaluation of a 50-year old model', Unpublished master's thesis, University of Bedfordhsire, Luton, UK.
Berardo, K. (2012) 'Manage cultural transitions', in K. Berardo and D.K. Deardorff (eds) *Building Cultural Competence: Innovative Activities and Models*, Sterling, VA: Stylus Publishing, pp. 183–9.
Berardo, K. and Deardorff, K.D. (eds) (2012) *Building Cultural Competence: Innovative Activities and Models*, Sterling, VA: Stylus Publishing.

References

Berry, J.W. (1997) 'Immigration, acculturation, and adaptation', *Applied Psychology: An International Review*, 46: 5–34. doi: 10.1111/j.1464-0597.1997.tb01087.x.

Berry, J.W. (2006) 'Contexts of acculturation', in D.L. Sam and J.W. Berry (eds) *The Cambridge Handbook of Acculturation Psychology*, Cambridge: Cambridge University Press, pp. 27–42.

Berry, J.W. (2010) 'Mobility and acculturation', in S.C. Carr (ed.) *The Psychology of Global Mobility*, New York: Springer, pp. 193–210.

Berry, J.W. (2015) 'Acculturation', in J.M. Bennett (ed.) *The Sage Handbook of Intercultural Competence, Volume 1*, Los Angeles: Sage Publications, pp. 1–4.

Berry, J.W., Poortinga, Y.H., Breugelmans, S.M., Chasiotis, A. and Sam, D.L. (2011) *Cross-Cultural Psychology: Research and Applications*, 3rd edn, Cambridge: Cambridge University Press.

Berthoz, A. (2009) *La Simplexité*, Paris: Odile Jacobs.

Bleistein, T. and Wong, M.S. (2015) 'Using qualitative research methods to assess education abroad', in V. Savicki and E. Brewer (eds) *Assessing Study Abroad: Theory, Tools, and Practice*, Sterling, VA: Stylus Publishing, pp. 103–21.

Block, D. (2003) *The Social Turn in Second Language Acquisition*, Edinburgh: Edinburgh University Press.

Block, D. (2007) *Second Language Identities*, London: Continuum.

Bloom, M. and Miranda, A. (2015) 'Intercultural sensitivity through short-term study abroad', *Language and Intercultural Communication*, 15(4): 567–80. doi: 10.1080/14708477.2015.1056795.

Bochner, S. (2006) 'Sojourners', in D.L. Sam and J.W. Berry (eds) *The Cambridge Handbook of Acculturation Psychology*, Cambridge: Cambridge University Press, pp. 181–97.

Bolen, M. (ed.) (2007a) *A Guide to Outcomes Assessment in Education Abroad*, Carlisle, PA: Forum on Education Abroad.

Bolen, M. (2007b) 'Introduction', in *A Guide to Outcomes Assessment in Education Abroad*, Carlisle, PA: Forum on Education Abroad, pp. 1–6.

Borghetti, C. (2016) 'Intercultural education in practice: Two pedagogical experiences with mobile students', *Language and Intercultural Education*, 16(3): 502–13. doi: 10.1080/14708477.2016.1168045.

Borghetti, C. and Beaven, A. (2018) 'Monitoring class interaction to maximise intercultural learning in mobility contexts', in J. Jackson and S. Oguro (eds) *Intercultural Interventions in Study Abroad*, Abingdon, UK and New York: Routledge, pp. 37–54.

Bosley, G.W. (2018) 'Developing a globally-prepared student body through an experiential constructivist-driven intervention during study abroad', in J. Jackson and S. Oguro (eds) *Intercultural Interventions in Study Abroad*, Abingdon, UK and New York: Routledge, pp. 155–74.

Bown, J., Dewey, D.P. and Belnap, R.K. (2015) 'Student interactions during study abroad in Jordan', in R. Mitchell, T. Tracy-Ventura and K. McManus (eds) *Social Interaction, Identity, and Language Learning During Residence Abroad*, Eurosla Monographs Series, 4, Amsterdam: The European Second Language Association, pp. 199–222.

Boye, S. (2016) *Intercultural Communicative Competence and Short Stays Abroad: Perceptions of Development*, Munster and New York: Waxmann.

Brah, A. and Phoenix, A. (2004) 'Ain't I a woman? Revisiting intersectionality', *Journal of International Women's Studies*, 5(3): 75–86. Online. Available: http://vc.bridgew.edu/jiws/vol5/iss3/8 (accessed 11 May 2017).

Brewer, E. and Moore, J. (2015) 'Where and how do students learn abroad? Using reflective writing for meaning-making and assessment', in V. Savicki and E. Brewer (eds) *Assessing Study Abroad: Theory, Tools, and Practice*, Sterling, VA: Stylus Publishing, pp. 145–61.

Brewer, E., Shively, R., Gozik, N., Doyle, D.M. and Savicki, V. (2015) 'Beyond the study abroad industry: Perspectives from other disciplines on assessing study abroad learning outcomes', in V. Savicki and E. Brewer (eds) *Assessing Study Abroad: Theory, Tools, and Practice*, Sterling, VA: Stylus Publishing, pp. 33–56.

Brewer, J. (2000) *Ethnography*, Buckingham, England: Open University Press.

British Council (2013) *The Future of the World's Mobile Students to 2014*. Online. Available: http://ihe.britishcouncil.org/educationintelligence/future-world-mobile-students-2024 (accessed 20 October 2016).

Brown, L. (2009) 'A failure to communication on the cross-cultural campus', *Journal of Studies in International Education*, 13(4): 439–54. doi: 10.1177/1028315309331913.

Brown, L. (2013) 'Identity and honorifics use in Korean study abroad', in C. Kinginger (ed.) *Social and Cultural Aspects of Language Learning in Study Abroad*, Amsterdam: John Benjamins, pp. 269–98.

Brux, J.M. and Fry, B. (2010) 'Multicultural students in study abroad: Their interests, their issues, and their constraints', *Journal of Studies in International Education*, 14(5): 508–27. doi: 10.1177/1028315309342486.

Bryant, K.M. and Soria, K.M. (2015) 'College students' sexual orientation, gender identity, and participation in study abroad', *Frontiers: The Interdisciplinary Journal of Study Abroad*, 25: 91–106. Online. Available: https://frontiersjournal.org/wp-content/uploads/2015/09/BRYANT-SORIA-FrontiersXXV-CollegeStudentsSexualOrientationGenderIdentityandParticipationinStudyAbroad.pdf (accessed 11 May 2017).

Burrell, G. and Morgan, G. (1988) *Sociological Paradigms and Organizational Analysis*, Portsmouth, NH: Heinemann.

Byram, M. (1997) *Teaching and Assessing Intercultural Communicative Competence*, Clevedon: Multilingual Matters.

Byram, M. (2006) 'Language teaching for intercultural citizenship: The European situation', Paper presented at the New Zealand Association of Language Teachers (NZALT) Conference, University of Auckland, July 2006.

Byram, M. (2009) 'The intercultural speaker and the pedagogy of foreign language education', in D.K. Deardorff (ed.) *The Sage Handbook of Intercultural Competence*, Thousand Oaks, CA: Sage Publications, pp. 321–2.

Byram, M. (2012) 'Conceptualizing intercultural (communicative) competence and intercultural citizenship', in J. Jackson (ed) *The Routledge Handbook of Language and Intercultural Communication*, Abingdon: Routledge, pp. 85–97.

Byram, M. and Dervin, F. (eds) (2008) *Students, Staff, and Academic Mobility*, Newcastle, UK: Cambridge Scholars Publishing.

Byram, M. and Feng, A. (eds) (2006) *Living and Studying Abroad: Research and Practice*, Clevedon: Multilingual Matters.

Byram, M., Gribkova, B. and Starkey, H. (2002) *Developing the Intercultural Dimension in Language Teaching: A Practical Introduction for Teachers*, Strasbourg: Council of Europe Publishing.

Byram, M. and Parmenter, L. (eds) (2012) *The Common European Framework of Reference: The Globalisation of Language Education Policy*, Bristol: Multilingual Matters.

Byram, M. and Parmenter, L. (2015) 'Global citizenship', in J.M. Bennett (ed.) *The Sage Handbook of Intercultural Competence, Volume 1*, Los Angeles: Sage Publications, pp. 346–48.

Byram, M. and Zarate, G. (1997) 'Defining and assessing intercultural competence: Some principles and proposals for the European context', *Language Teaching*, 29: 14–18. doi: 10.1017/S0261444800008557.

Byrnes, F.C. (1966) 'Role shock: An occupational hazard of American technical assistants abroad', *The Annals*, 368: 95–108. Online. Available: www.jstor.org/stable/1036924?seq=1#page_scan_tab_contents (accessed 11 May 2017).

Canagarajah, S. (2014) *Translingual Practice: Global Englishes and Cosmopolitan Relations*, New York: Routledge.

Canale, M. and Swain, M. (1980) 'Theoretical bases of communicative approaches to second language teaching and testing', *Applied Linguistics* (1): 1–47. doi: 10.1093/applin/I.1.1.

Carbaugh, E.M. and Doubet, K.J. (2016) *The Differentiated Flipped Classroom*, Thousand Oaks, CA: Corwin.

Carroll, J.B. (1967) 'Foreign language proficiency levels attained by language majors near graduation from college', *Foreign Language Annals*, 1(2): 131–51. doi: 10.1111/j.1944-9720.1967.tb00127.xl.

Carroll, J.B. (2015) *Tools for Teaching in an Educationally Mobile World*, London and New York: Routledge.

Cavana, M.L.P. (2009) 'Closing the circle: From Dewey to Web 2.0', in C.R. Payne (ed.) *Information Technology and Constructivism in Higher Education: Progressive Learning Frameworks*, London and Hershey, PA: IGI Global, pp. 1–13.

Chambers, A. and Chambers, K. (2008) 'Tuscan dreams: Study abroad student expectation and experiences in Siena', in V. Savicki (ed.) *Developing Intercultural Competence and Transformation: Theory, Research, and Application in International Education*, Sterling, VA: Stylus Publishing, pp. 128–53.

Chen, G.M. and Starosta, W.J. (2000) 'The development and validation of the intercultural communication sensitivity scale', *Human Communication*, 3: 1–15. Online. Available: http://digitalcommons.uri.edu/cgi/viewcontent.cgi?article=1035&context=com_facpubs (accessed 11 May 2017).

Chen, G.M. and Starosta, W.J. (2006) 'Intercultural awareness', in L.A. Samovar, R.E. Porter and E.R. McDaniel (eds) *Intercultural Communication: A Reader*, Belmont, CA: Wadsworth, pp. 357–66.

Chik, A. and Benson, P. (2008) 'Frequent flyer: A narrative of overseas study in English', in P. Kalaja, V. Menezes and A.M.F. Barcelos (eds) *Narratives of Learning and Teaching EFL*, Basingstoke: Palgrave Macmillan, pp. 155–68.

Chiu, C.-Y and Hong, Y.-Y. (2006) *Social Psychology of Culture*, New York: Psychology Press.

Church, A.T. (1982) 'Sojourner adjustment', *Psychological Bulletin*, 91: 540–72. doi: 10.1037/0033-2909.91.3.540.

Clark, V.L.P. and Ivankova, N.V. (2016) *Mixed Methods Research: A Guide to the Field*, Thousand Oaks, CA: Sage Publications.

Cohen, A.D., Paige, R.M., Shively, R.L., Emert, H. and Hoff, J. (2005) 'Maximizing study abroad through language and culture strategies: Research on students, study abroad program professionals, and language instructors', Final Report to the International Research and Studies Program, Office of International Education, DOE, Center for Advanced Research on Language Acquisition, University of Minnesota, Minneapolis.

Coleman, J.A. (2009) 'Study abroad and SLA: Defining goals and variables', in A. Berndt and K. Kleppin (eds) *Sprachlehrforschung: Theorie und Empire, Festschrift fur Rudiger Grotjahn*, Frankfurt am Main: Peter Lang Publishing Group, pp. 181–96.

Coleman, J.A. (2013) 'Researching whole people and whole lives', in C. Kinginger (ed.) *Social and Cultural Aspects of Language Learning in Study Abroad*, Amsterdam: John Benjamins, pp. 17–44.

Coleman, J.A. and Chafer, T. (2010) 'Study abroad and the Internet: Physical and virtual context in an era of expanding telecommunications', *Frontiers: The Interdisciplinary Journal of Study Abroad*, 19: 151–67. Online. Available: https://frontiersjournal.org/wp-content/uploads/2015/09/COLEMAN-CHAFER-FrontiersXIX-StudyAbroadandtheInternet.pdf (accessed 11 May 2017).

Collins, R. (1990) *Culture, Communication, and National Identity: The Case of Canadian Television*, Toronto: University of Toronto Press.

Cortazzi, M. and Jin, L. (2011) 'Conclusions: What are we learning from research about Chinese learners?', in L. Jin and M. Cortazzi (eds) *Researching Chinese Learners: Skills, Perceptions and Intercultural Adaptations*, Basingstoke: Palgrave MacMillan, pp. 314–18.

Council of Europe (2001) *Common European Framework of Reference for Languages (CEFR)*, Strasbourg: Council of Europe Publishing.

Creswell, J.W. (2014) *Research Design: Qualitative, Quantitative, and Mixed Methods Approaches*, 4th edn, Thousand Oaks, CA: Sage Publications.

Creswell, J.W. (2015) *A Concise Introduction to Mixed Methods Research*, Thousand Oaks, CA: Sage Publications.

Cuenat, M. (2018) 'Plurimobil: Pragmatic enhancement of intercultural learning in study abroad contexts', in J. Jackson and S. Oguro (eds) *Intercultual Interventions in Study Abraod*, Abingdon, UK and New York: Routledge, pp. 175–89.

Cushner, K. and Karim, A.U. (2004) 'Study abroad at the university level', in D. Landis, J.J.M. Bennett and M.J. Bennett (eds) *Handbook of Intercultural Training*, 3rd edn, Thousand Oaks, CA: Sage Publications, pp. 289–308.

Dahl, Ø, Jensen, I. and Nynäs, P. (2006) *Bridges of Understanding: Perspectives on Intercultural Communication*, Oslo: Unipub.

Dasli, M. and Díaz, A.R. (2017a) 'Tracing the "critical" trajectory of language and intercultural communication pedagogy', in M. Dasli and A. Díaz (eds) *The Critical Turn in Language and Intercultural Communication Pedagogy: Theory, Research and Practice*, London: Routledge, pp. 3–21.

Dasli, M. and Díaz, A.R. (eds) (2017b) *The Critical Turn in Language and Intercultural Communication Pedagogy: Theory, Research and Practice*, London: Routledge.

Deardorff, D.K. (2004) 'The identification and assessment of intercultural competence as a student outcome of internationalization at institutions of higher education in the United States', Unpublished dissertation, North Carolina State University, Raleigh, NC.

Deardorff, D.K. (2006) 'Identification and assessment of intercultural competence as a student outcome of internationalization', *Journal of Studies in International Education*, 10(3): 241–66. doi: 10.1177/1028315306287002.

Deardorff, D.K. (2008) 'Intercultural competence: A definition, model, and implications for education abroad', in V. Savicki (ed.) *Developing Intercultural Competence and Transformation: Theory, Research, and Application in International Education*, Sterling, VA: Stylus Publishing, pp. 32–52.

Deardorff, D.K. (ed.) (2009a) *The Sage Handbook of Intercultural Competence*, Thousand Oaks, CA: Sage Publications.

Deardorff, D.K. (2009b) 'Synthesizing conceptualizations of intercultural competence: A summary and emerging themes', in D.K. Deardorff (ed.) *The Sage Handbook of Intercultural Competence*, Thousand Oaks, CA: Sage Publications, pp. 264–9.

Deardorff, D.K. (2009c) 'Implementing intercultural competence assessment', in D.K. Deardorff (ed.) *The Sage Handbook of Intercultural Competence*, Thousand Oaks, CA: Sage Publications, pp. 477–91.

Deardorff, D.K. (2009d) 'Preface', in D.K. Deardorff (ed.) *The Sage Handbook of Intercultural Competence*, Thousand Oaks, CA: Sage Publications.

Deardorff, D.K. (2010) 'Understanding the challenges of assessing global citizenship', in R. Lewin (ed) *The Handbook of Practice and Research in Study Abroad: Higher Education and the Quest for Global Citizenship*, New York: Routledge, pp. 346–64.

Deardorff, D.K. (2015a) *Demystifying Outcomes Assessment for International Educators: A Practical Approach*, Sterling, VA: Stylus Publishing.

Deardorff, D.K. (2015b) 'Assessments of intercultural competence', in J.M. Bennett (ed.) *The Sage Encyclopedia of Intercultural Competence, Volume 1*, Thousand Oaks, CA: Sage, pp. 17–20.

Deardorff, D.K. (2015c) 'Definitions: Knowledge, skills, attitudes', in J.M. Bennett (ed.) *The Sage Encyclopedia of Intercultural Competence, Volume 1*, Thousand Oaks, CA: Sage, pp. 217–20.

Deardorff, D.K. (2016) 'How to assess intercultural competence', in H. Zhu (ed.) *Research Methods in Intercultural Communication*, Chichester: John Wiley and Sons, pp. 120–34.

Deardorff, D.K. and Arasaratnam-Smith, L. (eds) (2017) *Intercultural Competence in International Higher Education: International Approaches, Assessment and Application*, London: Routledge.

Deardorff, D.K. and Hunter, W.D. (2006) 'Educating global-ready graduates', *International Educator*, 15(3): 72–83.

Deardorff, D.K. and Jones, E. (2012) 'Intercultural competence: An emerging focus in post-secondary education', in D.K. Deardorff, H. de Wit, J.D. Heyl and T. Adams (eds) *The Sage Handbook of International Higher Education*, Thousand Oaks, CA: Sage Publications, pp. 283–304.

Delanty, G., Wodak, R. and Jones, P. (eds) (2008) *Migration, Identity, and Belonging*, Liverpool: Liverpool University Press.

Delanty, J. (2009) *The Cosmopolitan Imagination:The Renewal of Critical Social Theory*, Cambridge and New York: Cambridge.
Deller, J. and Stahl, G. (2015) 'Assessment centers', in J.M. Bennett (ed.) *The Sage Handbook of Intercultural Competence, Volume 1*, Los Angeles: Sage Publications, pp. 11–17.
Dervin, F. (2008) *Métamorphoses Identitaires en Situation de Mobilité*, Turku: Humanoria.
Dervin, F. (2012) 'Cultural identity, representation and othering', in J. Jackson (ed.) *Routledge Handbook of Language and Intercultural*, Communication, Abingdon: Routledge, pp. 181–94.
Dervin, F. (2013) 'Researching identity and interculturality: Moving away from methodological nationalism for good?', in R. Machart, C.B. Lim, S.N. Lim and E. Yamamoto (eds) *Intersecting Identities and Interculturality: Discourse and Practice*, Newcastle-upon-Tyne, UK: Cambridge Scholars Publishing, pp. 8–21.
Dervin, F. (2016) *Interculturality in Education: A Theoretical and Methodological Toolbox*, London: Palgrave MacMillan.
Dervin, F. (2017) 'Critical turns in language and intercultural communication pedagogy: The simple-complex continuum (simplexity) as a new perspective', in M. Dasli and A. Díaz (eds) *The Critical Turn in Language and Intercultural Communication Pedagogy: Theory, Research and Practice*, London: Routledge, pp. 58–71.
Dervin, F. and Dirba, M. (2006) 'On liquid interculturality: Finnish and Latvian student teachers' perceptions of intercultural competence', in P. Pietilä, P. Lintunen and H.-M. Järvinen (eds) *Language Learners of Today, Jyväskylä: Suomen soveltavan kielitieteen yhdistyksen (AFinLA) julkaisuja*, 64: 257–73. Online. Available: https://journal.fi/afinlavk/article/view/59960 (accessed 11 May 2017).
Dervin, F. and Gross, Z. (2016) *Intercultural Competence in Education: Alternative Approaches for Different Times*, London: Palgrave MacMillan.
Dervin, F. and Härkönen, A. (2018) 'I want to be able to understand each and every person that I come into contact with: Critical interculturality training, student mobility and perceptions of the "intercultural"', in J. Jackson and S. Oguro (eds) *Intercultural Interventions in Study Abroad*, Abingdon, UK and New York: Routledge, pp. 55–70.
Dervin, F. and Layne, H. (2013) 'A guide to interculturality for international and exchange students: An example of Hostipitality?', *Journal of Multicultural Discourses*, 6(1): 37–52. doi: 10.1080/17447143.2012.753896.
Dervin, F. and Risager, K. (2015) *Researching Identity and Interculturality*, London: Routledge.
de Singly, F. (2003) *Les Uns et les Autres*, Paris: Armand Collin.
Devlin, A.M. (2014) *The Impact of Study Abroad on the Acquisition of Sociopragmatic Variation Patterns: The Case of Non-Native Speaker English Teachers*, New York: Peter Lang.
Dewey, D.P., Bown, J. and Eggett, D. (2012) 'Japanese language proficiency, social networking, and language use during study abroad', *The Canadian Modern Language Review*, 68(2): 111–37.
Dewey, D.P., Ring, S., Gardner, D. and Belnap, R.K. (2013) 'Social network formation and development during study abroad in the Middle East', *System*, 41(2): 269–82.

de Wit, H., Hunter, F., Howard, L., and Egron-Polak, E. (2015) *Internationalisation of Higher Education*, Brussels: European Parliament.

Diao, W. (2011) 'Study abroad, participation, and turn-taking', in G. Granena, J. Koeth, S. Lee-Ellis, A. Lukyanchenko, G.P. Botano and E. Rhoades (eds) *Selected Proceedings of the 2010 Second Language Research Forum*, Somerville, MA: Cascadilla Proceedings Project, pp. 1–17.

Diao, W., Freed, B. and Smith, L. (2011) 'Confirmed beliefs or false assumptions? A study of home stay experiences in the French study abroad context', *Frontiers: The Interdisciplinary Journal of Study Abroad*, 21: 109–42. Online. Available: https://frontiersjournal.org/wp-content/uploads/2015/09/DIAO-FREED-FrontiersXXI-ConfirmedBeliefsorFalseAssumptions.pdf (accessed 11 May 2017).

Díaz, A.R. (2013) *Developing Critical Languaculture Pedagogies in Higher Education: Theory and Practice*, Bristol: Multilingual Matters.

Dill, B.T. and Zambrana, R.E. (2009) *Emerging Intersections: Race, Class, and Gender in Theory, Policy, and Practice*, New Brunswick, NJ: Rutgers University Press.

Dolby, N. (2004) 'Encountering an American self: Study abroad and national identity', *Comparative Education Review*, 48(2), 150–73. doi: 10.1086/382620.

Dolby, N. (2005) 'Globalisation, identity, and nation: Australian and American undergraduates abroad', *The Australian Educational Researcher*, 32(1): 101–17. doi: 10.1007/BF03216815.

Dolby, N. (2007) 'Reflections on nation: American undergraduates and education abroad', *Journal of Studies in International Education*, 11: 141–56. doi: 10.1177/1028315306291944.

Donatelli, L. (2010) '"The impact of technology on study abroad", in W. Hoffa and S. DePaul (eds) A history of U.S. study abroad: 1965-present', *Frontiers: The Interdisciplinary Journal of Study Abroad*, Special Issue: 295–320.

Dörnyei, Z. (2005) *The Psychology of the Language Learner: Individual Differences in Second Language Acquisition*, Mahwah, NJ: Lawrence Erlbaum Associates, Inc.

Dörnyei, Z. (2009) 'The L2 motivational self system', in Z. Dörnyei and E. Ushioda (eds) *Motivation, Language Identity and the L2 Self*, Bristol: Multilingual Matters, pp. 9–42.

Dörnyei, Z., MacIntyre, P. and Henry, A. (2015) 'Introduction: Applying complex dynamic systems principles to empirical research on L2 motivation', in Z. Dörnyei, H. Alastair, and P. MacIntyre (eds) *Motivational Dynamics in Language Learning*, Bristol: Multilingual Matters, pp. 1–10.

Driscoll, A. and Wood, S. (2007) *Developing Outcomes-Based Assessment for Learner-Centered Education: A Faculty Introduction*, Sterling, VA: Stylus Publishing.

Duff, P.A. (2007) 'Second language socialization as sociocultural theory: Insights and issues', *Language Teaching*, 40: 309–19. doi: 10.1017/S0261444807004508.

Duff, P.A. (2010) 'Language socialization', in N.H. Hornberger and S.L. McKay (eds) *Sociolinguistics and Language Education*, Bristol: Multilingual Matters, pp. 427–52.

DuFon, M. and Churchill, E. (2006) *Language Learners in Study Abroad Contexts*, Clevedon: Multilingual Matters.

Duke, S.T. (2014) *Preparing to Study Abroad: Learning to Cross Cultures*, Sterling, VA: Stylus Publishing.

Dwyer, M.M. (2004, Fall) 'More is better: The impact of study abroad program duration', *Frontiers', the Interdisciplinary Journal of Study Abroad*, 10: 151–63. Online. Available: https://frontiersjournal.org/wp-content/uploads/2015/09/DWYER-FrontiersX-MoreIsBetter.pdf (accessed 11 May 2017).

Eckert, P. and McConnell-Ginet, S. (1992) 'Think practically and look locally: Language and gender as community: Based practice', *Annual Review of Anthropology*, 21: 461–90. doi: 10.1146/annurev.an.21.100192.002333.

Egron-Polak, E. and Marmolejo, F. (2017) 'Higher education internationalization: Adjusting to new landscapes', in H. de Wit, J. Gacel-Avila, E. Jones and N. Jooste (eds) *The Globalization of Internationalization: Emerging Voices and Perspectives*, London and New York: Routledge, pp. 7–17.

Ehrenreich, S., Woodman, G. and Perrefort, M. (eds) (2008) *Auslandsaufenthalte in Schule und Studium—Bestandsaufnahmen aus Forschung und Praxis*, Münster: Waxmann.

Ehrman, M.E. (1996) *Understanding Second Language Acquisition*, Oxford: Oxford University Press.

Ellis, R. (1997) *The Study of Second Language Acquisition*, Oxford: Oxford University Press.

Ellwood, C. (2009) 'Uninhabitable identifications: Unpacking the production of racial difference in a TESOL classroom', in R. Kubota and A. Lin (eds) *Race, Culture, and Identities in Second Language Education: Exploring Critically Engaged Practice*, New York: Routledge, pp. 101–17. doi: 10.4324/9780 203876657.

Ellwood, C. (2011) 'Undoing the Knots: Identity transformations in a study abroad programme', *Educational Philosophy and Theory*, 43: 960–78. doi: 10.1111/j.1469-5812.2009.00559.x.

Engberg, M.E. and Davidson, L.M. (2015) 'Quantitative approaches to study abroad assessment', in V. Savicki and E. Brewer (eds) *Assessing Study Abroad: Theory, Tools, and Practice*, Sterling, VA: Stylus Publishing, pp. 122–41.

Erikson, E.H. (1968) *Identity, Youth and Crisis*, New York: W.W. Norton Company.

European Commission (2015) *A Statistical Overview of the Erasmus Programme in 2012–2013*. Online. Available: http://ec.europa.eu/dgs/education_culture/repository/education/library/publications/erasmus-stat-2012-13_en.pdf (accessed 4 September 2016).

Fantini, A.E. (2009) 'Assessing intercultural competence: Issues and tools', in D. Deardorff (ed.) *The Sage Handbook of Intercultural Competence*, Thousand Oaks, CA: Sage Publications, pp. 456–76.

Fantini, A.E. (2012a) 'Language: An essential component of intercultural communicative competence', in J. Jackson (ed.) *Routledge Handbook of Language and Intercultural*, Communication, Abingdon, UK: Routledge, pp. 263–78.

Fantini, A.E. (2012b) 'Multiple strategies for assessing intercultural communicative competence', in J. Jackson (ed.) *Routledge Handbook of Language and Intercultural*, Communication, Abingdon, UK: Routledge, pp. 390–405.

Fantini, A.E. and Tirmizi, A. (2006) *Exploring and Assessing Intercultural Competence*. World Learning Publications. Paper 1. Online. Available: http://digitalcollections.sit.edu/worldlearning_publications/1 (accessed 12 May 2017).

References

Fine, M. (1994) 'Working the hyphens: Reinventing self and other in qualitative research', in N.K. Denzin and Y.S. Lincoln (eds) *Handbook of Qualitative Research*, London: Sage Publications.

Fink, L.D. (2013) *Creating Significant Learning Experiences: An Integrated Approach to Designing College Courses*, San Francisco: Jossey-Bass.

Forbush, E. and Foucault-Welles, B. (2016) 'Social media use and adaptation among Chinese students beginning to study in the United States', *International Journal of Intercultural Relations*, 50, 1–12. htpp://dx.doi.org/10.1016/j.ijintrel.2015.10.007.

Forum on Education Abroad (FEA) (2011) *Education Abroad Glossary*, 2nd edn, Carlisle, PA: Forum on Education Abroad.

Fraenkel, J.R. and Wallen, N.E. (2008) *How to Design and Evaluate Research in Education*, 7th edn, New York: McGraw-Hill.

Freed, B.F. (ed.) (1995) *Second Language Acquisition in a Study Abroad Context*, Amsterdam and Philadelphia: John Benjamins Publishing Company.

Furnham, A. (2010) 'Human mobility in a global era', in S. Carr (ed.) *The Psychology of Global Mobility*, New York: Springer, pp. 23–46.

Furnham, A. (2015) 'Mobility in a global era', in J.M. Bennett (ed.) *The Sage Handbook of Intercultural Competence, Volume 2*, Los Angeles: Sage Publications, pp. 630–4.

Furnham, A. and Bochner, S. (1986) *Culture Shock: Psychological Reactions to Unfamiliar Environments*, New York: Methuen.

Gallagher, S. (2011) 'A philosophical epilogue on the question of autonomy', in H. Hermans and T. Gieser (eds) *Handbook of the Dialogical Self Theory*, Cambridge: Cambridge University Press, pp. 488–96.

Gao, G. (2015) 'Anxiety and uncertainty management', in J.M. Bennett (ed.) *The Sage Handbook of Intercultural Competence, Volume 1*, Los Angeles: Sage Publications, pp. 5–8.

García, O. (2009) *Bilingual Education in the 21st Century: A Global Perspective*, Oxford: Wiley-Blackwell.

García, O. and Li, W. (2014) *Translanguaging: Language, Bilingualism and Education*, New York: Palgrave MacMillan.

Gardner, R.C. (1985) *Social Psychology and Second Language Learning: The Role of Attitudes and Motivation*, London: Edward Arnold.

Gardner, R.C. (2010) *Motivation and Second Language Acquisition: The Socio-Educational Model*, New York: Peter Lang.

Gareis, E. (2012) 'Intercultural friendship: Effects of home and host region', *Journal of International and Intercultural Communication*, 5(4): 309–28. doi: 10.1080/17513057.2012.691525.

Garrett, P. (2010) *Attitudes to Language*, Cambridge: Cambridge University Press.

Garrett-Rucks, P. (2012) 'Byram versus Bennett: Discrepancies in the assessment of learners' intercultural development', in B. Dupuy and L. Waugh (eds) *Aiming for the Third Place: Proceedings of the Second International Conference on the Development and Assessment of Intercultural Competence, Volume 2*, pp. 11–33. Online. Available: http://cercll.arizona.edu/_media/development/conferences/2012_ICC/garrett_rucks_byram_versus_bennett_ic2012.pdf (accessed 11 May 2017).

Gaw, K.F. (2000) 'Reverse culture shock in students returning from overseas', *International Journal of Intercultural Relations*, 24: 83–104. doi: 10.1016/S0147-1767(99)00024-3.

Gebhard, J.G. (2010) *What Do International Students Think and Feel?: Adapting to U.S. College Life and Culture*, Ann Arbor: University of Michigan Press.

Geertz, H. (1973) *The Interpretation of Cultures*, New York: Basic Books.

Gelman, S.A. (2003) *The Essential Child: Origins of Essentialism in Everyday Thought*, New York: Oxford University Press.

Giles, H., Bonilla, D. and Speer, R.B. (2012) 'Acculturating intergroup vitalities, accommodation and contact', in J. Jackson (ed.) *Routledge Handbook of Language and Intercultural*, Communication, Abingdon: Routledge, pp. 244–59.

Ginsberg, M.B. and Wlodkowski, R. (2015) 'Motivation and culture', in J.M. Bennett (ed.) *The Sage Handbook of Intercultural Competence, Volume 2*, Los Angeles: Sage Publications, pp. 634–7.

Giovanangeli, A., Oguro, S. and Harbon, L. (2018) 'Mentoring students' intercultural learning during study abroad', in J. Jackson and S. Oguro (eds) *Intercultural Interventions in Study Abroad*, Abingdon, UK and New York: Routledge, pp. 88–102.

Gozik, N. (2015) 'Closing the loop: Linking stages of the assessment cycle', in V. Savicki and E. Brewer (eds) *Assessing Study Abroad: Theory, Tools, and Practice*, Sterling, VA: Stylus Publishing, pp. 57–79.

Graham, S. and Weiner, B. (1995) 'Theories and principles of motivation', in D. Berliner and R. Calfee (eds) *Handbook of Educational Psychology*, New York: Macmillan, pp. 63–84.

Gregersen, T. and MacIntyre, P.D. (2014) *Capitalizing on Language Learners' Individuality: From Premise to Practice*, Bristol: Multilingual Matters.

Griffith, R.L., Wolfeld, L., Armon, B.K., Rios, J. and Liu, O.L. (2016) 'Assessing intercultural competence in higher education: Existing research and future directions', *Educational Testing Service (ETS) Research Report No. RR-16-25*. doi: 10.1002/ets2.12112.

Groen, J. and Kawalilak, C. (2014) *Pathways of Adult Learning: Professional and Educational Narratives*, Toronto: Canadian Scholars' Press Inc.

Grove, C.N. (2015) 'Culture distance: Value orientations', in J.M. Bennett (ed) *The Sage Handbook of Intercultural Competence, Volume 2*, Los Angeles: Sage Publications, pp. 195–200.

Guba, E.G. and Lincoln, Y.S. (1994) 'Competing paradigms in qualitative research', in N.K. Denzin and Y.S. Lincoln (eds) *Handbook of Qualitative Research*, Thousand Oaks: Sage Publications, pp. 105–17.

Gudykunst, W.B. (2004) *Bridging Differences: Effective Intergroup Communication*, 4th edn, Thousand Oaks: Sage Publications.

Gudykunst, W.B., Lee, C.M., Nishida, T. and Ogawa, N. (2005) 'Theorizing about intercultural communication', in W.B. Gudykunst (ed.) *Theorizing about Intercultural Communication*, Thousand Oaks: Sage Publications, pp. 3–32.

Guilherme, M. (2002) *Critical Citizens for an Intercultural World: Foreign Language Education as Cultural Politics*, Clevedon: Multilingual Matters.

Guilherme, M. (2004) 'Intercultural competence', in M. Byram (ed.) *Routledge Encyclopedia of Language Teaching and Learning*, London: Routledge, pp. 297–300.

Gullahorn, J.T. and Gullahorn, J.E. (1963) 'An extension of the U-curve hypothesis', *Journal of Social Issues*, 19: 33–47. doi: 10.1111/j.1540-4560.1963.tb00447.x.
Gumperz, J.J. and Hymes, D.H. (eds) (1972) *Directions in Sociolinguistics*, New York: Holt, Rinehart, and Winston.
Guth, S. and Helm, F. (eds) (2010) *Telecollaboration 2.0: Language, Literacies and Intercultural Learning in the 21st Century, Volume 1*, Berlin: Peter Lang.
Hail, H.C. (2015) 'Patriotism abroad: Overseas Chinese students' encounters with criticisms of China', *Journal of Studies in International Education*, 19(4): 311–26.
Hall, E.T. (1959/1973) *The Silent Language*, New York: Doubleday.
Hall, E.T. (1966/1990) *The Hidden Dimension*, New York: Doubleday.
Hall, E.T. (1976) *Beyond Culture*, 1st edn, New York: Doubleday.
Hall, S. (1980) 'Cultural studies: Two paradigms', *Media, Culture and Society*, 2(1): 57–72. doi: 10.1177/016344378000200106.
Hall, S. (1990) 'Cultural identity and diaspora', in J. Rutherford (ed.) *Identity, Community, Culture, Difference*, London: Lawrence and Wishart, pp. 222–37.
Hall, S. (1991) 'The local and the global: Globalization and ethnicity', in A.D. King (ed.), *Culture, Globalization and the World-System*, New York: Palgrave, pp. 19–39.
Hammer, M.R. (2011) 'Additional cross-cultural validity testing of the intercultural development inventory', *International Journal of Intercultural Relations*, 35(4), 474–87. doi: 10.1016/j.ijintrel.2011.02.014.
Hammer, M.R. (2012) 'The intercultural development inventory: A new frontier in. assessment and development of intercultural competence', in M. Vande Berg, R.M. Paige and K.H. Lou (eds) *Student Learning Abroad: What Our Students Are Learning, What They're Not and What We Can Do about It*, Sterling, VA: Stylus Publishing, pp. 115–36.
Hammer, M.R. (2015) 'Intercultural competence development', Vande Berg, M. (2015a) 'Developmentally appropriate pedagogy', in J.M. Bennett (ed.) *The Sage Encyclopedia of Intercultural Competence, Volume 2*, Thousand Oaks, CA: Sage, pp. 483–6.
Hammer, M.R., Bennett, M.J. and Wiseman, R. (2003) 'Measuring intercultural sensitivity: The intercultural development inventory', *International Journal of Intercultural Relations*, 27: 421–43. doi: 10.1016/S0147-1767(03)00032-4.
Hampden-Turner, C. and Trompenaars, F. (1998) *Riding the Waves of Culture: Understanding Diversity in Global Business*, New York: McGraw-Hill.
Hansel, B. (2007) *The Exchange Student Survival Kit*, 2nd edn, Boston: Intercultural Press.
Härkönen, A. and Dervin, F. (2015) 'Talking just about learning languages and getting to know cultures is something that's mentioned in very many applications: Student and staff imaginaries about study abroad', in F. Dervin and R. Machart (eds) *The New Politics of Global Academic Mobility and Migration*, Frankfurt am Main: Peter Lang Publishing Group, pp. 101–18.
Härkönen, A. and Dervin, F. (2016) 'Study abroad beyond the usual "imagineering"? The benefits of a pedagogy of imaginaries', *East Asia*, 33(1): 41–58. doi: 10.1007/s12140-015-9247-1.
Harsch, C. and Poehner, M.E. (2016) 'Enhancing student experiences abroad: The potential of dynamic assessment to develop student interculturality',

Language and Intercultural Communication, 16(3): 470–90. doi: 10.1080/14708477.2016.1168043.

Harvey, L. (2016) '"I am Italian in the world": A mobile student's story of language learning and ideological becoming', *Language and Intercultural Communication*, 16(3): 368–83. doi: 10.1080/14708477.2016.1168049.

Hendershot, K. and Sperandio, J. (2009) 'Study abroad and development of global citizen identity and cosmopolitan ideals in undergraduates', *Current Issues in Comparative Education*, 12(1): 45–55. Online. Available: http://files.eric.ed.gov/fulltext/EJ879768.pdf (accessed 11 May 2017).

Hendrickson, B., Rosen, D. and Aune, R.K. (2010) 'An analysis of friendship networks, social connectedness, homesickness, and satisfaction levels of international students', *International Journal of Intercultural Relations*, 34(1): 34–46. doi: 10.1016/j.ijintrel.2010.08.001.

Hepple, E. (2018) 'The first step in embedding intercultural learning through study abroad within an Australian University: Designing and implementing pre-departure intercultural workshops', in J. Jackson and S. Oguro (eds) *Intercultural Interventions in Study Abroad*, Abingdon, UK and New York: Routledge, pp. 18–36.

Higgins, E.T. (1987) 'Self-discrepancy: A theory relating self and affect', *Psychological Review*, 94: 319–40. doi: 10.1037/0033-295X.94.3.319.

Hile, P. (1979) *Language Shock, Culture Shock and How to Cope*. Abilene Christian University Mission Strategy Bulletin 7.2. Online. Available: www.bible.acu.edu/ministry/centers_institutes/missions/page.asp?ID=486 (accessed 2 December 2016).

Hittleman, D.R. and Simon, A.J. (2006) *Interpreting Educational Research: An Introduction for Consumers of Research*, Upper Saddle River, NJ: Pearson Merrill Prentice Hall.

Hoffa, W.W. (2007) *A History of US Study Abroad: Beginnings to 1965*, Carlisle, PA: Frontiers: The Interdisciplinary Journal of Study Abroad and the Forum on Education Abroad.

Hofstede, G.H. (1980) *Culture's Consequences: International Differences in Work-Related Values*, Beverly Hills, CA: Sage Publications.

Hofstede, G.H. (1991) *Cultures and Organizations: Software of the Mind*, London: McGraw-Hill.

Hofstede, G.H. (2001) *Culture's Consequences: International Differences in Work-Related Values*, 2nd edn, Beverly Hills: Sage Publications.

Holliday, A. (1999) 'Small cultures', *Applied Linguistics*, 20(2): 237–64. doi: 10.1093/applin/20.2.237.

Holliday, A. (2010) 'Complexity in cultural identity', *Language and Intercultural Communication*, 10(2): 165–77. doi: 10.1080/14708470903267384.

Holliday, A. (2011) *Intercultural Communication and Ideology*, London: Sage Publications.

Holliday, A. (2012) 'Culture, communication, context and power', in J. Jackson (ed.) *The Routledge Handbook of Language and Intercultural Communication*, Abingdon: Routledge, pp. 37–51.

Holliday, A. (2018) 'Commentary', in J. Jackson and S. Oguro (eds) *Intercultural Interventions in Study Abroad*, Abingdon, UK and New York: Routledge, pp. 206–11.

Holliday, A.R., Hyde, M. and Kullman, J. (2004) *Intercultural Communication: An Advanced Resource Book for Students*, London: Routledge.

Holmes, P. (2012) 'Business and management education', in J. Jackson (ed.) *Routledge Handbook of Language and Intercultural*, Communication, Abingdon, UK: Routledge, pp. 464–80.
Holmes, P., Bavieri, L. and Ganassin, S. (2015) 'Developing intercultural understanding for study abroad: Students' and teachers' perspectives on pre-departure intercultural learning', *Intercultural Education*, 26(1): 16–30. doi: 10.1080/14675986.2015.993250.
Holmes, P., Bavieri, L., Ganassin, S. and Murphy, J. (2016) 'Interculturality and the study abroad experience: Students' learning from the IEREST materials', *Language and Intercultural Communication*, 16(3): 452–69. doi: 10.1080/14708477.2016.1168054.
Houghton, S.A. (2012) *Intercultural Dialogue in Practice: Managing Value Judgment through Foreign Language Education*, Bristol: Multilingual Matters.
Houghton, S.A. and Yamada, E. (2012) *Developing Criticality in Practice through Foreign Language Education*, Frankfurt am Mein: Peter Lang Publishing Group.
Hoult, S. (2018) 'Aspiring to postcolonial engagement with the Other: Deepening intercultural learning through reflection on a South India sojourn', in J. Jackson and S. Oguro (eds) *Intercultural Interventions in Study Abroad*, Abingdon, UK and New York: Routledge, pp. 71–87.
Howarth, C. (2002) 'Identity in whose eyes? The role of representations in identity construction', *Journal of the Theory of Social Behaviour*, 32(2): 145–62. doi: 10.1111/1468-5914.00181.
Hudzik, J.K. (2015) *Comprehensive Internationalization: Institutional Pathways to Success*, London and New York: Routledge.
Hunter, W.D. (2004) 'Knowledge, skills, attitudes, and experience necessary to become globally competent', Unpublished Ph.D. dissertation, Lehigh University, Bethlehem, Pennsylvania.
Hymes, D.H. (1966) 'Two types of linguistic relativity', in W. Bright (ed.) *Sociolinguistics*, The Hague: Mouton, pp. 114–58.
Hymes, D.H. (1972) 'On communicative competence', in J. Pride and J. Holmes (eds) *Sociolinguistics*, Harmondsworth: Penguin, pp. 269–93.
Hymes, D.H. (1974) *Foundations in Sociolinguistics: An Ethnographic Approach*, Philadelphia: University of Pennsylvania Press.
Iedema, R. and Caldas-Coulthard, C.R. (2008) 'Introduction: Identity trouble: Critical discourse and contested identities', in C. Caldas-Coulthard and R. Iedema (eds) *Identity Trouble: Critical Discourse and Contested Identities*, Basingstoke: Palgrave MacMillan, pp. 1–14.
Institute of International Education (2016) *Open Doors Report on International Educational Exchange*. Online. Available: www.iie.org/Research-and-Publications/Open-Doors/Data/US-Study-Abroad#.WLSUoTt97D4 (accessed 28 February 2017).
Isabelli-García, C. (2006) 'Study abroad social networks, motivation, and attitudes: Implications for second language acquisition', in M.A. Dufon and E. Churchill (eds) *Language Learners in Study Abroad Contexts*, Clevedon: Multilingual Matters, pp. 231–58.
Iwasaki, N. (2013) 'Getting over the hedge: Acquisition of mitigating language in L2 Japanese', in C. Kinginger (ed.) *Social and Cultural Aspects of Language*

Learning in Study Abroad, Philadelphia and Amsterdam: John Benjamins, pp. 239–67.
Jackson, J. (2006) 'Ethnographic preparation for short-term study and residence in the target culture', *The International Journal of Intercultural Relations*, 30(1): 77–98. doi: 10.1016/j.ijintrel.2005.07.004.
Jackson, J. (2008) *Language, Identity, and Study Abroad*, London: Equinox.
Jackson, J. (2010) *Intercultural Journeys: From Study to Residence Abroad*, Hampshire, UK: Palgrave MacMillan.
Jackson, J. (2011) 'Cultivating cosmopolitan, intercultural citizenship through critical reflection and international, experiential learning', *Language and Intercultural Communication*, 11(2): 80–96. doi: 10.1080/14708477.2011.556737.
Jackson, J. (2012) 'Education abroad', in J. Jackson (ed.) *Routledge Handbook of Language and Intercultural, Communication*, Abingdon: Routledge, pp. 449–63.
Jackson, J. (2013) 'Adjusting to differing cultures of learning: The experience of semester-long exchange students from Hong Kong', in L. Jin and M. Cortazzi (eds) *Researching Intercultural Learning*, Basingstoke, UK: Palgrave MacMillan, pp. 235–52.
Jackson, J. (2014) *Introducing Language and Intercultural Communication*, Abingdon, UK: Routledge.
Jackson, J. (2015a) 'Intercultural communication and language', in J.M. Bennett (ed.) *The Sage Handbook of Intercultural Competence, Volume 2*, Los Angeles: Sage Publications, pp. 453–8.
Jackson, J. (2015b) '"Unpacking" international experience through blended intercultural praxis', in R.D. Williams and A. Lee (eds) *Internationalizing Higher Education: Critical Collaborations across the Curriculum*, Rotterdam/Boston/Taipei: Sense Publishers, pp. 231–52.
Jackson, J. (2015c) 'Becoming interculturally competent: Theory to practice in international education', *International Journal of Intercultural Relations*, 48: 91–107. doi: 10.1016/j.ijintrel.2015.03.012.
Jackson, J. (2015d, November) 'National identity and intercultural engagement: Mainland Chinese students abroad, Keynote address', The 8th International Conference on Intercultural Communication (ICIC 2015), Ethnic communication, National Image and Intercultural Communication, Wuhan University, Wuhan, 20–22 November 2015.
Jackson, J. (2016a) 'Ethnography', in H. Zhu (ed.) *Research Methods in Intercultural Communication: A Practical Guide*, Hoboken, NJ: Wiley and Sons, pp. 239–54.
Jackson, J. (2016b) 'Encountering unfamiliar educational practices abroad: Opportunities or obstacles?', in D. Vellaris and D. Coleman-George (eds) *Handbook of Research on Study Abroad Programs and Outbound Mobility*, Hershey, PA: IGI Global, pp. 137–62.
Jackson, J. (2016c) 'The language use, attitudes, and motivation of Chinese students prior to a semester-long sojourn in an English-speaking environment', *Study Abroad Research in Second Language Acquisition and International Education*, 1(1): 4–33. doi: 10.1075/sar.1.1.01jac.
Jackson, J. (2016d) '"Breathing the smells of native-style English": A narrativised account of a L2 sojourn', *Language and Intercultural Communication*, 16(3): 332–48. doi: 10.1080/14708477.2016.1168047.

References

Jackson, J. (2017a) 'The personal, linguistic, and intercultural development of Chinese sojourners in an English-speaking country: The impact of language attitudes, motivation, and agency', *Study Abroad Research in Second Language Acquisition and International Education*, 2(1): 80–106. doi: 10.1075/sar.1.1.01jac.

Jackson, J. (2017b) 'Interculturality in study abroad research and practice', Presentation at the Criticality in Education (Research): Definitions, Discourses and Controversies Conference, University of Helsinki, Finland, 31 August–1 September 2017.

Jackson, J. (2017c) 'Intervening in the intercultural learning of L2 study abroad students: From research to practice', *Language Teaching*, 1–18 doi: 10.1017/S0261444816000392.

Jackson, J. (2017d) 'Intercultural communication and engagement abroad', in D.K. Deardorff and L.A. Arasaratnam-Smith (eds) *Intercultural Competence in Higher Education: International Approaches, Assessment and Application*, London: Routledge.

Jackson, J. (2018a) 'Optimizing intercultural learning and engagement abroad through online mentoring', in J. Jackson and S. Oguro (eds) *Intercultural Interventions in Study Abroad*, Abingdon, UK and New York: Routledge.

Jackson, J. (2018b) 'Training for study abroad', in Y.Y. Kim (ed.) *The Wiley-Blackwell Encyclopedia of Intercultural Communication*, Hoboken, NJ: Wiley-Blackwell.

Jackson, J. (forthcoming a) '"Cantonese is my own eyes and English is just my glasses": The evolving language and intercultural attitudes of a Chinese study abroad student', in M. Howard (ed.) *Study Abroad, Second Language Acquisition and Interculturality: Contemporary Perspectives*, Bristol: Multilingual Matters.

Jackson, J. (forthcoming b) 'Intercultural competence and L2 pragmatics', in N. Taguchi (ed.) *The Routledge Handbook of SLA and Pragmatics*, London and New York: Routledge.

Jackson, J. (forthcoming c) 'Building an online community to contest stereotyping and Otherization during study abroad', in M.D. López-Jiménez and J. Sánchez Torres (eds) *Issues in Intercultural Learning and Teaching across L2 Contexts and Situations*, New York: Springer.

Jackson, J. (in preparation) *Online Intercultural Education and Study Abroad: Theory into Practice*, Abingdon, UK and New York: Routledge.

Jackson, J. and Chen, X. (2017) 'Discussion-based pedagogy through the eyes of Chinese international exchange students', *Pedagogies: An International Journal*. https://doi.org/10.1080/1554480X.2017.1411263

Jackson, J. and Oguro, S. (eds) (2018a) *Intercultural Interventions in Study Abroad*, Abingdon, UK and New York: Routledge.

Jackson, J. and Oguro, S. (2018b) 'Introduction: Enhancing and extending study abroad learning through intercultural interventions', in J. Jackson and S. Oguro (eds) *Intercultural Interventions in Study Abroad*, Abingdon, UK and New York: Routledge, pp. 1–17.

Jacobone, V. and Moro, G. (2014) 'Evaluating the impact of the Erasmus programme: Skills and European identity', *Assessment and Evaluation in Higher Education*, 40(2): 309–28. doi: 10.1080/02602938.2014.909005.

Jandt, F. (2007) *An Introduction to Intercultural Communication: Identities in a Global Community*, 5th edn, Thousand Oaks, CA: Sage Publications.

Jandt, F. (2016) *An Introduction to Intercultural Communication: Identities in a Global Community*, 8th edn, Thousand Oaks, CA: Sage Publications.

Jenkins, J. (2013) *English as a Lingua Franca in the International University*, London: Routledge.

Jenks, C.J. (2016) 'Talking national identities into being in ELF interactions: An investigation of international postgraduate students in the UK', in P. Holmes and F. Dervin (eds) *The Cultural and Intercultural Dimensions of English as a Lingua Franca*, Bristol: Multilingual Matters, pp. 93–113.

Jin, L. and Cortazzi, M. (2006) 'Changing practices in Chinese cultures of learning', *Language, Culture and Curriculum*, 19(1): 5–20. doi: 10.1080/07908310608668751.

Jin, L. and Cortazzi, M. (2016) 'Practising cultures of learning in internationalising universities', *Journal of Multilingual and Multicultural Development*, Special Issue, 1–14. doi: 10.1080/01434632.2015.1134548.

Jones, E., Coelen, R., Beelen, J. and de Wit, H. (eds) (2016) *Global and Local Interntionalization*, Rotterdam: Sense Publications.

Joseph, J.E. (2016) 'Historical perspectives on language and identity', in S. Preece (ed.) *The Routledge Handbook of Language and Identity*, London and New York: Routledge, pp. 19–33.

Kanno, Y. (2003) *Negotiating Bilingual and Bicultural Identities: Japanese Returnees and Betwixt Two Worlds*, Mahwah, NJ: Lawrence Erlbaum Associates, Inc.

Kartoshkina, Y. (2015) 'Bitter-sweet re-entry after studying abroad', *International Journal of Intercultural Relations*, 44: 35–45. doi: 10.1016/j.ijintrel.2014.11.001.

Kaufmann, E.P. (2014) 'Introduction. Dominant ethnicity: From background to foreground', in E.P. Kaufmann (ed.) *Rethinking Ethnicity: Majority Groups and Dominant Minorities*, London and New York: Routledge, pp. 1–14.

Kecskes, I. (2012) 'Interculturality and intercultural pragmatics', in J. Jackson (ed) *Routledge Handbook of Language and Intercultural*, Communication, Abingdon, UK: Routledge, pp. 67–84.

Kecskes, I. (2014) *Intercultural Pragmatics*, Oxford: Oxford University Press.

Kelley, C. and Meyers, J. (1995) *The Cross-Cultural Adaptability Inventory: Manual*, Minneapolis: NCS Pearson.

Kelley, C. and Meyers, J. (1999) 'The cross-cultural adaptability inventory', in S.M. Fowler and M.G. Mumford (eds) *Intercultural Sourcebook: Cross-Cultural Training Methods, Volume 2*, Yarmouth, ME: Intercultural Press, pp. 53–60.

Kennedy, C., Díaz, A.R. and Dasli, M. (2017) 'Cosmopolitanism meets language education: Considering objectives and strategies for a new pedagogy', in M. Dasli and A. Díaz (eds) *The Critical Turn in Language and Intercultural Communication Pedagogy: Theory, Research and Practice*, London: Routledge, pp. 162–79.

Khan, A. (2005) *Ethnic Nationalism and the State in Pakistan*, New Delhi: Sage Publications.

Kim, M.-S. (2015) 'Intercultural verbal communication styles', in J.M. Bennett (ed.) *The Sage Handbook of Intercultural Competence, Volume 2*, Los Angeles: Sage Publications, pp. 530–5.

188 References

Kim, Y.Y. (2001) *Becoming Intercultural: An Integrative Theory of Communication and Cross-Cultural Adaptation*, Thousand Oaks, CA: Sage Publications.

Kim, Y.Y. (2005) 'Inquiry in intercultural and development communication', *Journal of Communication*, 55(3): 554–77. doi: 10.1111/j.1460-2466.2005.tb02685.x

Kim, Y.Y. (2012) 'Beyond cultural categories: Communication adaptation and transformation', in J. Jackson (ed.) *Routledge Handbook of Language and Intercultural*, Communication, Abingdon, UK: Routledge, pp. 229–43.

Kim, Y.Y. (2015a) 'Theory of acculturation', in J.M. Bennett (ed.) *The Sage Handbook of Intercultural Competence, Volume 2*, Los Angeles: Sage Publications, pp. 792–7.

Kim, Y.Y. (2015b) 'Integrative communication theory', in J.M. Bennett (ed.) *The Sage Handbook of Intercultural Competence, Volume 1*, Los Angeles: Sage Publications, pp. 438–41.

King, R. and Ruiz-Gelices, E. (2003) 'International student migration and the European "Year Abroad": Effects on European identity and subsequent migration behaviour', *Population, Space, and Place*, 9(3): 229–52. doi: 10.1002/ijpg.280.

Kinginger, C. (2004) 'Alice doesn't live here anymore: Foreign language learning and renegotiated identity', in A. Pavlenko and A. Blackledge (eds) *Negotiation of Identities in Multilingual Contexts*, Clevedon: Multilingual Matters, pp. 219–42.

Kinginger, C. (2008) 'Language learning in study abroad: Case studies of Americans in France', *The Modern Language Journal*, Special Issue, 92. doi: 10.1111/j.1540-4781.2008.00821.x.

Kinginger, C. (2009) *Language Learning and Study Abroad: A Critical Reading of Research*, Basingstoke: Palgrave MacMillan.

Kinginger, C. (2010) 'American students abroad: Negotiation of difference?', *Language Teaching*, 43: 216–27. doi: 10.1017/S0261444808005703.

Kinginger, C. (2011) 'National identity and language learning abroad: American students in the post-9/11 era', in C. Higgins (ed.) *Identity Formation in Globalizing Contexts: Language Learning in the New Millennium*, Berlin: Mouton de Gruyter, pp. 147–66.

Kinginger, C. (2013) 'Introduction', in C. Kinginger (ed.) *Social and Cultural Aspects of Language Learning in Study Abroad*, Amsterdam and Philadelphia: John Benjamins Publishing Company, pp. 3–16.

Kinginger, C. (2015) 'Student mobility and identity-related language learning', *Intercultural Education*, 26(1): 6–15. doi: 10.1080/14675986.2015.992199.

Kirkhart, E. and Kirkhart, L. (2015) 'Personality and culture', in J.M. Bennett (ed.) *The Sage Handbook of Intercultural Competence, Volume 2*, Los Angeles: Sage Publications, pp. 665–72.

Kirkpatrick, A. (2009) 'English as the international language of scholarship', in F. Sharifian (ed.) *English as an International Language*, Bristol: Multilingual Matters, pp. 254–70.

Kirshner, D.H. (2012) 'Enculturation and acculturation', in N.M. Seel (ed.) *Encyclopedia of the Sciences of Learning*, New York: Springer, pp. 1148–51.

Klopf, D.W. and McCroskey, J. (2007) *Intercultural Communication Encounters*, Boston: Pearson.

Kluckhohn, C. and Strodtbeck, F. (1961) *Variations in Value Orientations*, Evanston, IL: Row, Peterson.

Knight, J. (2004) 'Internationalization remodeled internationalization remodeled: Definition, approaches, and rationales', *Journal of Studies in International Education*, 8(1): 5–31. doi: 10.1177/1028315303260832.

Knight, J. (2008) *Higher Education in Turmoil: The Changing World of Internationalization*, Rotterdam: Sense Publishers.

Knight, J. (2015) 'Meaning, rationales and tensions in internationalization of higher education', in S. McGrath and Q. Gu (eds) *Routledge Handbook on International Education and Development*, London: Taylor Francis, pp. 325–39.

Knight, J. (2016) 'The internationalization of higher education: Motivations and realities', in P. Altbach (ed.) *Global Perspectives on Higher Education*, Baltimore: Johns Hopkins University, pp. 105–20.

Knight, S.M. and Schmidt-Rinehart, B.C. (2010) 'Exploring conditions to enhance student/host family interaction abroad', *Foreign Language Annals*, 43(1): 64–79. doi: 10.1111/j.1944-9720.2010.01060.x.

Kohls, L.R. (2001) *Survival Kit for Overseas Living*, 4th edn, Yarmouth, ME: Intercultural Press.

Kohls, L.R. with Brussow, H.L. (1995) *Training Know-How for Cross Cultural and Diversity Trainers*, Duncanville, TX: Adult Learning Systems, Inc.

Kohls, L.R. and Knight, J.M. (1994) *Developing Intercultural Awareness*, Yarmouth, ME: Intercultural Press.

Kolb, D.A. (1984) *Experiential Learning: Experience as a Source of Learning and Development*, Upper Saddle River, NJ: Prentice-Hall.

Komisarof, A. and Zhu, H. (2016) 'Introduction', in A. Komisarof and Z. Hua (eds) *Crossing Boundaries and Weaving Intercultural Work, Life and Scholarship in Globalizing Universities*, London and New York: Routledge, pp. 1–20.

Kraidy, M.M. (2005) *Hybridity, or the Cultural Logic of Globalization*, Philadelphia: Temple University Press.

Kramsch, C. (1993) *Context and Culture in Language Teaching*, Oxford: Oxford University Press.

Kroeber, A.L. and Kluckhohn, C. (1952) *Culture: A Critical Review of Concepts and Definitions*, Cambridge, MA: Harvard University Printing Office.

Krumer-Nevo, M. and Sidi, M. (2012) 'Writing against Othering', *Qualitative Inquiry*, 18(4): 299–309. http://dx.doi.org/10.1177/1077800411433546.

Krzaklewska, E. (2008) 'Why study abroad? An analysis of Erasmus students' motivations', in M. Byram and F. Dervin (eds) *Students, Staff and Academic Mobility in Hgher Education*, Newcastle: Cambridge Scholars Publishing, pp. 82–98.

Kuhn, T.S. (1970) *The Structure of Scientific Revolutions*, 2nd edn, Chicago: University of Chicago Press.

Kuhn, T.S. (2003) *The Road Since Structure*, Chicago: University of Chicago Press.

La Brack, B. (2003) *What's Up with Culture?* Online. Available: www2.pacific.edu/sis/culture/index.htm (accessed 5 January 2017).

La Brack, B. (2010) *Theory Reflections: Cultural Adaptations, Culture Shock and the 'Curves of Adjustment'*. NAFSA. Online. Available: www.nafsa.org/

Resource_Library_Assets/Networks/ICT/Cultural_Adaptation_Culture_Shock/ (accessed 7 February 2017).

La Brack, B. (2011) 'Theory connections, reflections, and applications for international educators', Paper presented at the 63rd Annual NAFSA: Association of International Educators Conference, Vancouver, BC, Canada.

La Brack, B. (2015) 'Reentry', in J.M. Bennett (ed) *The Sage Handbook of Intercultural Competence, Volume 2*, Los Angeles: Sage Publications, pp. 723–7.

La Brack, B. and Berardo, K. (2007) 'Is it time to retire the U-and W-curves of adjustment?', Paper presented at the Forum on Education Abroad Conference, Austin, Texas.

Laing, R.D. (1961) *The Self and Others*, London: Tavistock Publications.

Landis, D., Bennett, J.M. and Bennett, M.J. (eds) (2004) *Handbook of Intercultural Training*, 3rd edn, Thousand Oaks: Sage Publications.

Lantis, J.S. and DuPlaga, J. (2010) *The Global Classroom: An Essential Guide to Study Abroad*, Boulder, CO: Paradigm Press.

Lázár, I., Huber-Kriegler, M., Lussier, D., Matel, G.S. and Peck, C. (2007) *Developing and Assessing Intercultural Communicative Competence: A Guide for Language Teachers and Teacher Educators*, Strasbourg: Council of Europe Publishing.

Leask, B. (2009) 'Using formal and informal curricula to improve interactions between home and international students', *Journal of Studies in International Education*, 13(2): 205–21. doi: 10.1177/1028315308329786.

Leask, B., Green, W. and Whitsed, C. (2015) 'In Australia, internationalization of the curriculum at home', *Forum: Discussing International Education*, 34–5.

Lee, L. (2018) 'Extending the intercultural learning after study abroad through a telecollaborative exchange', in J. Jackson and S. Oguro (eds) *Intercultural Interventions in Study Abroad*, Abingdon, UK and New York: Routledge, pp. 137–54.

Lee, M.W. (2016) *Early Study Abroad and Identities: Korean Early Study-Abroad Undergraduates*, New York: Springer.

Leeds-Hurwitz, W. (1990) 'Notes on the history of intercultural communication: The Foreign Service Institute and the mandate for intercultural training', *The Quarterly Journal of Speech*, 76: 262–81. doi: 10.1080/00335639009383919.

Lewin, R. (ed.) (2009) *The Handbook of Practice and Research in Study Abroad: Higher Education and the Quest for Global Citizenship*, New York: Routledge.

Li, W. (2011) 'Moment analysis and translanguaging space: Discursive construction of identities by multilingual Chinese youth in Britain', *Multilingual Structures and Agencies*, 43(5): 1222–35. doi: 10.1016/j.pragma.2010.07.035.

Liddicoat, A.K. (2011) 'Language teaching and learning from an intercultural perspective', in E. Hinkel (ed.) *Handbook of Research in Second Language Teaching and Learning, Volume 2*, New York and London: Routledge, pp. 837–54.

Liddicoat, A.J. (2017) 'Language and intercultural communication pedagogy: A transnational turn?', in M. Dasli and A. Díaz (eds) *The Critical Turn in Language and Intercultural Communication Pedagogy: Theory, Research and Practice*, London: Routledge, pp. 22–39.

Liddicoat, A.J., Papademetre, L., Scarino, A. and Kohler, M. (2003) *Report on Intercultural Language Learning*, Canberra: Department of Education, Science and Training.

Lifton, R.J. (1993) *The Protean Self*, New York: Basic Books.

Light, G., Cox, R. and Calkins, S. (2009) *Teaching and Learning in Higher Education: The Reflective Professional*, 2nd edn, Thousand Oaks, CA: Sage Publications.

LoCastro, V. (2003) *An Introduction to Pragmatics: Social Action for Language Teachers*, Ann Arbor: University of Michigan Press.

Lou, K.H. and Bosley, G.W. (2012) 'Facilitating intercultural learning abroad: The intentional, targeted intervention model', in M. Vande Berg, R.M. Paige and K.H. Lou (eds) *Student Learning Abroad, What Our Students Are Learning, What They're Not, and What We Can Do about It*, Sterling, VA: Stylus Publishing, pp. 335–59.

Lou, K.H., Vande Berg, M. and Paige, R.M. (2012) 'Intervening in study learning abroad: Closing insights', in M. Vande Berg, R.M. Paige and K.H. Lou (eds) *Student Learning Abroad, What Our Students Are Learning, What They're Not, and What We Can Do about It*, Sterling, VA: Stylus Publishing, pp. 411–19.

Lysgaard, S. (1955) 'Adjustment in a foreign society: Norwegian Fulbright grantees visiting the United States', *International Social Science Bulletin*, 7: 45–51.

MacDonald, M.N. and O'Regan, J.P. (2012) 'A global agenda for intercultural communication research and practice', in J. Jackson (ed.) *Routledge Handbook of Language and Intercultural*, Communication, Abingdon: Routledge, pp. 553–67.

Machart, R. and Lim, S.N. (2014) 'Mobilité académique et ajustement au contexte d'accueil: La fin du choc culturel?', in R. Machart and F. Dervin (eds) *Les Nouveux Enjeux des Mobilités et Migrations Académiques*, Paris: L'Harmattan, pp. 149–82.

MacIntyre, P.D., Clément, R., Dörnyei, Z. and Noels, K.A. (1998) 'Conceptualizing willingness to communicate in a second language: A situational model of second language confidence and affiliation', *The Modern Language Journal*, 82(4): 545–62. doi: 10.1111/j.1540-4781.1998.tb05543.x.

MacIntyre, P.D. and Gardner, R. (1994) 'The subtle effects of language anxiety on cognitive processing in the second language', *Language Learning*, 44(2): 283–305. doi: 10.1111/j.1467-1770.1994.tb01103.x.

Maffesoli, M.(1988) *Le Temps des Tribus*, Paris: Klincksieck.

Magnan, S.S. and Back, M. (2007) 'Social interaction and linguistic gain during study abroad', *Foreign Language Annals*, 40(1): 43–61. doi. 10.1111/j.1944-9720.2007.tb02853.

Marginson, S. and Sawir, E. (2011) *Ideas for Intercultural Education*, Basingstoke: Palgrave MacMillan.

Markus, H. and Nurius, P. (1986) 'Possible selves', *American Psychologist*, 41: 954–69. doi: 10.1037/0003-066X.41.9.954.

Martin, J.N. and Harrell, T. (2004) 'Intercultural reentry of students and professionals: Theory and practice', in D. Landis, J.M. Bennett and M.J. Bennett (eds) *Handbook of Intercultural Training*, 3rd edn, Thousand Oaks, CA: Sage Publications, pp. 309–36.

Martin, J.N. and Nakayama, T.K. (2008) *Experiencing Intercultural Communication: An Introduction*, 3rd edn, Boston: McGraw-Hill.

Martin, J.N. and Nakayama, T.K. (2013) *Intercultural Communication in Contexts*, 6th edn, New York: McGraw Hill.

Martin, J.N., Nakayama, T.K. and Carbaugh, D. (2012) 'The history and development of the study of intercultural communication and applied linguistics', in

J. Jackson (ed.) *The Routledge Handbook of Language and Intercultural Communication*, Abingdon: Routledge, pp. 17–36.

Matsuo, C. (2012) 'A critique of Michael Byram's intercultural communicative competence model from the perspective of model type and conceptualization of culture', *Fukuoka University Review of Literature & Humanities*, 4: 347–80.

Mazak, C.M. (2017) 'Introduction: Theorizing translanguaging practices in higher education', in C.M. Mazak and K.S. Carroll (eds) *Translanguaging in Higher Education: Beyond Monolingual Ideologies*, Bristol: Multilingual Matters.

McKinnon, S. (2018) 'Foregrounding intercultural learning during study abroad as part of a degree in Modern Languages', in J. Jackson and S. Oguro (eds) *Intercultural Interventions in Study Abroad*, Abingdon, UK: Routledge.

Medina, A. (2008) *Intercultural Sensitivity Development in Study Abroad: Is Duration a Decisive Element in Cultural Learning Outcomes?* Saarbrücken: Verlag.

Mercer, S. and Williams, M. (2014) 'Concluding reflections', in S. Mercer and M. Williams (eds) *Multiple Perspectives on the Self in SLA*, Bristol: Multilingual Matters, pp. 177–85.

Merino, M. and Tileag, C. (2011) 'The construction of ethnic minority identity: A discursive psychological approach to ethnic self-definition in action', *Discourse and Society*, 22(1): 86–101. doi: 10.1177/0957926510382834.

Merriam, S. and Bierema, L.L. (2014) *Adult Learning: Theory and Practice*, San Francisco: Jossey-Bass.

Meyer-Lee, E. (2005) 'Bringing it home: Follow-up courses for study abroad returnees', in *Internationalizing Undergraduate Education: Integrating Study Abroad into the Curriculum*, Minneapolis, MN: University of Minnesota, pp. 114–16.

Meyers-Scotton, C. (2006) *Multiple Voices: An Introduction to Bilingualism*, Oxford: Oxford University Press.

Mezirow, J. (1994) 'Understanding transformative theory', *Adult Education Quarterly*, 44: 222–32. doi: 10.1177/074171369404400403.

Mezirow, J. (1996) 'Contemporary paradigms of learning', *Adult Education Quarterly*, 46: 158–72. doi: 10.1177/074171369604600303.

Mezirow, J. (2009) 'Transformative learning theory', in J. Mezirow, E.W. Taylor and Associates (eds) *Transformative Learning in Practice: Insights from Community, Workplace and Higher Education*, San Francisco: Jossey-Bass, pp. 18–30.

Mikal, J.P., Yang, J. and Lewis, A. (2015) 'Surfing USA: How internet use prior to and during study abroad affects Chinese students' stress, integration, and cultural learning while in the United States', *Journal of Studies in International Education*, 19(3): 203–24. doi: 10.1177/1028315314536990.

Mikk, B.K. (2015) 'Training for education abroad', in J.M. Bennett (ed.) *The Sage Handbook of Intercultural Competence, Volume 2*, Los Angeles: Sage Publications, pp. 803–10.

Mikk, B.K., Cohen, A.D., & Paige, R.M. with Chi, J. C., Lassegard, J.P., Meagher, M., and Weaver, S. (2009) *Maximizing Study Abroad: An Instructional Guide to Strategies for Language and Culture Learning and Use* (CARLA Working Paper Series), Minneapolis: University of Minnesota, Center for Advanced Research on Language Acquisition.

Miller, R. and Leskes, A. (2005) *Level of Assessment: From the Student to the Institution*, Washington, DC: Association of American Colleges and Universities.

Mills, N. (2014) 'Self-efficacy in second language acquisition', in S. Mercer and M. Williams (eds) *Multiple Perspectives on the Self in SLA*, Bristol: Multilingual Matters, pp. 6–22.

Mitchell, R. (2015) 'The development of social relations during residence abroad', *Innovation in Language Learning and Teaching*, 9(1): 22–33. doi: 10.1080/17501229.2014.995762.

Mitchell, R., Tracy-Ventura, N. and McManus, K. (2017) *Anglophone Students Abroad: Identity, Social Relationships and Language Learning*, London and New York: Routledge.

Montgomery, C. (2010) *Understanding the International Student Experience*, Basingstoke, UK: Palgrave MacMillan.

Moon, J.A. (2000) *Reflection in Learning and Professional Development: Theory and Practice*, London: Routledge.

Moon, J.A. (2004) *A Handbook of Reflective and Experiential Learning: Theory and Practice*, London: Routledge.

Moscovici, S. (1961/1976) *Ls Psychoanalyse, on Image et Son Public*, London: Academic Press.

Mukherjee, S. (2016, 2 May) 'Same but different: How epigenetics can blur the line between nature and nurture', *Annals of Science*. Online. Available: www.newyorker.com/magazine/2016/05/02/breakthroughs-in-epigenetics (accessed 1 May 2017).

Müller, M. and Schmenk, B. (2017) 'Narrating the sound of self: The role of pronunciation in learners' self-constructions in study-abroad contexts', *The International Journal of Applied Linguistics*, 27(1): 132–51. doi: 10.1111/ijal.12109.

Mumby, D.K. (1997) 'Modernism, postmodernism, and communication studies: A rereading of an ongoing debate', *Communication Theory*, 7: 1–28. doi: 10.1111/j.1468-2885.1997.tb00140.x.

Murphy-Lejeune, E. (2002) *Student Mobility and Narrative in Europe: The New Strangers*, London: Routledge.

Murphy-Lejeune, E. (2008) 'The student experience of mobility, a contrasting score', in M. Byram and F. Dervin (eds) *Students, Staff and Academic Mobility in Higher Education*, Newcastle, UK: Cambridge Scholars Publishing, pp. 12–30.

Nam, K.-A. (2015) 'High-context and low-context communication', in J.M. Bennett (ed.) *The Sage Handbook of Intercultural Competence, Volume 2*, Los Angeles: Sage Publications, pp. 377–81.

Nash, D. (1976) 'The personal consequences of a year of study abroad', *The Journal of Higher Education*, 47(2): 191–203. doi: 10.2307/1980421.

Nerlich, S. (2016) 'Counting outward mobility: The data sources and their constraints', in D. Vellaris and D. Coleman-George (eds) *Handbook of Research on Study Abroad Programs and Outbound Mobility*, Hershey, PA: IGI Global, pp. 40–65.

Nguyen, A.M.D. and Benet-Martínez, V. (2010) 'Multicultural identity: What it is and why it matters', in R. Crisp (ed.) *The Psychology of Social and Cultural Diversity*, Hoboken, NJ: Wiley-Blackwell, pp. 87–114.

Niesen, C.C. (2010) 'Navigating reentry shock: The use of communication as a facilitative tool', Unpublished M.A. thesis, Alberque, New Mexico: The University of New Mexico.

Nolan, R.W. (1999) *Communicating and Adapting across Cultures: Living and Working in the Global Culture*, Westport, CT: Greenwood Publishing Group.

Norton, B. and Toohey, K. (2002) 'Identity and language learning', in R. Kaplan (ed) *The Oxford Handbook of Applied Linguistics*, Oxford: Oxford University Press, pp. 115–23.

Oberg, K. (1960) 'Cultural shock: Adjustment to new cultural environments', *Practical Anthropology*, 7: 177–82. doi: 10.1177/009182966000700405.

Ochs, E. and Capps, L. (2001) *Living Narrative: Creating Lives in Everyday Storytelling*, Cambridge, MA: Harvard University Press.

Ochs, E. and Schieffelin, B. (1984) 'Language acquisition and socialization: Three developmental stories and their implications', in R. Shweder and R.A. LeVine (eds) *Culture Theory: Essays on Mind, Self, and Emotion*, New York: Cambridge University, pp. 276–320.

Oetzel, J.G. (2009) *Intercultural Communication: A Layered Approach*, International Edition, New York: Vango Books.

Ogden, A.C. (2015) *Toward a Research Agenda for U.S. Education Abroad*, Washington, DC: Association of International Education Administrators (AIEA). Online. Available: www.aieaworld.org/assets/docs/research_agenda/ogden_2015.pdf (accessed 5 January 2017).

Olson, C.L. and Kroeger, K.R. (2001) 'Global competency and intercultural sensitivity', *Journal of Studies in International Education*, 5(2): 116–37. doi: 10.1177/102831530152003.

Ornstein, A.C. and Hunkins, F.P. (2017) *Curriculum: Foundations, Principles and Issues*, 7th edn, Boston: Pearson.

Paige, R.M. (2004) 'Instrumentation in intercultural training', in D. Landis, J.M. Bennett and M.J. Bennett (eds) *Handbook of Intercultural Training*, 3rd edn, Thousand Oaks, CA: Sage Publications, pp. 85–128.

Paige, R.M. (2013) 'Factors impacting intercultural development in study abroad', Paper presented at Elon University, Elon, North Carolina, USA, 16 August 2013.

Paige, R.M. (2015a) 'Intensity factors', in J.M. Bennett (ed.) *The Sage Handbook of Intercultural Competence, Volume 2*, Los Angeles: Sage Publications, pp. 444–6.

Paige, R.M. (2015b) 'Interventionist models for study abroad', in J.M. Bennett (ed.) *The Sage Handbook of Intercultural Competence, Volume 2*, Los Angeles: Sage Publications, pp. 563–8.

Paige, R.M. and Bennett, J.M. (2015) 'Intercultural sensitivity', in J.M. Bennett (ed.) *The Sage Encyclopedia of Intercultural Competence, Volume 2*, Thousand Oaks, CA: Sage, pp. 519–25.

Paige, R.M., Cohen, A.D., Kappler, B., Chi, J.C. and Lassegard, J.P. (2006) *Maximizing Study Abroad: A Student's Guide to Strategies for Language and Culture Learning and Use*, 2nd edn, Minneapolis, MN: Center for Advanced Research on Language Acquisition, University of Minnesota.

Paige, R.M. and Goode, M.L. (2009) 'Cultural mentoring: International education professionals and the development of intercultural competence', in

D.K.Deardorff (ed.) *The Sage Handbook of Intercultural Competence*, Thousand Oaks, CA: Sage Publications, pp. 333–49.

Paige, R.M. and Stallman, E.M. (2007) 'Using instruments in education abroad outcomes assessment', in M. Bolen (ed.) *A Guide to Outcomes Assessment in Education Abroad*, Carlisle, PA: Forum on Education Abroad, pp. 137–61.

Paige, R.M. and Vande Berg, M. (2012) 'Why students are and are not learning abroad', in M. Vande Berg, R.M. Paige and K.H. Lou (eds) *Student Learning Abroad: What Our Students Are Learning, What They're Not and What We Can Do about It*, Sterling, VA: Stylus Publishing, pp. 29–59.

Papatsiba, V. (2006) *Des Etudiants Européens. 'Erasmus' et l'Aventure de l'Altérité*, Bern: Peter Lang.

Parra, M.L. (2016) 'Understanding identity among Spanish heritage learners: An interdisciplinary endeavor', in D.P. Cabo (ed.) *Advances in Spanish as a Heritage Language*, Amsterdam: John Benjamins, pp. 177–204.

Passarelli, A.M. and Kolb, D.A. (2012) 'Using experiential learning theory to promote student learning and development in programs of education abroad', in M. Vande Berg, R.M. Paige and K.H. Lou (eds) *Student Learning Abroad: What Our Students Are Learning, What They're Not and What We Can Do about It*, Sterling, VA: Stylus Publishing, pp. 137–61.

Patel, F., Li, M. and Sooknanan, P. (2011) *Intercultural Communication: Building a Global Community*, New Delhi, India: Sage Publications.

Patron, M.C. (2007) *Culture and Identity in Study Abroad Contexts: After Australia, French without France*, Berlin: Peter Lang.

Pedersen, E.R. (1991) 'Counselling international students', *The Counselling Psychologist*, 19: 10–58. doi: 10.1177/0011000091191002.

Pedersen, E.R., Neighbors, C., Larimer, M.E. and Lee, C.M. (2011) 'Measuring sojourner adjustment among American students studying abroad', *International Journal of Intercultural Relations*, 35(6): 881–9. doi: 10.1016/j.ijintrel.2011.06.003.

Pellegrino Aveni, V. (2005) *Study Abroad and Second Language Use: Constructing the Self*, Cambridge: Cambridge University Press.

Penman, C. and Ratz, S. (2015) 'A module-based approach to foster and document the intercultural process before and during the residence abroad', *Intercultural Education*, 26(1): 49–61. doi: 10.1080/14675986.2015.993529.

Pennycook, A. (2001) *Critical Applied Linguistics: A Critical Introduction*, Mahwah, NJ: Lawrence Erlbaum Associates, Inc.

Pérez-Vidal, C. and Howard, M. (2014, August) 'Study abroad and language learning: The role of social networks, integration and identity', ReN (Research Network) Session at the AILA Conference in Brisbane, Australia.

Phakiti, A. and Paltridge, B. (2015) 'Approaches and methods in applied linguistics research', in B. Paltridge and A. Phakiti (eds) *Research Methods in Applied Linguistics: A Practical Resource*, London: Bloomsbury, pp. 5–25.

Phipps, A.M. (2006) *Learning the Arts of Linguistic Survival: Languaging, Tourism, Life*, Clevedon: Multilingual Matters.

Phipps, A.M. (2013) 'Intercultural ethics: Questions of methods in language and intercultural communication', *Language and Intercultural Communication*, 13(1): 10–26. doi: 10.1080/14708477.2012.748787.

Phipps, A.M. and Gonzalez, M. (2004) *Modern Languages: Learning and Teaching in an Intercultural Field*, Thousand Oaks, CA: Sage Publications.

Piller, I. (2010) *Intercultural Communication: A Critical Introduction*, 1st edn, Edinburgh: Edinburgh University Press.

Piller, I. (2017) *Intercultural Communication: A Critical Introduction*, 2nd edn, Edinburgh: Edinburgh University Press.

Plews, J.L. and Jackson, J. (2017) 'Editorial: Study abroad to, from, and within Asia', *Study Abroad Research in Second Language Acquisition and International Education*, 2(2).

Plews, J.L. and Misfeldt, K. (2018) *Second Language Study Abroad: Programming, Pedagogy, and Participant Engagement*, New York: Springer International Publishing.

Pollock, D.C. and Van Reken, R.E. (2009) *Third Culture Kids: Growing Up Among Worlds*, Boston: Nicholas Brealey Publishing.

Pritchard, A. and Woollard, J. (2010) *Psychology for the Classroom: Constructivism and Social Learning*, Abingdon, UK: Routledge.

Pusch, M.D. (2004) 'Intercultural training in historical perspective', in D. Landis, J.M. Bennett and M.J. Bennett (eds) *Handbook of Intercultural Training*, 3rd edn, London: Sage Publications, pp. 13–36.

Raymond, P.M. and Parks, S. (2004) 'Chinese students' enculturation into an MBA program: Issues of empowerment', *Critical Inquiry in Language Studies*, 1(4): 187–202. doi: 10.1207/s15427595cils0104_1.

Regan, V., Howard, M. and Lemée, I. (2009) *The Acquisition of Sociolinguistic Competence in a Study Abroad Context*, Bristol: Multilingual Matters.

Reid, E. (2013) 'Models of intercultural competences in practice', *International Journal of Language and Linguistics*, 1(2): 44–53. doi: 10.11648/j.ijll.201 30102.12.

Rhodes, G. (2011) *Global Scholar: Online Learning for Study Abroad*. Online. Available: www.globalscholar.us (accessed 5 November 2016).

Riazi, A.M. (2016) *The Routledge Encyclopaedia of Research Methods in Applied Linguistics: Quantitative, Qualitative, and Mixed-Methods Research*, Abingdon, UK: Routledge.

Rienties, B. and Jindal-Snape, D. (2016a) 'Multiple and multi-dimensional transitions of international students to higher education: A way forward', in D. Jindal-Snape and B. Rienties (eds) *Multi-Dimensional Transitions of International Students to Higher Education*, Abingdon, UK: Routledge, pp. 259–81.

Rienties, B. and Jindal-Snape, D. (2016b) 'A social network perspective on the affect, behaviour and cognition of international and host-national students', in D. Jindal-Snape and B. Rienties (eds) *Multi-Dimensional Transitions of International Students to Higher Education*, Abingdon, UK: Routledge, pp. 53–70.

Risager, K. (2007) *Language and Culture Pedagogy: From a National to a Transnational Paradigm*, Clevedon: Multilingual Matters.

Roberts, C., Byram, M., Barro, A., Jordan, S. and Street, B. (2001) *Language Learners as Ethnographers*, Clevedon: Multilingual Matters.

Rodriguez, S.R. and Chornet-Roses, D. (2014) 'How "family" is your host family?: An examination of student-relationships during study abroad', *International Journal of Intercultural Relations*, 39(2): 164–74. doi: 10.1016/j.ijintrel.2013.11.004.

Roy, P., Wandschneider, E. and Steglitz, I. (2014) *Assessing Education Abroad Outcomes: A Review of the BEVI, IDI, and GPI*, International Studies and Programs, Office of Study Abroad, East Lansing, MI: Michigan State University. Online Pdf. Available: http://studyabroad.isp.msu.edu/research/documents/Assessing_EA_Outcomes_WhitePaper.pdf

Ryan, J. (2013) 'Comparing learning characteristics in Chinese and Anglophone cultures: Pitfalls and insights', in M. Cortazzi and L. Jin (eds) *Researching Cultures of Learning: International Perspectives on Language Learning and Education*, Basingstoke: Palgrave MacMillan, pp. 41–58.

Ryan, R.M. and Deci, E.L. (2002) 'Overview of self-determination theory: An organismic dialectical perspective', in E.L. Deci and R.M. Ryan (eds) *Handbook of Self-Determination Research*, Rochester: The University of Rochester Press, pp. 3–33.

Salisbury, M. (2015) 'How we got to where we are (and aren't) in assessing study abroad learning', in V. Savicki and E. Brewer (eds) *Assessing Study Abroad: Theory, Tools, and Practice*, Sterling, VA: Stylus Publishing, pp. 15–32.

Samovar, L.A., Porter, R.E. and McDaniel, E.R. (2010) *Communication between Cultures*, 7th edn, Boston: Wadsworth Cengage Learning.

Sampasivam, S. and Clément, R. (2014) 'The dynamics of second language confidence: Contact and interaction', in S. Mercer and M. Williams (eds) *Multiple Perspectives on the Self in SLA*, Bristol: Multilingual Matters, pp. 23–40.

Sandel, T.L. (2014) '"Oh, I'm here!": Social media's impact on the cross-cultural adaptation of students studying abroad', *Journal of Intercultural Communication Research*, 43(1): 1–29. htpp://dx.doi.org/10.1080/17475759.2013.865662.

Saunders, K.P., Hogan, J. and Olson, C.L. (2015) 'Contextualizing the assessment journey and tools for the trek', in V. Savicki and E. Brewer (eds) *Assessing Study Abroad: Theory, Tools, and Practice*, Sterling, VA: Stylus Publishing, pp. 83–102.

Savicki, V. (ed.) (2008) *Developing Intercultural Competence and Transformation: Theory, Research, and Application in International Education*, Sterling, VA: Stylus Publishing.

Savicki, V. (2015) 'Stress, coping, and adjustment', in J.M. Bennett (ed.) *The Sage Handbook of Intercultural Competence, Volume 2*, Los Angeles: Sage Publications, pp. 776–80.

Savicki, V. and Brewer, E. (eds) (2015a) *Assessing Study Abroad: Theory, Tools, and Practice*, Sterling, VA: Stylus Publishing.

Savicki, V. and Brewer, E. (2015b) 'Introduction', in V. Savicki and E. Brewer (eds) *Assessing Study Abroad: Theory, Tools, and Practice*, Sterling, VA: Stylus Publishing, pp. 1–12.

Savicki, V. and Selby, R. (2008) 'Synthesis and conclusions', in V. Savicki (ed.) *Developing Intercultural Competence and Transformation: Theory, Research and Application in International Education*, Sterling, VA: Stylus Publishing, pp. 342–52.

Scannell, P. (2015) 'Cultural studies: Which paradigm?', *Media, Culture and Society*, 37(4): 645–54. doi: 10.1177/0163443715580948.

Schaetti, B.F. (2015) 'Third-culture kids/Global nomads', in J.M. Bennett (ed.) *The Sage Handbook of Intercultural Competence, Volume 2*, Los Angeles: Sage Publications, pp. 797–800.

Schartner, A. (2016) 'The effect of study abroad on intercultural competence: A longitudinal case study of international postgraduate students at a British university', *Journal of Multilingual and Multicultural Development*, 37(4): 402–18. doi: 10.1080/01434632.2015.1073737.

Selby, R. (2008) 'Designing transformation in international education', in V. Savicki (ed.) *Developing Intercultural Competence and Transformation: Theory, Research, and Application in International Education*, Sterling: Stylus, pp. 1–12.

Sen, A. (2006) *Identity and Violence: The Illusion of Destiny*, New York: Norton and Co.

Shames, W. and Alden, P. (2005) 'The impact of short-term study abroad on the identity development of college students with learning disabilities and/or AD/HD', *Frontiers: The Interdisciplinary Journal of Study Abroad*, 11: 1–31. Online. Available: http://files.eric.ed.gov/fulltext/EJ891461.pdf (accessed 6 August 2017).

Shiri, S. (2015) 'The homestay in intensive language study abroad: Social networks, language socialization, and developing intercultural competence', *Foreign Language Annals*, 48(1): 5–25. doi: 10.1111/flan.12127.

Shively, R.L. (2010) 'From the virtual world to the real world: A model of pragmatics instruction for study abroad', *Foreign Language Annals*, 43(1): 105–37.

Shively, R.L. (2016) 'Heritage language learning in study abroad: Motivation, identity work, and language development', in D.P. Cabo (ed.) *Advances in Spanish as a Heritage Language*, Amsterdam: John Benjamins, pp. 259–80.

Shively, R.L. and Cohen, A.D. (2008) 'Development of Spanish requests and apologies during study abroad', *Íkala*, 13(2): 57–118.

Shi-xu (2001) 'Critical pedagogy and intercultural communication: Creating discourses of diversity, equality, common goals and rational moral motivation', *Journal of Intercultural Studies*, 22(3): 279–93. doi: 10.1080/07256860120094000.

Sinicrope, C., Norris, J. and Watanabe, Y. (2007) 'Understanding and assessing intercultural competence: A summary of theory, research, and practice (Technical report for the Foreign Language Program Evaluation Project)', *Second Language Studies*, 26(1): 1–58. Online. Available: https://scholarspace.manoa.hawaii.edu/bitstream/10125/40689/1/Sinicrope%20et%20al.%20(2007)_26(1).pdf (accessed 11 May 2017).

Smalley, W. (1963) 'Culture shock, language shock, and the shock of self-discovery', *Practical Anthropology*, 10: 49–56.

Smith, S. (2002) 'The cycle of cross-cultural adaptation and reentry', in J.N. Martin, T.K. Nakayama and L.A. Flores (eds) *Readings in Intercultural Communication*, Boston: McGraw Hill, pp. 246–59.

Smolic, E. and Martin, D. (2018) 'Structured reflection and immersion in Ecuador: Expanding Teachers' intercultural and linguistic competencies', in J. Jackson and S. Oguro (eds) *Intercultural Interventions in Study Abroad*, Abingdon, UK and New York: Routledge, pp. 190–205.

Sorrells, K. (2012) 'Intercultural training in the global context', in J. Jackson (ed.) *Routledge Handbook of Language and Intercultural Communication*, Abingdon: Routledge, pp. 372–89.

Sorrells, K. (2013) *Intercultural Communication: Globalization and Social Justice*, Thousand Oaks, CA: Sage Publications.

Sorrells, K. (2015) 'Essentialism', in J.M. Bennett (ed.) *The Sage Handbook of Intercultural Competence, Volume 1*, Los Angeles: Sage Publications, pp. 297–9.

Sorrells, K. (n.d.) 'Ethical intercultural praxis', *Eye on Ethics: SIETAR USA Website*. Online. Available: www.sietarusa.org/page-1382650 (accessed 20 December 2017).

Sorrells, K. and Sekimoto, S. (2016) 'Globalizing intercultural communication: Traces and trajectories', in H. Sorrells and S. Sekimoto (eds) *Globalizing Intercultural Communication: A Reader*, Thousand Oaks, CA: Sage Publications, pp. 2–12.

Spencer, S. and Tuma, K. (eds) (2008) *The Guide to Successful Short-Term Programs Abroad*, 2nd edn, Washington, DC: NAFSA: Association of International Educators.

Spencer-Oatey, H. (2012) *What Is Culture? A Compilation of Quotations*. GlobalPAD Core Concepts. Online. Available: GlobalPAD Open House http://go.warwick.ac.uk/globalpadintercultural (accessed 5 December 2016).

Spitzberg, B.H. and Changnon, G. (2009) 'Conceptualizing multicultural competence', in D.K. Deardorff (ed.) *Handbook of Intercultural Competence*, Thousand Oaks, CA: Sage Publications, pp. 2–52.

Stemler, S.E. and Sorkin, C.K. (2015) 'A closer look at the Wesleyan intercultural competence scale', in V. Savicki and E. Brewer (eds) *Assessing Study Abroad: Theory, Tools, and Practice*, Sterling, VA: Stylus Publishing, pp. 246–61.

Stevens, D. and Levi, A.J. (2013) *Introduction to Rubrics: An Assessment Tool to Save Grading Time, Convey Effective Feedback, and Promote Student Learning*, Sterling, VA: Stylus Publishing.

Storti, C. (2009) 'Intercultural competence in human resources', in D. Deardorff (ed.) *The Sage Handbook of Intercultural Competence*, Thousand Oaks, CA: Sage Publications, pp. 272–86.

Sung, C.C.M. (2014a) 'English as a lingua franca and global identities: Perspectives from four second language learners of English in Hong Kong', *Linguistics and Education*, 26: 31–9. doi: 10.1016/j.linged.2014.01.010.

Sung, C.C.M. (2014b) 'Hong Kong university students' perceptions of their identities in English as a Lingua Franca contexts: An exploratory study', *Journal of Asian Pacific Communication*, 24(1): 94–112. doi: 10.1075/japc.24.1.06sun.

Suskie, L. (2009) *Assessing Student Learning: A Common Sense Guide*, San Francisco: Jossey-Bass.

Swann, J., Deumert, A., Lillis, T. and Mesthrie, R. (2004) *A Dictionary of Sociolinguistics*, Edinburgh: Edinburgh University Press.

Szkudlarek, B. (2010) 'Reentry: A review of the literature', *International Journal of Intercultural Relations*, 34(1): 1–21. doi: 10.1016/j.ijintrel.2009.06.006.

Taguchi, N. (2015) *Developing Interactional Competence in a Japanese Study Abroad Context*, Clevedon: Multilingual Matters.

Taguchi, N. (2018) 'Contexts and pragmatics learning: Problems and opportunities of the study abroad research', *Language Teaching*, 51(1), 124–37. doi: 10.1017/S0261444815000440.

Tajfel, H. (1981) *Human Groups and Social Categories: Studies in Social Psychology*, Cambridge: Cambridge University Press.

Tajfel, H. and Turner, J.C. (1979) 'An integrative theory of intergroup conflict', in W.G. Austin and S. Worchel (eds) *The Social Psychology of Intergroup Relations*, Belmont, CA: Wadsworth, pp. 33–53.

Tajfel, H. and Turner, J.C. (1986) 'An integrative theory of intergroup conflict', in S. Worchel and W.G. Austin (eds) *Psychology of Intergroup Relations*, Chicago, IL: Nelson-Hall, pp. 2–24.

Tarrant, M.A., Rubin, D.L. and Stoner, L. (2013) 'The added value of study abroad: Fostering a global citizenry', *Journal of Studies in International Education*, 18(2): 141–61. doi: 10.1177/1028315313497589.

Taylor, C. (2004) *Modern Social Imaginaries*, Durham and London: Duke University Press.

Taylor, E.W. (2015) 'Transformative learning', in J.M. Bennett (ed.) *The Sage Handbook of Intercultural Competence, Volume 2*, Los Angeles: Sage Publications, pp. 818–20.

Taylor, P.C. and Medina, M.N.D. (2013) 'Educational research paradigms: From positivism to multiparadagmatic', *Meaning Centered Education*, 1(1). Online. Available: http://patrickblessinger.com/meaningcentered//journal/volume-01/educational-research-paradigms-from-positivism-to-multiparadigmatic (accessed 15 September 2016).

Thebodo, S.W. and Marx, L.E. (2005) 'Predparture orientation and reentry programming', in J.L. Brockington, W.H. Hoffa and P.C. Martin (eds) *NAFSA' Guide to Education Abroad for Advisors and Administrators*, Washington, DC: NAFSA, pp. 293–312.

Thomas, J. (1983) 'Cross-cultural pragmatic failure', *Applied Linguistics*, 4(2): 91–112. doi: 10.1093/applin/4.2.91.

Timpe, V. (2014) *Assessing Intercultural Language Learning: The Dependence of Receptive Sociopragmatic Competence and Discourse Competence on Learning Opportunities and Input*, Frankfurt: Peter Lang.

Ting-Toomey, S. (2005) 'The matrix of face: An updated face-negotiation theory', in W.B. Gudykunst (ed.) *Theorizing about Intercultural Communication*, Thousand Oaks, CA: Sage Publications, pp. 71–92.

Ting-Toomey, S. (2012) 'Understanding conflict competence: Multiple theoretical insights', in J. Jackson (ed.) *Routledge Handbook of Language and Intercultural*, Communication, Abingdon, UK: Routledge, pp. 279–95.

Ting-Toomey, S. (2015) 'Identity negotiation theory', in J.M. Bennett (ed.) *The Sage Encyclopedia of Intercultural Competence, Volume 1*, Thousand Oaks, CA: Sage, pp. 418–23.

Ting-Toomey, S. and Chung, L.C. (2012) *Understanding Intercultural Communication*, 2nd edn, Oxford: Oxford University Press.

Trentman, E. (2013) 'Imagined communities and language learning during study abroad: Arabic learners in Egypt', *Foreign Language Annals*, 46(4): 543–64. doi: 10.1111/flan.12054.

Trentman, E. (2015) 'Negotiating gendered identities and access to social networks during study abroad in Egypt, social interaction, identity and language learning during residence abroad', in R. Mitchell, T. Tracy-Ventura and K. McManus (eds) *Social Interaction, Identity, and Language Learning During Residence Abroad*, Eurosla Monographs Series, 4, Amsterdam: The European Second Language Association, pp. 263–80.

Tucker, M.F. (2015) 'Expatriates', in J.M. Bennett (ed.) *The Sage Encyclopedia of Intercultural Competence, Volume 1*, Thousand Oaks, CA: Sage, pp. 315–18.

Turner, Y. and Robson, S. (2008) *Internationalizing the University*, London and New York: Continuum.

Ulysse, B.K. and Lukenchuk, A. (2013) 'Presaging educational inquiry: Historical development of philosophical ideas, traditions, and perspectives', in A. Lukenchuk (ed.) *Paradigms of Research for the 21st Century: Perspectives and Examples from Practice*, New York: Peter Lang, pp. 3–30.

Ushioda, E. (2014) 'Motivational perspectives on the self in SLA: A developmental view', in S. Mercer and M. Williams (eds) *Multiple Perspectives on the Self in SLA*, Bristol: Multilingual Matters, pp. 127–41.

Van de Vijver, F.J.R. and Leung, K. (2009) 'Methodological issues in measuring intercultural competence', in D.K. Deardorff (ed.) *The Sage Handbook of Intercultural Competence*, Thousand Oaks, CA: Sage Publications, pp. 456–76.

van Lier, L. (2011) 'Language learning: An ecological-semiotic approach', in E. Hinkel (ed.) *Handbook of Research in Second Language Teaching and Learning, Volume II*, New York and London: Routledge, pp. 383–94.

Van Mol, C. (2013) 'Intra-European student mobility and European identity: A successful marriage?', *Population, Space and Place*, 19(2): 209–22. doi: 10.1002/psp.1752.

Van Selm, K., Sam, D.L. and Oudenhoven, J.P. (1997) 'Life satisfaction and competence of Bosnian refugees in Norway', *Scandinavian Journal of Psychology*, 38: 143–9. doi: 10.1111/1467-9450.00020.

Vande Berg, M. (2015a) 'Developmentally appropriate pedagogy', in J.M. Bennett (ed.) *The Sage Encyclopedia of Intercultural Competence, Volume 1*, Thousand Oaks, CA: Sage, pp. 229–33.

Vande Berg, M. (2015b) 'International education', in J.M. Bennett (ed.) *The Sage Handbook of Intercultural Competence, Volume 2*, Los Angeles: Sage Publications, pp. 546–9.

Vande Berg, M., Paige, R.M. and Lou, K.H. (eds) (2012a) *Student Learning Abroad: What Our Students Are Learning, What They're Not and What We Can Do about It*, Sterling, VA: Stylus Publishing.

Vande Berg, M., Paige, R.M. and Lou, K.H. (2012b) 'Student learning abroad: Paradigms and assumptions', in M. Vande Berg, R.M. Paige and K.H. Lou (eds) *Student Learning Abroad: What Our Students Are Learning, What They're Not and What We Can Do about It*, Sterling, VA: Stylus Publishing, pp. 3–28.

Vanderstoep, S.W. and Johnston, D.D. (2009) *Research Methods for Everyday Life: Blending Qualitative and Quantitative Approaches*, San Francisco: Jossey-Bass.

Virkkula, T. and Nikula, T. (2010) 'Identity construction in ELF contexts: A case study of Finnish engineering students working in Germany', *International Journal of Applied Linguistics*, 20(2): 251–73. doi: 10.1111/j.1473-4192.2009.00248.x.

Vögtle, E.M. (2014) *Higher Education Policy Convergence and the Bologna Process: A Cross-National Study*, New York: Palgrave MacMillan.

Walliman, N. (2011) *Research Methods: The Basics*, London: Routledge.

Walton, W. (2009) *Internationalism, National Identities, and Study Abroad: France and the United States, 1890–1970*, Redwood City, CA: Stanford University Press.

Wanner, D. (2009) 'Study abroad and language: From maximal to realistic models', in R. Lewin (ed.) *The Handbook of Practice and Research in Study Abroad: Higher Education and the Quest for Global Citizenship*, New York and London: Routledge, pp. 81–98.

Ward, C. (1996) 'Acculturation', in D. Landis & R. Bhagat (eds), *Handbook of Intercultural Training*, Thousand Oaks, CA: Sage, pp. 81–98.

Ward, C.A. (2015) 'Culture shock', in J.M. Bennett (ed.) *The Sage Handbook of Intercultural Competence, Volume 2*, Los Angeles: Sage Publications, pp. 207–10.

Ward, C.A., Bochner, S. and Furnham, A. (2001) *The Psychology of Culture Shock*, London: Routledge.

Ward, C.A., Okura, Y., Kennedy, A. and Kojima, T. (1998) 'The U-curve on trial: A longitudinal study of psychological and sociocultural adjustment during cross-cultural transition', *International Journal of Intercultural Relations*, 22(3): 277–91. doi: 10.1016/S0147-1767(98)00008-X.

Weaver, K. and Olson, J.K. (2006) 'Understanding paradigms used for nursing research', *Journal of Advanced Nursing*, 53(4): 459–69. doi: 10.1111/j.1365-2648.2006.03740.x.

Weimer, M. (2012) 'Learner-centered teaching and transformative learning', in E.W. Taylor and P. Cranton (eds) *The Handbook of Transformative Learning: Theory, Research, and Practice*, San Francisco: Jossey-Bass, pp. 439–54.

Welch, A. (2008) 'Myths and modes of mobility: The changing face of academic mobility in the global era', in M. Byram and F. Dervin (eds) *Students, Staff and Academic Mobility in Higher Education*, Newcastle, UK: Cambridge Scholars Publishing, pp. 292–311.

Wells, R. (2006) 'Nontraditional study abroad destinations: Analysis of a trend', *Frontiers: The Interdisciplinary Journal of Study Abroad*, 13: 113–33. Online. Available: https://frontiersjournal.org/wp-content/uploads/2015/09/WELLS-FrontiersXIII-NontraditionalStudyAbroadDestinations.pdf.

Wiersma, W. and Jurs, S.G. (2009) *Research Methods in Education: An Introduction*, 9th edn, Boston: Pearson Education, Inc.

Wilkinson, S. (1998) 'Study abroad from the participants' perspective: A challenge to common beliefs', *Foreign Language Annals*, 31: 23–39. doi: 10.1111/j.1944-9720.1998.tb01330.x.

Wimmer, A. and Glick Schiller, N.G. (2002) 'Methodological nationalism and beyond: Nation–state building, migration and the social sciences', *Global Networks: A Journal of Transnational Affairs*, 2(4): 301–34. doi: 10.1111/1471-0374.00043.

Wiseman, R.L. and Koester, J. (1993) *Intercultural Communication Competence*, Thousand Oaks, CA: Sage Publications.

Wolcott, T. (2013) 'An American in Paris: Myth, desire, and subjectivity in one student's account of study abroad in France', in C. Kinginger (ed.) *Social and Cultural Aspects of Language Learning in Study Abroad*, Amsterdam and Philadelphia: John Benjamins Publishing Company, pp. 127–55.

Woodin, J. (2016) 'How to research interculturally and ethically', in H. Zhu (ed.) *Research Methods in Intercultural Communication: A Practical Guide*, Chichester: John Wiley and Sons, pp. 103–19.

Xie, Y. (2018) 'The evolution of L2 identities during study abroad: multiple case studies of inbound international exchange students in Hong Kong'. Unpublished Ph.D. dissertation. Hong Kong: The Chinese University of Hong Kong.

Yang, M., Webster, B. and Prosser, M. (2011) 'Travelling a thousand miles: Hong Kong Chinese students' study abroad experience', *International Journal of Intercultural Relations*, 35(1): 69–78. doi: 10.1016/j.ijintrel.2010.09.010.

Yashima, T., Zenuk-Nishide, L. and Shimizu, K. (2004) 'The influence of attitudes and effect on willingness to communicate and second language communication', *Language Learning*, 54: 119–52. doi: 10.1111/j.1467-9922.2004.00250.x.

Young, V.A., Barrett, R., Young-Rivera, Y. and Lovejoy, Y. (2014) *Other People's English: Code-Meshing, Code-switching, and African American Literacy*, New York, NY: Teachers College Press.

Zaharna, R.S. (1989) 'Self-Shock: The double-binding challenge of identity', *International Journal of Intercultural Relations*, 13(4): 501–26. doi: 10.1016/0147-1767(89)90026-6.

Zamani-Gallaher, E.M., Leon, R. and Lang, J. (2016) 'Abroad as self-authorship: Globalization and reconceptualizing college and career readiness', in R.L. Raby and E.J. Valeau (eds) *International Education at Community Colleges: Themes, Practices and Case Studies*, Basingstoke: Palgrave MacMillan, pp. 111–25.

Zarate, G. and Gohard-Radenkovic, A. (eds) (2004) *La reconnaissance des compétences interculturelles*, De la grille á la carte, Paris: Didier.

Zhu, H. (2014) *Exploring Intercultural Communication: Language in Action*, London: Routledge.

Zhu, H. (2016a) '"Where are you from?": Interculturality and interactional practices', in A. Komisarof and H. Zhu (eds) *Crossing Boundaries and Weaving Intercultural Work, Life and Scholarship in Globalizing Universities*, London and New York: Routledge, pp. 147–59.

Zhu, H. (2016b) 'Identifying research paradigms', in H. Zhu (ed.) *Research Methods in Intercultural Communication: A Practical Guide*, Chichester: John Wiley and Sons, pp. 3–22.

Zhu, H. (ed.) (2016c) *Research Methods in Intercultural Communication: A Practical Guide*, Chichester: John Wiley and Sons.

Zubizarreta, J. (2009) *The Learning Portfolio: Reflective Practice for Improving Student Learning*, San Francisco: Jossey-Bass.

Zukroff, S., Ferst, S., Hirsch, J., Slawson, C. and Wiedenhoeft, M. (2005) 'Program assessment and evaluation', in J.L. Brockington, W.H. Hoffa and P.C. Martin (eds) *NAFSA' Guide to Education Abroad for Advisors and Administrators*, Washington, DC: NAFSA, pp. 445–78.

Zull, J.E. (2012) 'The brain, learning, and study abroad', in M. Vande Berg, R.M. Paige and K.H. Lou (eds) *Student Learning Abroad: What Our Students Are Learning, What They're Not, and What We Can Do about It*, Sterling, VA: Stylus Publishing, pp. 162–87.

Glossary

acceptance of difference According to the developmental model of intercultural sensitivity (DMIS), individuals in this phase accept the existence of culturally different ways of organising human existence, although they may not like or agree with them

accountability The furnishing of concrete evidence of learning to affirm the quality of a programme or pedagogical intervention

acculturation The process through which an individual is socialised into a new cultural environment

acculturation strategies The ways that individuals and ethnocultural groups respond to the process of acculturation

acculturative stress A negative psychological reaction to the experiences of acculturation, often characterised by anxiety, depression, and a variety of psychosomatic problems

adaptation The act or process of adjusting or adapting to a new cultural environment

adaptation to difference According to the developmental model of intercultural sensitivity (DMIS), individuals in this phase can expand their own worldviews to accurately understand other ways of being and are able to behave in culturally appropriate ways

adaptive stress The body's response to environmental stress that can arise when moving from one environment to another

agency The capacity of an individual to act in a given environment and situation

'appropriate' intercultural communication The actions and communication a person uses to achieve his or her communication goals are interpreted as meaningful by the interlocutor who has a different cultural background

ascribed identity The identity that others assign to us (or we give to someone else)

ascription The process of ascribing or assigning an identity to someone else

assessment The systematic collection, review, and use of information about student learning

assimilation The process whereby immigrants do not retain their original cultural identity and link to their heritage/culture; instead, they seek close interaction with the host culture and adopt the cultural values, norms, and traditions of the new society

attitude An emotional (positive or negative) response to people, ideas, and objects

avowal The process of conveying what identity(ies) one wishes to be acknowledged by others

avowed identity The identity that an individual wishes to present or claim in an interaction

bias A personal preference, like or dislike, which can interfere with one's ability to be objective, impartial, and without prejudice

bicultural An individual who is culturally competent in two cultural contexts (e.g., his or her original home environment and the host environment)

biculturalism A state that is characterised by proficiency and comfort with both one's original culture and the culture of the new country or region

bilingual Using or able to use two languages with equal or nearly equal fluency

case study The intensive study of a phenomenon, person, or group

communication style The way individuals or a group of individuals prefer to communicate with others

communicative competence What a speaker needs to know to be able to use language appropriately and effectively in specific social/cultural settings

community of practice (CoP) A group of people who share a concern or a passion for something they do and gradually learn how to do it better through interaction on a regular basis

co-national An individual from one's home nation

construct validity The degree to which a test measures what it claims, or purports, to be measuring

constructive marginality The development of an integrated multicultural self with the acceptance of an identity that is not based on a single cultural identity

constructivism A paradigm or worldview that posits that learning is an active, constructive process that entails reflection on personal experiences

constructivist pedagogy An approach to teaching that is based on the notion that learning (cognition) occurs when students develop their own understanding through reflection on their personal experiences and by making links with what they already know

content validity The degree to which an assessment or measurement tool taps into the knowledge or skill for which the instrument was developed

contested identity Facets or elements of one's identity that are not recognised or accepted by the people one is in contact with

206 *Glossary*

context The overall environment in which communication occurs (e.g., physical, psychological, sociocultural, political, sociorelational, etc.)

contextual evaluation The process of evaluating multiple cultural perspectives when deciding how best to proceed in intercultural situations

cosmopolitanism The ideology that all human beings belong to a single community, based on a shared morality

credit mobility A short period of study or traineeship abroad (in the framework of on-going studies at a home institution) for the purpose of gaining credits (see *study abroad*)

critical approach to intercultural communication The impact of power and power relations on intercultural communication are examined bearing in mind the sociopolitical, historical context

critical cosmopolitanism A sociological paradigm in which culture is viewed as being politically constructed and efforts are made to view the cultural Other with respect and empathy

critical cultural awareness/political education (*savoir s'engager*) The ability to critically evaluate perspectives, practices, and products in one's own and other cultures

critical discourse analysis An interdisciplinary, critical approach to the study of discourse that views language as a form of social practice which is loaded with cultural and ideological values

critical intercultural communication A critical examination of the role of power and positioning in language and intercultural communication within a particular context

critical intercultural speaker An individual (second language speaker) who is able to negotiate between his or her own cultural, social and political identifications and representations with those of the Other, and, in the process, become critically aware of the complex nature of cultural identities in an intercultural encounter (see also *intercultural speaker*)

critical pedagogy A social movement and philosophy of education that has developed and applied concepts from critical theory to the field of education and the study of culture

critical reflection The process of analysing, reconsidering, and questioning intercultural experiences with the aim of developing a better understanding of internal and external factors that influenced the outcome

critical theory A social theory oriented toward critiquing and changing society as a whole (e.g., to overcome social injustice)

critical thinking The ability to think clearly and rationally about what action to take or what to believe (e.g., the ability to engage in reflective and independent thinking)

criticality An approach to higher education which promotes critical thinking, critical self-reflection, and critical action

cultural awareness An understanding of how an individual's cultural background may inform his or her values, behaviour, beliefs, and basic assumptions

cultural disengagement The degree to which an individual or group feels a sense of disconnection from his or her primary cultural community

cultural identity A social identity that is influenced by one's membership or affiliation with particular cultural groups

cultural mentoring An intercultural pedagogy in which the mentor or facilitator provides ongoing support for and facilitation of intercultural learning

cultural norms Shared expectations of appropriate behaviours in certain situations and contexts

cultural script Representations of cultural norms which are widely held in a given society and which are reflected in language (e.g., a sequence of expressions and behaviours in certain situations)

cultural socialisation The process through which our primary cultural beliefs, values, norms, and worldviews are internalised, to varying degrees

cultural space A physical or virtual place where individuals have a sense of community and culture, e.g., a neighbourhood, region, virtual space

culture A community or group that is perceived to share a common history, traditions, norms, and imaginings in a particular cultural space (e.g., a neighbourhood, region, virtual space)

'culture as nation' perspective An orientation towards culture in which nations or communities are viewed as homogeneous and diversity within groups is largely ignored

'culture of learning' The norms, values, and expectations of teachers and learners that influence classroom activities in a particular cultural setting

culture shock Disorientation and discomfort that an individual may experience when entering an unfamiliar cultural environment

'dark' sides of identity The negative consequences of identification that can arise when individuals possess a high level of ethnocentrism such as prejudice, discrimination and racism

declarative knowledge Factual knowledge and information that an individual knows

defence against difference According to the developmental model of intercultural sensitivity (DMIS), individuals in this ethnocentric phase view their own culture/way of life as the best and overt negative stereotyping is common

defence/reversal According to the developmental model of intercultural sensitivity (DMIS), in this ethnocentric phase one's own culture is devalued and another culture or way of life is romanticised as superior

denial of difference According to the developmental model of intercultural sensitivity (DMIS), individuals in this ethnocentric phase experience their own culture as the only 'real' one and other cultures are either not noticed or are understood in a simplistic way

developmental model of intercultural sensitivity (DMIS) A framework developed by Milton Bennett to depict the process of becoming interculturally sensitive; it describes various ways that individuals perceive and react to cultural differences

digital portfolio An electronic collection of evidence that shows a student's learning journey over time

direct assessment Methods of assessment that provide evidence of actual learning or performance (e.g., tests, essays, portfolios)

direct communication The speaker's intentions and views are made clear by the use of explicit verbal messages and a forthright tone of voice

discourse competence The ability to understand and produce the range of spoken, written, and visual texts that are characteristics of a language

discrimination The prejudicial or unequal treatment of individuals based on their membership, or perceived membership, in a particular group or category

disequilibrium The loss or lack of stability in an unfamiliar situation

diversity Differences among humans in terms of such aspects as culture, language, race, ethnicity, gender, socio-economic status, age, physical/cognitive abilities, national origin, physical attributes, sexual orientation, ethnic affiliation, regional differences, religious beliefs, political beliefs, or other ideologies

education abroad Education outside one's home country (e.g., study abroad, internships, volunteering, directed travel with learning goals)

'effective' intercultural communication Communication with someone who has a different cultural background in which communication goals are achieved

emic perspective The perspective of an insider (member) in a particular culture

emotional intelligence The ability to understand and manage one's own emotions and display sensitivity to others' feelings

emotional resilience An individual's ability to adapt to stressful situations or crises

empathetic behaviour Verbal and nonverbal actions that indicate that one is attending to the messages of others

empathy The ability to understand another person's feelings and point of view

enculturation The primary socialisation process in one's home environment whereby one learns the cultural values and rules of behaviour that are prevalent in one's culture

Englishisation The spread of English throughout the world

environmental elements Factors in the environment (e.g., external programme features, host community elements)

epistemology A branch of philosophy that is concerned with the theory of knowledge and the assumptions or beliefs that we have about the nature of knowledge

eportfolio See *digital portfolio*

Glossary

essentialism The belief that the attributes and behaviour of socially-defined groups can be explained by reference to cultural and/or biological characteristics believed to be inherent to the group (see also *'culture as nation', reductionism*)

essentialist Presenting people's individual behaviour as entirely defined and constrained by the cultures in which they live so that the stereotype becomes the essence of who they are (Holliday 2011)

ethnicity A socially defined category based on such aspects as common ancestry, cuisine, dressing style, heritage, history, language or dialect, physical appearance, religion, symbols, traditions, or other cultural factors

ethics Principles of conduct that help govern the behaviour of individuals and groups

ethnocentric mindset A way of thinking which holds that one's cultural worldview and way of life are superior to all others

ethnocentricism A point of view that views one's group's standards as the best and judges all other groups in relation to them

ethnographic fieldwork Sustained observation and participation in a cultural setting to develop an understanding of how the members view their social and cultural world and interact with each other

ethnography The study and systematic recording of people in naturally occurring settings to create a detailed, in-depth description of everyday life and practice

ethnography of communication The study of the communication patterns of speech communities

ethnorelative mindset A way of thinking which tries to view another person's cultural worldview and way of life from that person's perspective

ethnorelativism The ability to understand a communication practice or worldview from another person's cultural frame of reference

etic perspective An outsider's (observer's) perspective on a particular culture

evaluation The process of critically examining a programme or course, which entails interpretation and judgment related to quality and effectiveness

experiential learning The process of learning through reflection on experience

external programme review An evaluation of a programme carried out by an outside agency

extrinsic motivation In a study abroad context, the learning of another language (and the enhancement of cultural knowledge) to meet an external requirement (e.g., admission standard for an international exchange programme)

fieldnotes Notes recorded by researchers in the course of field research (e.g., participant observation)

formative assessment The gathering of information about how students are performing in a course or programme to provide direction for changes to enhance learning

functionalism A psychological school of thought concerned with how the conscious is related to behaviour

geopolitics The study of the influence of economics, demography, and geography on the politics (e.g., foreign policy) of a state

global citizen An individual who identifies with being part of an emerging world community and whose actions contribute to building this community's values and practices

global citizenship Awareness of and commitment to societal justice for marginalised groups and care for the environment based on principles of equity, respect, and sharing

global competence Possessing an open mind while actively seeking to understand different cultural norms and expectations, and using this knowledge to interact, communicate, and work effectively outside one's environment

global competence model A framework developed by W. Hunter (2004) to help international educators prepare individuals for a diverse workforce and society that necessitates intercultural and global competencies

global identity An identity which affords an individual a sense of belonging in a worldwide culture and is often associated with the use of an international language

global-mindedness A worldview or mindset in which one perceives oneself as connected to the global community and feels a sense of responsibility to its members

global nomads Individuals who have an international lifestyle (e.g., live and work in more than one country for a long period of time), including those who have grown up in many different cultural contexts because their parents have frequently relocated (see also *third culture kids*)

global-ready graduates Individuals who are adequately prepared for a diverse workforce and society that necessitates intercultural and global competencies

globalisation The growing tendency towards international interdependence in business, media, and culture

hedging The use of a hedge, a mitigating word, sound or construction, to lessen the impact of an utterance (e.g., soften the blow, avoid being seen as arrogant or impolite) in accord with the sociocultural constraints on the interaction between the speaker and addressee

heritage student A student who studies abroad in a location that is linked in some way (e.g., linguistically, culturally, historically) to his/her family or cultural background

Hofstede's Value-Orientations Framework The identification of systematic differences in national cultures by Geert Hofstede: power distance (PDI), individualism (IDV), uncertainty avoidance (UAI) and masculinity (MAS), with Confucian Dynamism added later

homestay   Private housing provided for sojourners by a local family, usually with the aim of providing students with firsthand experience of family life in the host culture

host environment   The location where students study abroad

host family   A family in the host environment that provides lodging for student sojourners usually with the aim of affording them firsthand experience of family life in the host culture

host national   A person from the host country

host receptivity   The degree to which the host environment welcomes newcomers into its interpersonal networks and offers them support

hybrid (mixed) identity   A sense of self with elements from multiple cultures

hypothesis   A proposed explanation for a phenomenon made on the basis of limited evidence which serves as a starting point for further investigation

'ideal L2 self'   'the L2-specific facet of one's ideal self' in Dörnyei's (2009) L2 Motivational Self System

identity   An individual's self-concept or sense of self within a particular context

identity expansion   The broadening of one's sense of self through experience and reflection on that experience

identity reconstruction   The reshaping of one's sense of self through experience and reflection on that experience

identity salience   The degree to which an identity is prominent in a particular situation

identity shock   Confusing, and sometimes, conflicting self-images that may develop when one moves to a new environment

ideology   A system of ideas which promotes the interests of a particular group of people

imagined identity   An individual's perception or expectation of his or her sense of self in a particular context or situation

inclusion   General acceptance and appreciation of differences within a community or society

indirect assessment   Information about student perceptions of their learning (e.g., questionnaire surveys, interviews)

individual difference   Variable internal conditions or elements

inequality   Unequal access to power and resources

ingroup   A social or cultural group to which a person psychologically identifies as being a member

ingroup members   People to whom you feel emotionally connected

instrumental orientation   In a study abroad context, the learning of a language and the enhancement of cultural knowledge for instrumental rewards (e.g., to gain admission to an international exchange programme in a prestigious university abroad)

integration Immigrants take steps to maintain their cultural heritage and original cultural identity while developing harmonious relationships with host nationals

integration of difference According to the developmental model of intercultural sensitivity (DMIS), individuals in this phase do not have a definition of self that is central to any particular culture and they are able to shift from one cultural worldview to another

integrative communication theory of cross-cultural adaptation A theory proposed by Young Yun Kim (2001) to depict an individual's gradual adaption to a new environment

integrative orientation In a study abroad context, the learning of a language and the enhancement of one's intercultural communication skills to become closer to host nationals who speak that language

intensity The importance or strength of something (e.g., identity, value)

intercultural anxiety Feelings of tension and apprehension that arise when communicating with people who have a different language and intercultural background

intercultural attitudes (*savoir être*) Curiosity and openness, readiness to suspend disbelief about others' cultures and belief about one's own intercultural attitudes

intercultural communication Interpersonal communication which involves interaction between people from different cultural (and often linguistic) backgrounds

intercultural communication competence The ability to communicate appropriately and effectively with individuals who have a different cultural background

intercultural communication skills The skills needed to interact appropriately and effectively in intercultural interactions (e.g., adaptability, empathy, cross-cultural awareness, intercultural mediation, intercultural sensitivity)

intercultural communicative competence The abilities needed to communicate effectively and appropriately with people who are linguistically and culturally different from oneself

intercultural competence The ability to communicate effectively and appropriately in intercultural situations based on one's intercultural knowledge, skills and attitudes

intercultural education Education designed to help prepare students for responsible intercultural citizenship in our global community

intercultural effectiveness The ability to interact with people from a different cultural background in ways that are respectful and appropriate

intercultural friendship A personal connection or affiliation forged between people who have a different cultural background

intercultural intervention An educational approach that aims to enhance the intercultural development of students

intercultural knowledge Cognitive awareness that facilitates intercultural communication

intercultural mentor An educator who guides and facilitates the intercultural learning of a mentee (e.g., study abroad student)

intercultural mind/mindset An open mindset capable of understanding from within and from without both one's own culture and other cultures (see also *ethnorelativism*)

intercultural pedagogy An approach to teaching which aims to promote the intercultural awareness and competence of students

intercultural sensitivity A positive emotion that enables individuals to acknowledge and respect cultural differences

intercultural speaker A competent, flexible second language speaker who is able to establish positive intercultural relationships by drawing on/recognising multiple identities and ways of being in intercultural interactions

intercultural training A pedagogical intervention which is designed to increase the knowledge and skills required to adjust to an unfamiliar cultural environment

intercultural transformation A process of change in which border crossers develop a broadened sense of self that is more inclusive and intercultural

interculturality The forging of respectful, equitable links between individuals and groups from different cultural (and linguistic) backgrounds

interdisciplinary Scholars from multiple disciplines work together to examine an issue or topic of concern

internal assessment The assessment of various programme elements that are carried out by a campus or programme institutional review board

internal programme review A review of a programme conducted by personnel who are associated with the programme

international education Education that takes place outside one's home country

international educational exchange programme The exchange of students and scholars between educational institutions in different countries

internationalisation Any systematic sustained effort designed to make higher education more responsive to the requirements and demands of an interconnected, global world

'internationalisation at home' (IaH) The embedding of international/intercultural perspectives into local education systems to raise the global awareness, cultural understanding, and intercultural competence of faculty and students

interpretivism An approach to research which rejects positivism and seeks to understand the meaning of people's actions and behaviours (e.g., qualitative investigations)

intrinsic motivation In a study abroad context, the desire to learn a language and enhance one's intercultural competence because it is enjoyable and interesting

knowledge (saviors) Social groups and their products and practices in one's own country as well as one's interlocutor's country

language anxiety Feelings of tension and apprehension that arise when learning or using a second language

language attitude The feelings that people have about their own language variety (e.g., dialect or the language varieties of others)

language identity The relationship between one's sense of self and the language one uses to communicate

language shock The challenge of understanding and communicating in a second language in an unfamiliar environment

language socialisation The acquisition of linguistic, pragmatic, and other cultural knowledge through social experience

languaging The process whereby learners make use of their second language to make sense of and shape the world around them

'large culture' Prescribed ethnic, national and international entities

learner-centred teaching An approach to teaching in which the focus is on the student as a learner and ways to enhance student learning and engagement, rather than on the transmission of knowledge from teachers to students

learning aims The broad intentions and orientation of the course or programme of study

learning objectives (also called instructional objectives or performance objectives) The statements that describe what students will be able to do once they successfully complete a unit, course, or programme

learning outcomes Statements that indicate what learners will know or be able to do as a consequence of a learning activity

lingua franca A language which is used as the medium of communication between speakers who have no native language in common

linguistic competence The ability to apply knowledge of the rules of a standard version of the language to produce and interpret spoken and written language

liquid identity The perception of one's sense of self as evolving and dynamic

local self A regional or national identity

longitudinal study A research method in which data is gathered for the same participants over a period of time, sometimes lasting more than a year

marginality A cultural lifestyle at the edges where two or more cultures meet, which can be either encapsulating or constructive (see also *constructive marginality*)

micro-term sojourner People who stay abroad for less than three weeks

mindfulness Being aware of our own assumptions, ideas, and emotions and those of our communication partners

minimisation of difference According to the developmental model of intercultural sensitivity (DMIS), elements of one's own cultural world view are experienced as universal in this phase

mixed-methods research A study that involves the collection of both quantitative and qualitative data to develop a deeper understanding of the phenomenon under investigation

motivation The capacity to direct energy and effort towards the pursuit of a goal

multidisciplinary Drawing on several academic disciplines or professional specialisations in an approach to a topic or issue

multilingual The ability to speak more than two languages

multilingual identity A hybrid sense of self linked to the use of multiple languages

national identity An individual's affiliation with and sense of belonging to a state or nation

neo-essentialism The dominant approach within the sub-discipline of intercultural communication studies which follows the essentialist and highly influential work of theorists such as Hofstede while claiming a more liberal, non-essentialist vision

objectivity The state or quality of being objective

ontology The philosophical study of the nature of being, becoming, existence or reality

openness An internal posture that is receptive or open to new practices

Other A construction of what is different from the Self

Othering The labeling and degrading of individuals or particular group of people who are perceived as different from oneself

Otherisation See *Othering*

'Ought-to-L2 self' In Dörnyei's (2009) L2 Motivational Self System, the attributes that one believes on ought to possess to avoid possible negative consequences

outcomes-based assessment (OBA) An approach to assessment in which information is collected from learners to determine if the stated learning goals and objectives for a course or programme were achieved

paradigm Philosophical framework or worldview

participant observation A method in which the researcher participates in the daily life of the people under study

perceptual acuity The ability to recognise and interpret cultural cues

personal autonomy Strength and confidence in one's identities, values, and beliefs

personal growth Improvements in all aspects of one's life to move closer to achieving one's true potential (e.g., enhanced self-awareness, maturity)

personal identity An individual's sense of self, which differentiates him or her from others (e.g., our age, personal interests, gender, personality)

personality The relatively enduring cognitive and behavioural traits of an individual

personality openness An individual's state of mind that is open to new ideas and ways of being

personality strength The quality of resilience, persistence, and patience when facing challenges

portfolio A compilation of academic work and achievements assembled for the purpose of evaluating coursework quality, learning progress, and academic achievement and providing a lasting record of work

positivism A research paradigm that emphasises the use of empirical data and scientific methods; objective reality is believed to be identifiable and predictable

positivity An optimistic outlook that enables an individual to cope better in stressful situations

postmodernism Within the context of social science, perceiving that the subjects in a study as well as the methodology are ideologically constructed

post-positivism A milder form of positivism, which recognises that all observation is fallible and has error and that all theory is revisable

post-sojourn A period of time after an individual has returned home from a stay abroad

power Authority or strength

power distance The degree to which less powerful members of a society or organisation expect and accept the unequal distribution of power among members

power relations An imbalance of power between individuals or groups

pragmatic competence The ability to comprehend and produce communicative acts in a culturally appropriate and effective manner

pragmatic failure The inability to comprehend and produce situationally appropriate language behaviour

pragmatics The study of the relationships between linguistic forms and the users of those forms

pragmatism A practically-oriented research paradigm which advocates the use of any of the techniques, methods, and procedures associated with quantitative and qualitative research in order to address research problems

prejudice Dislike or hatred of a person or group formed without reason that is often rooted in a person's early socialisation

preparedness The degree of readiness of an individual to undertake the process of cross-cultural adaptation

pre-sojourn A period of time immediately before a short stay abroad

primary socialisation The learning and acceptance of social norms, values, and practices in one's home environment from an early age (see also *cultural socialisation*)

programme evaluation A systematic method for collecting, analysing, and using information to answer questions about the effectiveness and efficiency of programmes

programme review The comprehensive evaluation of a programme based on a critical examination of its component parts'
psychological adaptation Feelings of personal well-being and self-esteem
psychological adjustment The ability to adapt to new situations
psychological health Mental well-being
qualitative research A mode of inquiry employed in many different academic disciplines, including in the social sciences and natural sciences, which involves the collection and analysis of non-numerical data through observations, conducting interviews, conducting document analysis, and/or analysing participant products such as journals, diaries, images, or blogs, etc.
quantitative research Informed by the (post-) positivist paradigm, this mode of inquiry involves the collection and analysis of numerical data
quality assurance The systematic review of an educational programme to ensure that acceptable standards of education and scholarship are being maintained
race A contested concept that refers to the classification of humans into groups based on ancestry, genetics, physical traits, or social relations
racism The belief in the inherent superiority of a particular race and the perceived inferiority of other races
racist discourse Talk which has the effect of sustaining racist practices
reductionism The tendency to ignore variations within cultures (see also *essentialism*)
re-entry The process of returning home after spending time abroad
re-entry culture shock The process of re-adjusting and re-acculturating to one's own home environment after living in a different cultural setting for a significant period of time
reflective mindset The ability to revisit and make meaning from one's experience
reflexivity The qualitative researcher's awareness of his or her role in research and how it might influence the research process and outcomes
regional identity The part of an individual's identity that is rooted in his or her region of residence
reliability The extent to which an experiment, test, or measuring procedure yields the same results on repeated trials
research design How researchers plan their studies with the aim of answering their research questions
research ethics The application of fundamental ethical issues and principles to a variety of topics involving research (e.g., protection of the rights and well-being of participants in a study)
research methodology The process used by researchers to collect data for the purpose of describing, explaining, and predicting the phenomena under study
resilience An individual's ability to cope with stress and adversity

resocialisation The process of re-adjusting one's attitudes and behaviours to feel at ease in one's home environment after a period away

respect The display of positive regard for an individual from a different cultural background

respondent faking The respondents in a questionnaire survey distort the results by providing erroneous or inaccurate information

reverse culture shock See *re-entry culture shock*

role shock Lack of knowledge and confusion about the norms of behaviour in a new cultural setting

rubric A scoring guide used to evaluate the quality of students' work

saviors Cultural knowledge in Byram's framework of intercultural competence

scientific method The principles and procedures employed to systematically seek knowledge, which includes the recognition and formulation of a research problem, the collection of relevant data through observation and experiment, and the formulation and testing of related hypotheses

second language socialisation The process by which novices in an unfamiliar linguistic and cultural context gain intercultural communicative competence by acquiring linguistic conventions, sociopragmatic norms, cultural scripts, and other behaviours that are associated with the new culture

segregation The acculturation strategy in which individuals strive to maintain their cultural heritage and avoid participation in the larger society of their new country

self An image or construction of what is deemed to be different from the Other

self-awareness Knowledge about one's identities, strengths and weaknesses

self-efficacy An individual's beliefs about his or her capacity to perform well

self-identities One's conception of oneself and one's place in the world

self-reports A method which involves asking a participant about his/her attitudes, feelings, beliefs and so on

self shock Inconsistent, conflicting self-images, which can involve the loss of communication competence and self-confidence in a new environment

service learning (community-engaged learning) A structured learning experience which combines community service with guided reflection

short-term sojourner An individual who stays abroad for a few months or less

skills of discovery and interaction (*savoir apprendre/faire*) The ability to acquire new knowledge of a culture and to operate this knowledge in real-time communication

skills of interpreting and relating (*savoir comprendre*)   The ability to interpret a document or event from another culture, to explain it and relate it to documents or events from one's own

'small culture'   The notion of culture is attached to small social groupings or activities wherever there is cohesive behaviour rather than large groups (e.g., ethnic groups)

social categorisation   The way we group people into conceptual categories in order to make sense of our increasingly complex social environment

social identity   How we identify ourselves in relation to others based on what we have in common

social identity theory (SIT)   A theory developed by Tajfel and Turner (1979, 1986) that suggests that individuals tend to categorise people in their social environment into ingroups and outgroups

social justice   The equal and fair distribution of resources and opportunities with no discrimination based on such categories as ethnicity, gender, and sexual orientation, etc.

social media   Internet-based applications that build on the ideological and technological foundations of Web 2.0 and permit the creation and exchange of content generated by users

social network   The multiple web of relationships an individual forms in a society with other people who he or she is bound to directly or indirectly through friendship or other social relationships

social networking site (SNS)   Online platform that is used by people to build a social network or relationships with other people who share similar personal or career interests, activities, backgrounds or affiliations

social responsibility   An ethical orientation that suggests that organisations and individuals have an obligation to act for the benefit of society as a whole

socialisation   The process by which individuals internalise the conventions of behaviour imposed by a society or social group (see also *primary socialisation*)

sociocultural adaptation   Competence in dealing with life in the larger society

socio-emotional support   The psychological assistance provided by friendship circles, intracultural, and intercultural relationships, and family members

sociolinguistic competence   The ability to give to the language produced by an interlocutor—whether native speaker or not—meanings which are taken for granted by the interlocutor or which are negotiated and made explicit with the interlocutor

sociopragmatic competence   The ability to communicate appropriately in social situations in a particular cultural context

sociopragmatic norms   Rules governing the appropriate use of discourse in social situations

sojourn A period of time spent living in a cultural setting different from one's home environment

sojourn duration The length of the stay abroad

sojourner An individual who is in the new environment temporarily for a specific purpose (e.g., study, work, business) and often for a specific length of time (e.g., several days, months, or years)

solid identity The association of an individual with static cultural elements (e.g., traits and behaviours associated with a national, cultural, gender category)

speech community A group of individuals who use the same variety of a language and share specific rules for speaking and for interpreting speech

stereotype A preconceived idea that attributes certain characteristics (e.g., personality traits, level of intelligence), intentions, and behaviours to all the members of a particular social class or group of people

stereotyping A strong tendency to characterise people from other cultural backgrounds unfairly, collectively, and usually negatively

stress-adaptation-growth dynamic Young Yun Kim's (2001) notion that acculturative stress (e.g., language and culture shock) can gradually lead to adaptation in border crossers

structured reflection Prompts, questions, activities, or organised discussions that aim to help individuals think more deeply about an issue or problem

summative assessment The evaluation of student learning at the end of an instructional unit by comparing it against some standard or benchmark

study abroad A subtype of education abroad that leads to progress toward an academic degree at a student's home institution; typically, this may include such activities as classroom study, research, internships, and service learning

study abroad cycle The period before, during, and after study abroad

subjectivity How an individual's judgment is influenced by personal opinions, beliefs, and feelings

teacher-centred teaching An approach to teaching in which the focus is on the knowledge being transmitted to students by the teacher

telecollaboration The use of online communication tools to link language and culture learners in different countries for intercultural exchange and the development of collaborative projects

third culture kid (TCK) A person who has spent a significant part of his or her developmental years outside the parent's culture (see also *global nomad*)

tolerance for ambiguity One's ability to cope with situations that are not clear

transformation The act or process of change

transformative learning theory A theory developed by Jack Mezirow (1994, 2009) which posits that adults who engage in critical reflection and self-examination may experience a dramatic transformation

transition shock The state of loss, disorientation, and identity confusion that can occur when one enters a new situation, job, relationship, or physical location and is confronted with the strain of adjusting to the unfamiliar

translanguaging The constant, active envisioning of new realities through social action and the use of a second language

transnationalism Multiple ties and interactions linking people and institutions across the borders of nation-states

U-curve adjustment model A theory of cultural adaption which suggests that border crossers go through several phases as they adjust to a new cultural environment

uncertainty avoidance Feeling threatened by ambiguous situations, one takes steps to avoid uncertainty

validity How well a test or other assessment instrument measures what it is purported to measure

value Shared ideas about what is right or wrong

value orientations framework Models that identify, describe, and contrast the dominant value system in various cultures

voluntary migrant An individual who willingly chooses to settle abroad

W-curve adjustment model An extended version of the U-curve model of adjustment that suggests that sojourners go through predictable phases when adapting to a new cultural situation and returning home

ways of being The manner or means of a way of life/a way of knowing

willingness to communicate (WTC) An individual's readiness to enter into discourse at a particular time with a specific person or persons

world citizen An individual with a global or international identity

worldview Our overall way of looking at the world, which serves as a filter to help us make sense of humanity

xenophobia An irrational fear of foreigners or strangers

Index

AAC&U Intercultural Knowledge and Competence Value Rubric 121
acceptance of difference 113, 114, 204
acculturation 23–4, 38–62, 89, 90, 92, 98, 99, 104, 113, 132, 135–6, 141–3, 148–9, 204; *see also* acculturative stress; culture shock; second language socialisation
acculturation strategies 40, 204; *see also* acculturation
acculturative stress 40, 44, 48–52, 59, 71, 92, 98–9, 113, 121, 136, 142, 146, 204
adaptation to difference *112*, 113, 204
adjustment *see* acculturation
Affect-Behaviour-Cognition model (ABC model) 40
agency 23, 28, 50, 66, 91–2, 204
American Association for Applied Linguistics (AAAL) 10
Angelo, Thomas A. 117–20, 139
assessment 17, 102–27, 138–9, 141, 151, 162, 165–6, 168; *see also* evaluation; programme evaluation
Association of American Colleges and Universities (AAC&U) 116, 121

Bandura, Albert 96
Beaven, Ana 26–7, 92, 137, 155
Beliefs, Events and Values Inventory (BEVI) 123
Bennett, Janet M. 43–4, 93, 105, 136, 140, 144
Bennett, J. Milton 111–14, 121, 122, 137; *see also* development model of intercultural sensitivity
Benson, Philip 60, 63, 75–7, 83, 91, 92–3, 146
Berry, John W. 39–40, 57

biculturalism 56–7, 205
blended learning 132, 139, 152, 166
Block, David 75, 153, 160
blogging 76, 145, 147, 148
Bologna Process 85
Borghetti, Claudia 137, 155
British Council 6
Byram, Michael 94, 105–6, 107–9, 110, 114, 116, 145

Center for Advanced Research on Language Acquisition (CARLA) 154–5
Center for Educational Resources in Culture, Language, and Literacy (CERCLL) 9
Coleman, James 18, 59, 60, 83, 84, 89, 93, 96, 152
Common European Framework of Reference for Languages: Learning, Teaching, Assessment (CEFR) 108
community of practice 70, 205
comprehensive intercultural interventions 154–5
congruence of communication style 49
constructive marginality 113, 205
constructivism 21, 27–9, 205
contextual evaluation 113, 206
contextual relativism 137
Council of Europe's *Common European Framework of Reference for Languages: Learning, Teaching Assessment* (CEFR) 108
credit mobility 4, 206
critical (transformative) paradigm 21, 29–31; *see also* critical theory; criticality
critical cosmopolitanism 29, 30, 206

critical cultural awareness (savoir s'engager) 108, 206
critical ethnography 30
critical intercultural speaker 105, 206
criticality 1, 117, 134–5, 148, 159
critical perspectives on interculturality 117, 134–5, 148
critical theory 29–31, 41, 137–8, 167, 206
Cross-Cultural Adaptability Inventory (CCAI) 121–2
cross-cultural pragmatics 22
cultural awareness 104, 121, 134, 142, 148, 155; *see also* critical cultural awareness
cultural difference 5, 22, 27, 29, 48, 54, 56, 91, 98, 104, 106, 111–15, 135, 137, 148, 151, 159, 167
cultural disengagement 114, 207
cultural mentoring *see* mentoring
cultural norms 21, 25, 54, 116, 207; *see also* enculturation
cultural similarity 48
culture, conceptions of 21, 130, 133–5, 138, 159, 166, 167
'culture as nation' perspective 41, 60, 135, 137, 207; *see also* essentialism; Othering; reductionism; stereotyping
culture of learning 48, 55, 56, 207
culture shock 44–60, 136, 142, 146, 151; *see also* adjustment; curve of adjustment models; reverse culture shock
curve of adjustment models 53, 54, 53–60, 135–6, 142

Dasli, Maria 103, 105, 108–9, 130, 135, 137, 148, 158, 159
Deardorff, Darla K. 8, 94, 104, 106–7, 115, 116, 121, 126, 137, 165
debriefing 2, 60, 78, 86, 89, 148–9, 150–1; *see also* mentoring
defence of difference *112*, 112–13, 207
denial of difference *112*, 112, 113, 114, 207
Dervin, Fred 5, 8, 12, 23, 48, 59, 60, 63–80, 103, 104, 105, 108–9, 117, 126, 130, 134–5, 137–8, 143, 148, 158, 159, 167
development model of intercultural sensitivity (DMIS) 111–15, *112*; *see also* intercultural development continuum

Dewey, Dan P. 69, 70, 164
de Wit, Hans 3–4, 84–5
Diao, Wenhao 83, 146
Díaz, Adriana R. 105, 108–9, 117, 130, 134–5, 137, 148, 158, 159
digital portfolios *see portfolios*
discourse competence 107, 109
duration of sojourn 12, 51, 86, 141, 143, 147, 158, 161, 220

enculturation 39, 44, 65, 110
Englishisation 30, 208
environmental factors 12, 60, 82, 85–90, 100, 134, 161, 208
epistemology 18–19, 21, 208
essentialism 23, 39, 41, 66–7, 72, 74, 135, 137, 142–3, 159, 167, 209; *see also* Othering; reductionism; stereotyping
ethical intercultural praxis 135
ethics 36, 103, 109, 145, 159, 160, 162
ethnocentric mindset *see* ethnocentrism
ethnocentrism 69, *112*, 112, 113, 114, 159, 167, 209
ethnography 25–6; *see also* critical ethnography; ethnography of communication
ethnography of communication 26, 30, 209
ethnorelative mindset *see* ethnorelativism
ethnorelativism *112*, 112–13, 114, 116, 209
European Centre for Modern Languages (ECML) 108, 155
European Commission 4, 6, 83, 85
European Cooperation in Science and Technology (COST) 10
European Region Action Scheme for the Mobility of University Students (ERASMUS) 4, 6, 26, 70, 73, 74, 83, 85, 154, 155
evaluation 113, 116, 118–19, 126–7, 135, 138–9, 209; *see also* assessment; programme evaluation
experiential learning 132, 136, 141, 145, 150
external factors *see* environmental factors
external programme review 126–7, 139, 168, 209; *see also* internal programme review; programme review
extrinsic motivation 95, 209

Fantini, Alvino E. 33, 110–11, 121, 123, 124–5, 138
Forum on Education Abroad (FEA) 4, 8, 58–9, 60, 83, 85, 86, 87, 118–19, 126, 136
Freed, Barbara 7

generalisation 22, 25, 41
geopolitical dimensions 51, 210
global citizenship 3, 5–6, 59, 103, 104, 129, 130, 135, 154, 157, 158, 159, 161, 162, 165, 168
Global Competence Aptitude Assessment (GCAA) 123
global-mindedness 6, 17, 61, 103, 138, 165, 168, 210
global mindset *see* global-mindedness
Global Perspectives Inventory (GPI) 122
guided critical reflection *see* mentoring

Hall, Edward T. 20, 25, 26
Hall, Stuart 64, 159
Hammer, Mitchell, R. 113, 114–15, 122, 137, 153
heritage study abroad students 58–9, 163
Hofstede, Geert H. 23, 135, 167
Holliday, Adrian R. 4–5, 23, 29–30, 41, 66, 74, 117, 130, 134, 135, 137, 143, 153, 158, 159, 167
Holmes, Prue 135, 137–8, 141
homestay 12, 25, 41, 51, 69, 70, 87, 90, 146
honeymoon stage 54, 55
hostility phase 55–6
host receptivity 44, 60, 79, 90, 97, 100, 134, 161, 211
humourous stage 56

'ideal L2 self' 95–6, 211
identity: ascription 67–9, 75, 204; avowal 67–9, 75, 205; confusion 43–4, 57–8, 59, 78, 151, 211; contested 47–8, 63, 68, 73, 205; 'dark' sides 12, 63, 69, 167, 207; global 77, 79, 129, 152, 210; hybrid 12, 58, 64, 211; imagined 63, 64, 67, 72–4, 75, 80, 91, 92–3, 167, 211; multicultural 58, 59, 78, 97, 105; multilingual 43, 64, 78, 215; national 65–7, 69, 72, 215; reconstruction 12, 43, 64, 65, 70, 72, 78, 79, 82, 211; salience 65, 211; shock (*see* identity, confusion; self shock); social 40, 64, 69, 219
ideology 29, 30, 42, 73, 104, 211
imaginaries about identity in study abroad 6, 60–1, 72–4, 82, 141, 182; *see also* identity, imagined
immersion 6, 12, 50, 89, 96, 114, 129, 161, 165
individual differences 90–101, 211
integration 54, 73, 112, *112,* 113, 114, 147, 212
intensity of experience 49–50, 101, 212
intentional targeted intervention (ITI) 140
interaction between domestic and international students 30, 50, 51, 56, 68, 70, 71, 86, 88, 90, 91, 92, 133, 147, 161
international education (definition) 4, 213
intercultural attitudes 93–4, 107, 132, 141, 143, 212
intercultural communication 5, 19, 23, 29, 212; *see also* intercultural communication competence; intercultural communicative competence; intercultural competence
intercultural communication apprehension 97
intercultural communication competence 23, 104, 212
Intercultural Communication Institute (ICI) 123
intercultural communicative competence (ICC) 105, 106–8, 117, 128, 212
intercultural competence 5, 9, 33, 94, 103–17, 121–7, 134, 135, 136–9, 155, 156, 162, 163, 166, 212
intercultural competence assessment 104, 119–27, 138–9; *see also* assessment
intercultural competence assessment tools 121–3; *see also* intercultural competence assessment
intercultural competencies dimensions model 110–11
intercultural development continuum (IDC) 114–15, 122
intercultural development inventory (IDI) 113, 122, 138
Intercultural Education Resources for Erasmus Students and their Teachers (IEREST) 155

Intercultural Effectiveness Scale (IES) 122–3
intercultural intervention 129–56, 213
interculturality 4–5, 33, 64, 69, 74, 79, 80–1, 103–6, 114, 116, 117, 125, 130, 137, 141, 155, 158, 159, 162, 166, 213
(inter)cultural mentoring *see* mentoring
intercultural personhood 77
intercultural praxis 135
intercultural sensitivity 5, 23, 32, 53, 59, 94, 103, 111, 112, 158, 161, 168
intercultural speaker 105, 107, 213; *see also* critical intercultural speaker
internal programme review 126–7, 139, 168, 213; *see also* external programme review; programme review
International Academy for Intercultural Research (IAIR) 9
International Association for Languages and Intercultural Communication (IALIC) 9
International Association of Applied Linguistics (AILA) 10
international education 1, 3–4, 213
internationalisation at home (IaH) 133, 168, 213
internationalisation of the curriculum (IoC) 133, 168
interpretivism 21, 24–7, 213
intrinsic motivation 95, 214
investment 87, 94–6, 97

Jackson, Jane 7, 8, 18, 44, 45, 46, 47, 49, 50, 52, 53, 55, 59, 60, 61, 63, 66, 67, 68, 70, 76, 77, 81, 83, 88, 91, 92, 93, 94, 96, 105, 117, 130, 132, 134, 135, 136, 137, 138, 140, 141, 143, 145, 147, 148, 149, 150, 151, 152, 153, 154, 156
journal (diary) writing 26–7, 31, 32, 114, 124, 139, 145, 147–8

Kim, Young Yun 23, 39, 50, 52, 60, 77, 90, 92, 99, 140, 142
Kinginger, Celeste 7, 8, 18, 40, 50, 52, 59, 60, 70, 72, 76, 83, 160, 164
Knight, Jane 3
knowledge (savoirs) 107, 116, 214
Kolb, David A. 132, 136, 141, 145, 147, 148, 150; *see also* experiential learning

L2 motivational self system 95–6
La Brack, Bruce 45, 52, 57, 58–9, 136, 140, 150, 151, 153
language attitudes 93–4, 214
language identity 64, 69–70, 75–7
language shock 46–7
languaging 41–2; *see also* translanguaging
'large culture' **21**, 23, 41, 137, 153, 167
Leask, Betty 133
Liddicoat, Anthony J. 113, 114, 135
lingua franca 6, 28–9, 71, 77, 88, 95, 164, 214
linguistic competence 107
linguistic similarity 49
local students *see* interaction between domestic and international students

Martin, Judith N. 20, 29, 36, 41, 78, 131, 134
Maximizing Study Abroad (MAXSA) 154–5
mentoring 78, 87, 122, 132, 136, 141, 148, 153, 213
Mezirow, Jack 47, 52, 65, 136–7, 148, 153
mindfulness 149, 215
minimisation *112*, 112, 113, 114, 215
Mitchell, Rosamond 71, 74, 76, 77
mixed-methods research **21**, 31–2, 33, 34, 59, 60, 82, 126, 155, 160, 166
monocultural mindset 69, 114, 159
Moon, Jennifer A. 132, 148
motivation 89, 94–6, 97, 100, 111

narrative analysis 31, 34, 77, 79, 80–1, 92, 145, 154
nationalism 66, 80

Oberg, Karl 45, 51, 142
objectivity 20, **21**, 22, 31–2, 215
online intercultural learning and teaching 120, 132, 147, 148, 150–4, 155
ontology 18–19, **21**, 215
Othering 12, 23, 79, 137, 142–3, 146, 167, 215; *see also* essentialism; stereotyping
Otherisation *see* Othering
'ought-to L2 self' 95–6, 215
outcomes-based Assessment (OBA) 102, 117–18, 128, 215

Paige, R. Michael 7, 17, 18, 37, 49–50, 51, 52, 61, 69, 78, 112, 113, 121, 123, 132, 136, 141, 153, 155, 165
patience 98–9, 110, 149, 216
pedagogy 46, 56, 107–8, 118, 130–3, 135, 138, 140–56, 158, 165–8, 213; *see also* 'culture of learning'
personality 47, 49, 60, 74, 91, 95, 96, 99, 104, 216
personality strength 104, 216
Phipps, Alison 41–2
Plews, John 8, 18, 61, 130, 138, 156
PluriMobil: Plurilingual and intercultural learning through mobility 140, 155
polarisation: defense/reversal *112*, 113, 114
portfolios 114, 120, 124, 139, 208, 216
positivism 20, 22, 216; *see also* (post-)positivism
(post-)positivism 20–4, **21**, 216
post-post sojourn phase 17
post-sojourn interventions 151–2
poststructuralism 29, 41, 64–5, 91, 153
power 5, 12, 23, 29–30, 51, 60, 63, 66, 70, 71, 72, 79, 80–1, 90–1, 134, 216
pragmatic failure 22, 216
pragmatism (multi-paradigmatic research) **21**, 31–3, 216
prejudice 80, 205, 216; *see also* identity, 'dark' sides; stereotyping
pre-sojourn interventions 140–6
privilege 29, 71, 72, 134, 137, 149
process model of intercultural competence 94, *115*, 115–16
professional organisations in international/intercultural education 8–10
programme evaluation 126–7, 138, 216; *see also* external programme review; internal programme review
programme review 126–7, 139, 168, 217; *see also* external programme review; internal programme review; programme evaluation
Project for Learning Abroad, Training & Outreach (PLATO) 153
psychological adjustment 23–4, 104, 217

qualitative research 21, 24–6, 33, 34, 60, 75, 79, 80–1, 82–3, 114, 139, 160, 217; *see also* ethnography; mixed-methods research

reductionism 41, 100, 137, 143, 159, 217; *see also* essentialism
re-entry 54, 57–9, 60, 139, 150–2, 154–5, 162, 217; *see also* reverse culture shock
reflective learning 32, 114, 120, 124, 132, 134–5, 136, 141, 151
reflexivity1, 2, 79, 80–1, 137, 159, 217
research design 33–4, 62, 160, 217
research methodology 18, 36, 80–1, 160, 162, 217
research network (International Association of Applied Linguistics) (ReN) 10
research paradigm 18, 19–34, **21**, 36, 37, 82, 156, 160–1, 215
resocialisation stage 54, 58, 218; *see also* re-entry; reverse culture shock
reversal 113, 207
reverse culture shock 151, 218; *see also* re-entry; resocialisation stage

Savicki, Victor 4, 7, 8, 17, 92, 102, 128, 138, 156
scientific method 20, 218
second language socialisation 39–41, 70, 218; *see also* acculturation; translanguaging
self-awareness 65, 79, 106, 113, 143–2, 218
self-confidence 56, 96–7, 136, 144
self-efficacy 96–7, 136, 218
self shock 44, 47–8, 218; *see also* identity, confusion
Shively, Rachel 90, 142, 144, 147, 155, 162, 163
skills of discovery and interaction (savoir apprendre/faire) 108, 218
skills of interpreting and relating (savoir comprendre) 108, 219
'small and large cultures' *see* essentialism; 'small culture'; 'large culture'
'small culture' **21**, 41, 153, 219
social categorisation 68, 219; *see also* stereotyping
socialisation *see* acculturation; second language socialisation
social justice 5, 30, 63, 80, 135, 219
social media 7, 72–3, 89, 132, 152, 160, 166, 219
social network 10, 12, 50, 58, 62, 64, 69–71, 73, 76, 77, 81, 91, 140, 161, 164; *see also* social networking site

social networking site (SNS) 73, 219
social responsibility 36, 219
Society for International Education, Training and Research (SIETAR) 9
socio-emotional support 44, 50, 71, 86, 87, 148–9, 219
sociolinguistic competence 107, 219
sociopragmatics 22, 40, 44, 56, 75, 77, 90, 94, 105, 142, 144, 146, 162–3, 219
sojourn expectations 12, 44, 46, 55, 79, 92–3, 94, 97, 129, 131, 142–3, 151; *see also* assessment
sojourn interventions 147–51
Sorrells, Kathryn 5, 30, 131, 134, 135, 143
Spencer-Oatey, Helen 26–7, 92, 130, 133
stereotyping 5, 12, 23, 41, 59, 69, 73, 79, 80, 94, 105, 137, 142–3, 144, 146, 167, 220; *see also* essentialism; Othering; reductionism
study abroad definitions 4, 158, 220
study abroad goals 4, 24, 70, 86, 92–3, 94, 99, 118, 120, 126, 132, 137, 138, 140, 141, 142–3, 146, 149, 151, 152, 168
study abroad outcomes 2, 7, 17, 24, 35, 60, 61, 67, 75, 82, 83, 86, 91, 92, 100, 102, 116, 117–23, 125, 128, 133, 138, 139, 141, 161, 165; *see also* outcomes-based assessment
study abroad participation rates 6, 60
Study Abroad Research in European Perspective (SAREP) 10
subjectivity **21**, 23, 220

Taguchi, Naoko 8, 40, 56, 144, 162
Tajfel, Henri 69
teacher education 125, 155

technology 89, 120, 130, 132, 140, 152–4, 160, 166
technology and assessment 120; *see also* assessment; intercultural competence assessment
telecollaborative intercultural exchange 153, 220
third culture kid (TCK) 59, 220
tolerance for ambiguity 46, 49, 91–2, 98–9, 110, 220
transformative learning theory 52, 136–7, 166
transition shock 43–61, 221
translanguaging 38, 41–3, 53, 59, 62, 70–1, 221; *see also* languaging
Trentman, Emma 70, 71, 164

U-curve adjustment model 53, 53–4, 58–60, 135–6, 221; *see also* W-curve adjustment model

Vande Berg, Michael 7, 17, 18, 37, 61, 62, 115, 131, 132, 140, 153, 156, 165

Ward, Colleen 39, 40, 43–4, 45, 48, 49, 50, 51, 52, 58, 90, 93, 140, 142, 148
W-curve adjustment model 54, 54, 60, 135–6, 142, 221; *see also* U-curve adjustment model
willingness-to-communicate (WTC) 97, 98, 221
Workshop on Intercultural Skills Enhancement (WISE) 9
worldview 18, 19, 31, 33–4, 36, 43, 44, 47, 112, 113, 114, 133, 151, 162, 221; *see also* research paradigm

Zhu, Hua 20, 27, 28, 34, 37, 40, 41, 137, 158, 159, 167

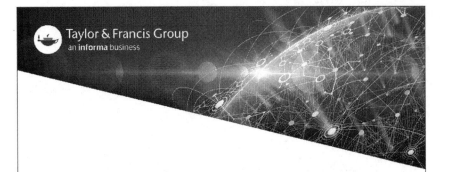